The Great Migration

The Great Migration

Rural–Urban Migration in China and Indonesia

Edited by

Xin Meng
Australian National University, Australia

Chris Manning
Australian National University, Australia

with

Li Shi
Beijing Normal University, China

Tadjuddin Noer Effendi
Gadjah Mada University, Indonesia

Edward Elgar
Cheltenham, UK • Northampton, MA, USA

Published by
Edward Elgar Publishing Limited
The Lypiatts
15 Lansdown Road
Cheltenham
Glos GL50 2JA
UK

Edward Elgar Publishing, Inc.
William Pratt House
9 Dewey Court
Northampton
Massachusetts 01060
USA

A catalogue record for this book
is available from the British Library

Library of Congress Control Number: 2009941235

ISBN 978 1 84844 644

Printed and bound by MPG Books Group, UK

Contents

PART II   INDONESIA

Figures

Tables

Contributors

Armida Alisjahbana, Professor, Faculty of Economics, University of Padjadjaran, Bandung

Danang Arif Darmawan, Lecturer, Social Development Department, Faculty of Social and Political Sciences, Gadjah Mada University, Yogyakarta

Deng Quheng, Assistant Professor, Chinese Academy of Social Sciences, Beijing

Tadjuddin Noer Effendi, Professor, Sociology Department, Faculty of Social and Political Sciences, Gadjah Mada University, Yogyakarta

Paul Frijters, Professor, School of Economics and Finance, Queensland University of Technology, Brisbane

Fina Itriyati, Lecturer, Sociology Department, Faculty of Social and Political Sciences, Gadjah Mada University, Yogyakarta

Sherry Tao Kong, Research Fellow, Economics Program, Research School of Social Sciences, The Australian National University, Canberra

Leng Lee, Doctoral Candidate, Oxford University Centre for the Environment, Oxford University, United Kingdom

Li Shi, Professor, Department of Economics, School of Economics and Business Administration, Beijing Normal University, Beijing

Chuliang Luo, Associate Professor, School of Economics and Business Administration, Beijing Normal University, Beijing

Chris Manning, Associate Professor, Arndt-Corden Division of Economics, Research School of Pacific and Asian Studies, The Australian National University, Canberra

Xin Meng, Professor, Economics Program, Research School of Social Sciences, The Australian National University, Canberra

Mujiyani, Research Associate, Rural–Urban Migration in China and Indonesia Project, Gadjah Mada University, Yogyakarta

Raden M. Purnagunawan, PhD candidate, Arndt-Corden Division of Economics, Research School of Pacific and Asian Studies, The Australian National University, Canberra

Budy P. Resosudarmo, Research Fellow, Arndt-Corden Division of Economics, Research School of Pacific and Asian Studies, The Australian National University, Canberra

Asep Suryahadi, Director, SMERU Research Institute, Jakarta

Derajad S. Widhyharto, Lecturer, Sociology Department, Faculty of Social and Political Sciences, Gadjah Mada University, Yogyakarta

Chikako Yamauchi, Research Fellow, Economics Program, Research School of Social Sciences, The Australian National University, Canberra

Ximing Yue, Professor, School of Finance, Renmin University of China, Beijing

Athia Yumna, Researcher, SMERU Research Institute, Jakarta

Asri Yusrina, Researcher, SMERU Research Institute, Jakarta

Acknowledgments

This book is the first major publication of the Rural–Urban Migration in China and Indonesia (RUMiCI) project. It outlines the results of the first of five annual surveys on rural–urban migration in China and Indonesia to be undertaken from 2008 to 2012. At the outset we would like to acknowledge the financial support for our work of the Australian Research Council, the Australian Agency for International Development (AusAID) and the Ford Foundation.

In China, the surveys were conducted by professional survey company Datasea Marketing Research, and by the Department of Rural Social and Economic Surveys and the Department of Urban Social and Economic Surveys at the National Bureau of Statistics. The success of our surveys relied heavily on their efforts. Ms Zhijing Wei managed the survey monitoring process and contributed significantly to the quality of the survey data.

In Indonesia, the project benefited from the support of the Faculty of Social and Political Sciences at Gadjah Mada University, especially the successive deans of the faculty during the survey period, Professors Mochtar Mas'oed and Pratikno. We would also like to thank the other members of the Indonesia Field Survey Project team at Gadjah Mada University, who undertook the field work for the study.

The Australian National University and Indonesia's National Development Planning Agency (Bappenas) hosted workshops in December 2008 and February 2009 at which most of the papers were presented. The comments received from both the discussants and the audience during these meetings proved very useful.

We appreciate the time and attention devoted by all those who read the draft manuscripts, which greatly assisted in the preparation of the final chapters. In particular, we would like to thank Tue Gorgens and Stephen Horn for reading through the two chapters on survey design (Chapters 7 and 11) several times, and for providing valuable suggestions on our sampling strategies.

Our thanks go to Hong Yu, manager of the RUMiCI project, for overseeing the flow of papers and arranging the preparation of supporting documents, including the two maps included in Chapter 1. Cartographic Services at the Australian National University did a fine job of preparing the maps. Finally, we would like to thank Beth Thomson for her meticulous and very patient copy editing of the draft papers, and for readying the book for print.

Xin Meng and Chris Manning

October 2009

1 The Great Migration in China and Indonesia: Trends and Institutions

Xin Meng and Chris Manning

1 THE RURAL–URBAN MIGRATION IN CHINA AND INDONESIA PROJECT

Economic growth almost inevitably leads to a substantial movement of labour from rural primary industry to secondary and tertiary industries in the cities. This movement is essential to foster growth and to spread rising income more evenly across the population. It is thought to benefit both those who migrate and those who remain behind. As a result, rural–urban migration is often regarded as one of the most effective ways to reduce rural poverty and increase agricultural productivity.

Industrialization and urbanization almost always go hand in hand. Most countries in the developed world experienced large-scale rural–urban migration during the process of economic growth. In the United Kingdom, for example, less than 27 per cent of the population lived in towns with more than 5,000 inhabitants in 1801, but 100 or so years later the proportion had increased to 60–70 per cent (Brown 1991). In Japan, more than 80 per cent of the labour force worked in the agricultural sector between 1878 and 1882, but by 1979 the ratio had dropped to 11 per cent (Moriya 1963: 238–9; Sorensen 2004).

A similar process is occurring in China and Indonesia at a much faster speed. Twenty to thirty years ago, both were largely agricultural societies. In 1980, only 19 per cent of the total population of China, and 22 per cent of the total population of Indonesia, inhabited cities; by 2005, the rates had reached 47 per cent and 43 per cent respectively.[1] But these percentages do not portray the precise dimension of the urbanization process, and the following absolute numbers may be more revealing. In the 10 years between 1995 and 2005, the number of rural-to-urban migrants in China increased from 40 million to around 130 million, to account for almost one-third of the total urban labour force. In comparison, at the height of the Industrial Revolution in Great

Britain, only 3 million people moved from rural to urban areas during the 60 years from 1841 to 1901 (Long 2005).

Over the course of the next two decades, both China and Indonesia are expected to make the transition from mainly rural-based to urban-based societies. In both countries, it is estimated that about two-thirds of the rural labour force will migrate to urban areas. The sheer size and speed of the urbanization process in the two countries should qualify as among the largest population movements ever.

Driving the speed of the urbanization process in China and Indonesia is their high economic growth rates, which are more than double those that prevailed in Europe and the United States during the Industrial Revolution. The unprecedented scale and pace of the movements of people that are taking place are confronting both governments with challenging policy questions, particularly in terms of properly managing the process of migration.

While China and Indonesia face similar challenges, the policies implemented in each country, and their consequences, have been very different. China has established an internal 'guest worker' system with tight controls on the migration process, both to prevent overly fast migration and to force migrants to maintain their ties with the home village. One positive outcome of this system has been very few slums, even though over 100 million rural migrants are currently employed in urban areas throughout China. However, the system has also led to large discrepancies in income between migrant and urban workers, partly due to constraints on the types of jobs that migrants have access to in the cities. Moreover, in the countryside, agricultural productivity has not improved as much as it should have in recent years. Restrictions on land trading and on the access of rural residents to urban facilities have prevented migrants from severing their ties with the land; this in turn has severely hindered progress in the rationalization of the agricultural sector. As a result, the income gap between rural and urban areas has increased significantly over the last 20 years, and migration has led to only modest reductions in rural poverty. In addition, the members of migrant families left behind in rural areas have suffered disproportionately from social problems caused by a lack of quality education and health care services for left-behind children and inadequate provision of care for the elderly.

In contrast to the situation in China, over the past 40 years the Indonesian government has placed few restrictions on rural–urban migration. Most of the migrants moving to the cities have been rural poor taking up jobs in the informal sector and living in urban slums, although there are also a considerable number of circular migrants who leave their families behind in the countryside while they work in the cities. The pace of rural-to-urban migration slowed after the Asian economic crisis of 1997–98 but has nevertheless continued to fuel urban population growth. Over the last three decades, the picture that has emerged is one of a country with rapidly growing urban agglomerations on the one hand, and a decline in rural and urban poverty on the other. In Indonesia, increased productivity in the agricultural sector, partly related to out-migration, has contributed to a relatively narrow rural–urban income gap (Thorbecke and van der Pluim 1993).

Given the contrasting strategies undertaken to manage rural–urban migration in China and Indonesia, and their consequences, Indonesia may serve as an excellent case study through which to contrast the benefits (and costs) of relatively free migration. At the same time, migration and its effect on economic development in Indonesia is an important issue in its own right.

This book reports on the findings of the first stage of a research project examining the effect of the unprecedented movements of people in China and Indonesia—on migrants and their families, on the rural communities they leave behind and on the urban communities they enter. The Rural–Urban Migration in China and Indonesia (RUMiCI) project was initiated by a group of researchers at the Australian National University, the Queensland University of Technology, the Beijing Normal University and Gadjah Mada University. The broad aim of the project is to gain an understanding of the comparative migration and urbanization processes in China and Indonesia, in order to inform policy makers about how to manage these processes most effectively.

The research project was designed to focus on the following three issues:

1 the effect of rural–urban migration on income mobility and poverty alleviation;
2 its long-term effect on the education, health and nutrition of migrants' children; and
3 the extent to which migrants assimilate into urban societies and the channels through which they do so.

To study these subjects, large-scale household surveys were planned in 2006–07, with the first wave of the surveys conducted in both countries in early 2008.

The Chinese surveys were carried out in 10 provinces identified as major migrant-sending or migrant-receiving regions, namely Shanghai, Jiangsu, Zhejiang, Guangdong, Sichuan, Chongqing, Henan, Anhui, Hubei and Hebei (see Figure 1.1). To capture the three populations of interest—rural–urban migrants, urban residents and rural residents—the researchers conducted three surveys: the Urban Migrant Survey (5,000 households in 15 cities), the Urban Household Survey (5,000 households, in 19 cities) and the Rural Household Survey (8,000 households in 10 provinces).

The Indonesian survey was conducted in four cities: Tangerang near Jakarta in Java; Medan in the northern part of Sumatra; Samarinda in the resource-rich region of Kalimantan; and Makassar in Sulawesi (see Figure 1.2). The total sample comprised 2,400 households: 900 non-migrant households, 900

Figure 1.1   Rural–Urban Migration in China and Indonesia Project: Survey Cities and Provinces in China

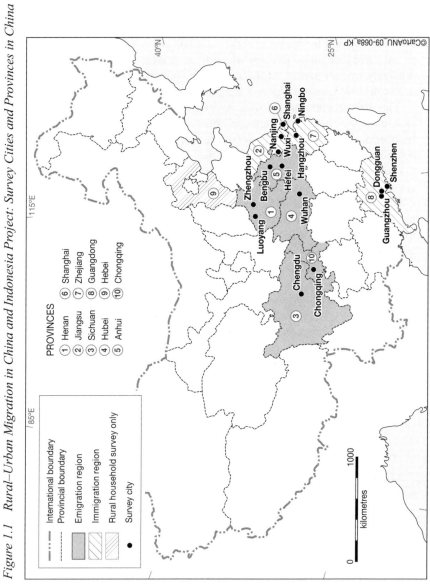

Figure 1.2   Rural–Urban Migration in China and Indonesia Project: Survey Cities and Provinces in Indonesia

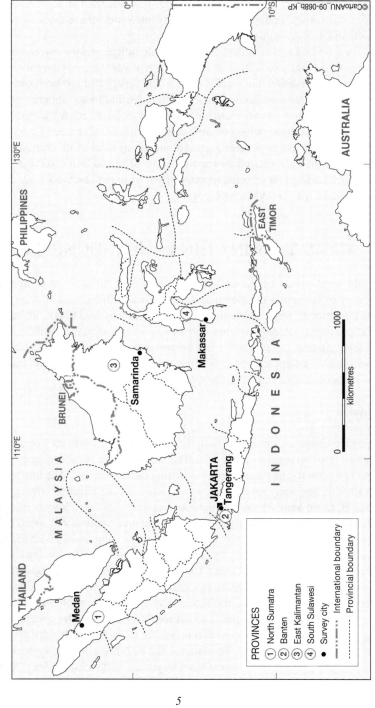

long-term migrant households (those that had migrated five or more years before the survey) and 600 recent migrant households (those that had migrated less than five years ago).

The RUMiCI survey is designed to be longitudinal, and the current plan is to conduct it annually in both countries over a five-year span. At the time of writing (September 2009), the second wave of the survey had just been completed. We hope that the comparative and dynamic methodology underpinning this research will allow us to investigate the important issues related to rural–urban migration and urban socio-economic change from a broader perspective.

This book seeks to present a general picture of rural-to-urban migration in China and Indonesia based on the first wave of the RUMiCI surveys. It also examines findings on selected topics and on the overall methodology adopted to undertake the surveys in each country.

2   MIGRATION IN CHINA AND INDONESIA

While rural–urban migration and urbanization commonly accompany the process of economic development, institutional differences in the regulation and operation of labour markets across countries may lead to considerable differences in the outcomes of rural–urban migration and in the challenges faced by governments in facilitating the urbanization process. It is therefore very important to understand the conditions under which rural-to-urban migration has proceeded in China and Indonesia.

China

After the Chinese Communist Party came to power in 1949, the economy was divided into two separate parts: a rural economy and an urban economy. For the next few decades, this dual-economy setting did not change. The initial reason for the division was closely related to China's industrialization strategy at the time. Because agricultural productivity was very low—too low to sustain the high levels of industrialization in the cities deemed necessary to speed up economic growth—the government tried to keep its rural population on the farms, where the sheer quantity of labour could compensate for the low productivity of agriculture (Perkins and Yusuf 1984). The rural–urban divide was also perpetuated by China's very generous social welfare system. Based on communist ideology, China decided to implement a system of full employment, lifetime employment and cradle-to-grave social welfare. However, the system was too expensive to cover all the population, so the government decided to restrict coverage to urban residents. To maintain the viability of such a system, it was necessary to prevent rural people from migrating to the cities (Meng 2000).

The restrictions on rural–urban migration were implemented through the household registration (*hukou*) system, which obliged individuals to live and work in the areas in which they were born. The cornerstone of the system was the food coupon scheme. During the pre-reform (pre-1978) period, urban residents had to use food coupons to purchase food. The coupons were distributed only to households with an urban *hukou*, and allocated according to the number and age of household members (Meng, Gregory and Wang 2005). Thus, even if they had moved to the cities, rural *hukou* holders would have had no means to survive.

These restrictions persisted for the next 40 years. It was not until the late 1980s and early 1990s, when demand for labour in the cities began to rise and the food coupon scheme was abolished, that the restrictions were gradually eased and the Great Migration began.

In 1978, the Chinese government initiated market-oriented economic reform in rural areas. Agricultural productivity increased considerably, allowing large numbers of rural workers to move out of agriculture. By the mid-1980s, the effects of reform were being felt in the cities. Urban incomes increased, creating demand for various types of services. At the same time, food became more readily available in the cities as agricultural production rose, and individuals were able to buy food products at markets, where food coupons were not required. Despite the restrictions on rural-to-urban migration, many rural *hukou* holders came to the cities to work illegally as domestic servants, labourers and street vendors. City governments periodically evacuated these workers to the countryside, but that did not stop them from returning (Wang and Wang 1995; Xiang 1996; Zhao 2000).

The huge flows of foreign direct investment into China in the early 1990s created further demand for labour, prompting the first large-scale rural-to-urban migrations. Although the government did not formally announce the relaxation of restrictions on rural–urban migration, in practice the controls were gradually eased.

Official statistics on the size of rural-to-urban migration have never been available. However, Zhao (2000) estimates that between 1980 and 1985 around 12 million rural migrants were working in Chinese cities. Based on national survey data from the Ministry of Agriculture, Du (2000) indicates that around 37 million rural workers were working in the cities by 1994. Figures from the World Bank (2009) point to a sharp increase in migration since the late 1990s, to reach around 130 million, or one-third of the urban labour force, by 2005 (see Figure 1.3).

Although rural–urban migration is one of the most important forces driving economic growth and urbanization in China, migrants continue to encounter widespread hostility and discrimination from local governments, employers and urban residents. Until recently, much of this discrimination was institutionalized

*Figure 1.3   China: Estimates of the Number of Rural–Urban Migrants,
            1980–2006*

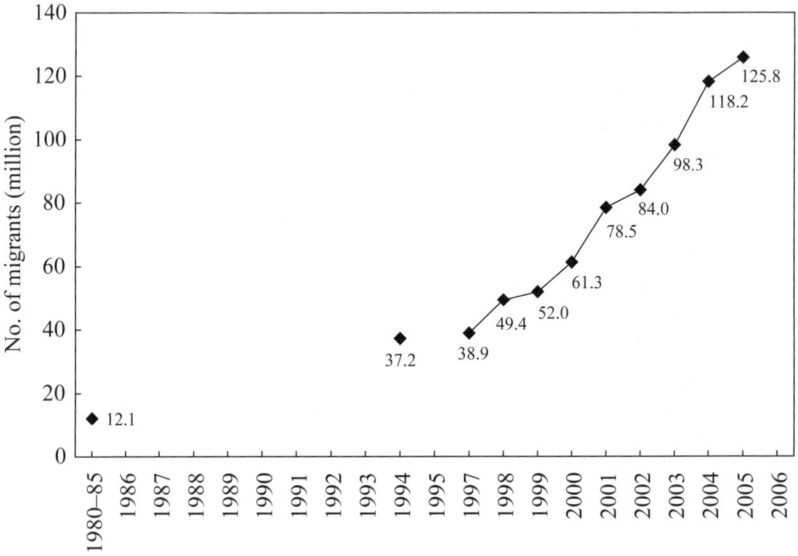

Source: 1980–85: Zhao (2000); 1994: Du (2000); 1996–2005: World Bank (2009).

(Zhao 2000). For example, migrant workers were only allowed to take certain types of jobs—normally the jobs that urban residents were unwilling to do themselves. Even if they were doing the same job as an urban *hukou* holder, they were not entitled to employer contributions to various insurance schemes. If they were sick or injured, they had no health cover. If they lost their jobs, they were not eligible for unemployment benefits. Unlike urban workers, they did not receive housing subsidies or pension contributions. And the children of migrant workers were not allowed to enrol in normal city schools without paying extra fees (West and Zhao 2000; Meng 2000; Meng and Zhang 2001; Du, Gregory and Meng 2006).

The rationale for not providing a social safety net for migrant workers was the view that land already served as a safety net for the rural population. When farmers migrated, their families were permitted to keep their land. If rural–urban migrants lost their jobs, they could always return to the countryside and work on the family farm. Similarly, if they fell ill, they could be cared for by family back in the rural home town, where the cost of living was much lower than in the cities, even though the quality of health care was worse and its cost still substantial (Du, Gregory and Meng 2006).

As a result of these institutional settings, internal rural–urban migration in China has taken place within a guest worker system. Most migrants come to the cities alone, leaving their families behind in the rural village of origin. Migrants do not envisage a future for themselves in the cities. Rather, they hope to earn as much as possible in the city before returning home with a nest egg that will secure their future in the countryside.

In recent years, the central government has introduced new laws and regulations to protect migrants' benefits and increase their access to urban services. These attempts to eliminate discrimination against migrants have had only limited success, however, for both systemic and institutional reasons. Urban stakeholders at every level lack the incentives and resources to treat migrants equally. Local governments, for instance, are evaluated on indicators such as economic growth, city image and the welfare of local constituents, so it is no surprise to find that they are prepared to sacrifice the interests of migrant workers in the process of achieving better performance. Over the years, local governments have repeatedly demolished the shanty towns where migrants live (Wang and Wang 1995; Xiang 1996), tightened employment restrictions on migrant workers when local employment conditions were tough (Zhao 2000) and ignored violations of labour laws by local employers. Employers, in turn, are unlikely to provide the requisite welfare insurance and working conditions for migrants as long as they are able to avoid serious scrutiny from the local government. Often, migrants are paid lower than minimum wages, receive no social security contributions from their employers and work extremely long hours. Urban residents are not usually sympathetic to the plight of migrants either; they see them as their competitors in the labour market, as a drain on local government services—both welfare and infrastructure—and as a source of crime, violence and overcrowding. They regularly call on their local governments to control migration and restrict migrants' access to the urban labour market (Zhao 2000).

The trends and challenges associated with migration have changed dramatically since the RUMiCI project was first envisaged, due to changes in both domestic policies and the international economic environment. In mid-2007, the People's Congress of China passed a new Labour Contract Law, which was implemented at the beginning of 2008. The law required employers to sign permanent contracts (under the same conditions as existing contracts) with all workers who had had one temporary fixed contract or who had been employed by the same employer for 10 years or more. In addition, employers were obliged to inform employees and unions of any lay-off or retrenchment plans at least one month in advance, with those plans to be approved by the local labour bureau. Employers were required to provide severance pay equal to one month's salary per year of employment to workers who were laid off.

Employers viewed these features of the new law as a return to the old 'iron-bowl' system under which wages were guaranteed to meet basic needs regardless of productivity. Labour-intensive manufacturing industries in particular had difficulty complying with the provisions of the new law. In late 2007 and early 2008, many export-oriented enterprises began to retrench large numbers of workers and some closed down. Thus, a policy that had been intended to protect migrant workers in practice turned into a policy that may actually have worsened their employment conditions.

The global financial crisis hit the Chinese exporting industry around this time. The combination of the introduction of the new Labour Contract Law and the financial downturn can be expected to have had a profound effect on the employment prospects and earnings of rural migrants. At the time of writing this chapter, however, the extent of the impact was unclear.[2]

Indonesia

Indonesia's migration has been smaller than China's, but it has nonetheless been substantial. Although the country has some features in common with China as a developing country, it has experienced a very different modern history of rural–urban migration, it has developed very different institutions, and its migration has extended over a longer time period. Apart from the desire to prevent 'overurbanization', successive governments have had no major reason to try and keep rural people in the countryside, and hence have imposed no systematic restrictions on population mobility since relative peace was restored to independent Indonesia in 1949. In any case, the early democratic governments, and even the more autocratic, quasi-military government of Soeharto, did not have the means to control the temporary or permanent migration of rural people to the cities, despite an extensive registration system.

Since independence, the rate of urbanization has been rapid by developing country standards, slowing only slightly in the past 20 years.[3] The urban population comprised approximately 15 per cent of Indonesia's total population of just under 100 million in 1961. It grew less quickly in the early years after independence, and especially in the period of slow economic growth during a good part of the 1960s (Hugo et al. 1987: 89). Urban population growth rates then accelerated to close to 5 per cent per annum—that is, to two to three times the rate of total population growth over the same period—through to the Asian economic crisis.[4] The share of the urban population doubled from just over 20 per cent of the total population in 1980 to 40 per cent in 2005, with the pace of urbanization slowing perceptibly (to a little under 2 per cent per annum) in the most recent period, 2000–05. Over the past 20–30 years, around one-quarter of urban population growth has been due to net migration to the larger cities, much of it from rural areas.[5]

Indonesia's national censuses differentiate between two kinds of migrants: lifetime and recent. Lifetime migrants are those who currently live in a province that is different from the province of birth. Recent migrants are migrants

*Figure 1.4   Indonesia: No. of Recent and Lifetime Migrants, and Migrants
             as a Share of the Total Urban Population, 1980–2005*

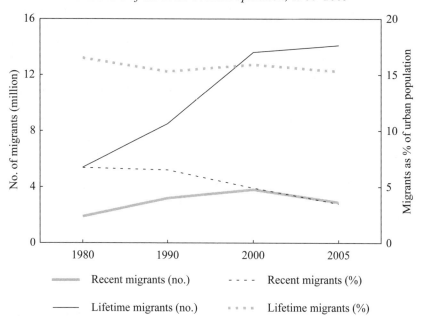

Source: 1980, 1990 and 2000 population censuses; 2005 intercensal population survey.

aged five years and above who reside in a province that is different from the province of residence five years ago. For both definitions, the published data are broken down by current place of residence in an urban or rural area.[6] The national data have historically defined migrants as persons who have moved across a provincial border, thereby missing much of the important intra-provincial movement between the countryside and nearby towns and cities.

Figure 1.4 presents census data on patterns of rural–urban migration in Indonesia over the 25-year period from 1980 to 2005, based on the official definitions given above. Lifetime migrants to urban areas (those people who were born in another province and moved to an urban area) accounted for around 16 per cent of the total urban population in 1980. This share has remained relatively constant, falling slightly in 2005. Recent migrants (those aged five years and above who moved to an urban area during the five years preceding the census) accounted for about 20–30 per cent of all urban migrants, with the share declining from around 1990.

The above figures refer to permanent migrants as defined in the official data. However, in the 1970s and 1980s a large proportion of all rural people working in the major cities were circular migrants whose families lived in the home village or a nearby small town, especially in Java where the majority of the urban population resided. It has been estimated that as much as half of the total working population in urban areas were circular migrants during this early period of accelerated growth (Hugo 1997). This was a time when rural labour supply pressures, together with rapid increases in labour demand and cheaper transport, were leading to large-scale movements of rural workers into the major cities. These circular migrants were typically engaged in wage employ-ment or the informal sector, and returned to their home villages on a monthly, three-monthly or irregular basis depending on economic circumstances.

As the focus of development shifted in the late 1980s and 1990s, a different kind of circular migrant emerged. These were the young, single and increas-ingly better-educated people, many of them women, who had benefited from improved access to schooling during the early years of growth. They became especially visible in the rapidly expanding export-oriented factories found in the major urban conurbations, and commonly returned to their home villages when they married.[7] The economic crisis of 1997–98 marked a turning point for these more educated people, many of whom had little choice but to return to their villages. Unlike their parents, who still had ties with agriculture, they were unable to fit easily back into rural life. Most of them probably drifted back to the cities as the economy underwent a slow but steady recovery over the next decade.[8]

As in other countries, Indonesia's migration has been accompanied by all the attendant opportunities and social and environmental challenges in the cit-ies, and the problems for families left behind. Major cities and urban conur-bations grew rapidly from the 1970s through to the Asian economic crisis. During this period the economy was expanding at 7–8 per cent per annum, initially as a result of the oil boom and later through export-oriented manufac-turing growth.

While Jakarta is by far the largest city, and the extended Jakarta region one of the most rapidly growing, Indonesia has experienced a visible but quite mild problem of urban 'primacy'—mild, that is, compared with some neighbouring countries, such as Thailand and the Philippines. The greater Jakarta region, with its population of around 25 million, accounted for approximately one-quarter of the total urban population in 2005, close to the share recorded in the 1990s (Firman 1997).[9] But migration has spread well beyond Jakarta to other major cities on the island of Java (especially Greater Surabaya in the east and Bandung in the west),[10] as well as the major Outer Island cities of Medan and Palembang in Sumatra, Samarinda in Kalimantan and Makassar in Sulawesi. The populations of these secondary cities expanded from a relatively small base to reach around 1–3 million by 2005, placing strains on urban services similar to those experienced in the larger cities. Three of these large Outer Island cities (Medan, Samarinda and Makassar) were chosen for this study, in addition to Tangerang, a major industrial centre on the outskirts of Jakarta (see Chapter 11 for details).

As noted, the movement of people from rural to urban areas has been a relatively uncontrolled process in Indonesia. Unlike in China, where the restrictions on mobility have been man-made, the main constraints to migration have typically been transport costs associated with poor infrastructure rather than government regulation, especially in the more isolated Outer Island regions. As both living standards and infrastructure improved, migrant flows increased significantly in the more densely populated regions from around the mid-1970s.

Although much easier than in China, movement to the cities has not always been smooth. Migrants moving from one residential address to another (whether from a rural to an urban area or from one urban area to another) are required to register with the local authorities and, if the move is permanent, to register their address on a new identity and family card.[11] Some city authorities have attempted to limit migration from rural areas by banning informal sector activities such as peddling and trishaw driving from the city centre and major highways. Conflicts between the authorities and migrant populations have been most publicized in the case of Jakarta, where successive governors (equivalent to mayors in other cities) have sought to improve the capital's image by removing unsightly and potentially congesting informal sector activities from the main thoroughfares.[12]

Nevertheless, these efforts to limit the spread of the informal sector, and by implication rural–urban migration, have probably had only a marginal effect in slowing the growth of the urban population. The illegal practice of holding multiple identity cards bearing different residential addresses has tended to undermine any controls that city authorities might seek to exert over the movement of people from rural areas. Unlike in China, urban slum areas have been a constant feature of the urban environment over the past half-century, and have increased in absolute size, even if they have spread from the urban centre to the urban periphery over time.[13]

At the same time, the urban informal sector has not always been so visible, or as constraining with regard to modern urban functions and social services, as at the present time. Tensions between the resident urban population and migrants are thus important in present-day Indonesia. Efforts to relocate slum dwellers have been more constrained under the democratic governments elected since 1999 than under the military-backed rule of Soeharto. Although demand for labour in the urban economy has grown less rapidly since the fall of Soeharto, the police and military have proved less able to prevent rural people from setting up stalls and selling their wares on crowded footpaths, contributing to major problems of congestion in the major cities. These stalls often compete directly with the formal sector shops and other services operated by long-term urban residents.

3 OUTLINE OF THE BOOK

The book is separated into two parts: the first on China and the second on Indonesia. The chapters in each section examine several important issues related to rural–urban migration in the respective countries.

China

The book contains six chapters examining rural–urban migration in China. The issues they investigate include who migrates and why, how migrants fare in the urban labour market, the effect of rural–urban migration on the education and health of the children of migrants and whether rural–urban migration contributes to poverty alleviation in rural areas. The final chapter in this section of the book is devoted entirely to the sampling methodology and survey details of the China component of the RUMiCI project. Below we outline the main issues raised in these chapters.

Although rural-to-urban migration has contributed significantly to Chinese economic growth in recent years, very little is known about why people do or do not migrate and to what extent government restrictions prevent rural workers from moving to the cities. Leng Lee and Xin Meng examine these two interrelated questions in Chapter 2. They find that in 2007, the year in which the number of migrants to cities reached its peak (around 135 million), only 22 per cent of the rural labour force had migrated. The analysis reveals that, while pure monetary push and pull factors form part of the reason for rural people to consider migration, these are much less important than family-related factors such as marriage, childbearing and the need to look after elderly household members. The results suggest that the special social service and welfare arrangements applying to migrants play an important role in discouraging migration among certain groups of rural people.

In Chapter 3, Paul Frijters, Leng Lee and Xin Meng look at the working conditions and remuneration of migrant workers versus incumbent urban residents in the urban labour market. They find that, on average, migrant wage and salary workers work 58 hours per week, or 35 per cent more hours than their urban counterparts. The average hourly compensation of an urban worker is more than double that of a rural migrant worker. Only 20 per cent or so of migrant workers benefit from the various insurance schemes—known as 'Five Insurances, One Fund'—provided for workers, whereas the ratio for urban workers is above 60 per cent. Around half of the hourly compensation difference between migrant and urban workers cannot be explained by differences in education, work experience or any of the other observable characteristics that are commonly used to explain wage differentials. The implication of this finding is that, even in 2008, migrant workers were still experiencing discrimination in the urban labour market.

The analysis presented in Chapter 3 also reveals strong differences between cities. In Wuxi and Bengbu, for example, total compensation is roughly the same for migrants as for the equivalent urban city dweller with the same characteristics. Yet in Shenzhen, Guangzhou, Shanghai and Dongguan, a migrant is paid less than half the equivalent urban city dweller. This suggests that some cities compete for migrants whilst others do not. It also suggests that there are many city dwellers who would be better off if they moved to another city.

Because there have been no previous household surveys of rural–urban migrants based on a randomly selected sample, to date studies of urban earnings inequality have never included migrant workers. Chapter 4 fills this gap in the literature. The authors, Deng Quheng and Li Shi, study the effect on wage inequality of including migrant workers in the urban labour market. They find that wage inequality is higher among urban workers than among rural migrant workers. The Gini coefficient of monthly and hourly earnings is 0.38 and 0.39 respectively for urban workers, but 0.29 and 0.31 for rural migrant workers—a 10 percentage point difference.

The inclusion of migrant workers in the urban labour force does little to monthly wage inequality but slightly increases hourly wage inequality. The more equal distribution of hours worked by urban workers, and the large variation in hours worked by migrant workers, may be the main reason for this discrepancy. Regional variations in earnings play a very important role in explaining wage inequality between migrant and urban workers.

The effect of rural–urban migration on the children of migrants is of interest to both academics and policy makers, not only because these children will be vital to social stability, but more importantly because they will play a crucial part in China's future economic and social performance. Sherry Tao Kong and Xin Meng inspect the effect of migration on the educational and health outcomes of migrants' children in Chapter 5. They find that left-behind and migrated children are less likely to have very good school performance relative to rural non-migrant children and urban children respectively. They also find that the long-term health of left-behind and migrated children, as measured by their height, is worse than that of rural non-migrant children and urban children respectively.

Based on the Rural Household Survey sample, in Chapter 6 Chuliang Luo and Ximing Yue evaluate the effect of rural–urban migration on poverty by estimating poverty indices as a function of many factors, including migration. The results suggest that migration plays an important role in alleviating poverty among rural households. On average, a household with one or more migrant members is around 31–46 per cent less likely to be poor. The length of time a migrant works in the destination city is also significant in reducing poverty among family members left behind in the rural village.

In Chapter 7, Sherry Tao Kong explains the sample and survey design for the data collected in China. The chapter highlights the innovative listing and sampling strategy developed by the RUMiCI project to address the lack of information on the distribution of the migrant population. This design provides a scientifically based sampling frame for random and representative sample selection.

Indonesia

What do the papers included in this volume tell us about rural–urban migration and migrants in Indonesia? Like the chapters in the first section of the book, the four chapters in the second section of the book focus on the differences between migrants and non-migrants. But the chapters on Indonesia also pay close attention to the duration of migration and the contrasts between recent and longer-term migrants. This topic is especially relevant in the case of Indonesia, because of its longer experience with rural–urban migration and because of the relatively unconstrained nature of mass migration to the cities in Indonesia. The topics covered include the characteristics of migrants and non-migrants; contrasts in perceptions, incomes and health outcomes; differences in occupation and earnings; and finally, the methodology employed in the Indonesian part of the study.

Three main themes stand out. First, it is clear that migrants fare no worse, and often fare better, than non-migrants in the four cities studied. Migrants record better results than non-migrants in relation to participation in formal sector occupations, wages and household incomes, and health. For example, longer-term migrants to the four Indonesian cities have done well compared with both non-migrants and recent migrants in terms of income and earnings, although the health and poverty status of recent migrants is as good as, or superior to, that of both longer-term migrants and non-migrants.

Second, although recent migrants are paid lower wages than longer-term migrants and non-migrants, they earn quite high household incomes and record lower incidences of poverty, partly because they are younger and have few dependants. Their health outcomes also tend to be superior to those of longer-term migrants and non-migrants. We are not certain whether the higher wages of longer-term migrants is a cohort effect or simply an outcome of the relative inexperience of younger labour market participants. Anecdotal evidence suggests a combination of both.

And third, location appears to be important for migration outcomes. Residence in the rapidly growing towns of Tangerang and Samarinda is important for relative incomes among recent migrants but much less so among long-term migrants. Employment outcomes appear to be superior among those who have settled in the more established cities of Medan and Makassar.

In Chapter 8, Tadjuddin Noer Effendi, Mujiyani, Fina Itriyati, Danang Arif Darmawan and Derajad S. Widhyharto describe the socio-demographic and employment characteristics of recent migrants, long-term migrants and non-migrants in the four Indonesian cities. They draw attention to the younger age of recent migrants, their better school performance and the significant share of females in this group. Poverty rates are also lower among recent migrants, although their housing conditions are worse. On the basis of the many similarities between longer-term migrants and non-migrants, the authors conclude that there appear to be quite high levels of social and economic mobility in the cities surveyed. At the same time, they draw attention to the dynamic growth in the newer cities of Tangerang and Samarinda, which has given recent migrants an edge in the urban labour market. In contrast, recent migrants have not always fared so well in the more established cities of Medan and Makassar, where urban growth has been more influenced by their administrative functions as regional capitals.

In Chapter 9, Budy P. Resosudarmo, Asep Suryahadi, Raden M. Purnagunawan, Athia Yumna and Asri Yusrina pose the provocative question: 'Do rural–urban migrants make it in the city?' Their answer is very much in the affirmative, especially among longer-term migrants who are able to invest in themselves and their children. But although migrants feel they have succeeded relative to the people in the rural communities they have left behind, they do not feel they have made it compared with non-migrants in the cities, even though their incomes are higher. Perhaps this is because of the greater (perceived?) wealth among the latter group. And perhaps it is because migrants are less optimistic, because they have had to work doubly hard to make it in the city. In contrast to the findings on wages and incomes, recent migrants report better levels of health than the lifetime migrant and non-migrant groups. The single marital status of many recent migrants may contribute to this result: a significant number are dependent students.

Armida Alisjahbana and Chris Manning take a close look at employment patterns and wages among migrants and non-migrants in Chapter 10. They, too, ask whether migrants make it in the city, but they place greater emphasis on the differences between recent and longer-term migrants than those between migrants and non-migrants. They find that long-term migrants in particular perform significantly better than non-migrants in terms of earnings. Especially for males, this difference is almost entirely explained by differences in human capital, employment and location. Higher levels of participation in the formal sector and in small business reward long-term migrants, again mainly among males, suggesting that productivity and job quality are important, although these effects are not well captured in the regression. Two other important findings are the higher earnings of long-term compared with recent migrants, reflecting the rewards for experience (among males) and age (among both males and females). Unlike in China, gender differentials in earnings are small among all groups, after taking a range of explanatory variables into account.

In general, the findings confirm our hypothesis that a relatively unconstrained migration process (as in Indonesia) brings greater gains to migrants relative to non-migrants than a highly controlled migration process (as in China).

The final chapter, by Budy P. Resosudarmo, Chikako Yamauchi and Tadjuddin Noer Effendi, describes the methodology employed in the Indonesian study. The 2007 National Socio-Economic Survey proved a valuable starting point for the implementation of a census in randomly selected census blocks in the four Indonesian cities, and the subsequent survey. The experience with sampling design and implementation provides insights into some of the pitfalls associated with trying to develop a set of quite sophisticated sampling procedures. This is especially true when enumerators may not stick to a sometimes difficult set of instructions on the substitution of new households for households in the original sample that had dropped out for various reasons.

CONCLUSION

The RUMiCI project and the chapters in this book have been inspired by the Great Migration that gathered pace in China towards the end of the twentieth century, and the smaller yet very substantial migration that has occurred in Indonesia over a longer period of time. In China, this massive movement of people has taken place under institutional arrangements that are very different to those in many other countries—including Indonesia—where there are less imposing barriers to the longer-term relocation of rural people to urban areas. In both countries, migration is connected with very high rates of economic growth. In China, it has been underpinned by extraordinarily high economic growth rates by world standards over a compressed time period. Indonesia's smaller yet still very substantial migration has been driven by a similar, if less dramatic, process of economic growth for most of the past half-century, though to a lesser extent over the past decade.

The chapters in this book allow us to see some of the striking differences and similarities between the two countries, and to test some of the conventional beliefs about rural–urban migration. Although migrants have benefited from the creation of new jobs in both countries, we find that the social and economic gap between the migrant and urban populations is much wider in China than in Indonesia.

Some of the differences between the two countries are explained by the cross-sectional analysis and models described in this book. The longitudinal study of households that we are undertaking in both countries, repeated annually through to 2012, should shed light on other differences. For instance, one important topic to be covered in future rounds of the surveys is the impact of the world economic crisis on the jobs and welfare of urban and rural households, both migrant and non-migrant.

We hope that the chapters in this book will provide important baseline findings for investigation of many other analytical and policy-related issues in the years to come, in addition to providing original data and the methodology to analyse these problems.

NOTES

1   The 1980 figure for China is from the 1989 *China Statistical Yearbook*; the 2005 figure is calculated from the 2005 intercensal population survey. The data for Indonesia are from the 1980 population census and the 2005 intercensal population survey.
2   The second round of the survey, conducted in March–July 2009, should shed considerable light on the impact of the global financial crisis on the employment situation for migrants and non-migrants.
3   In estimating the size of the urban population outside the areas officially classified as cities (*kota*), Statistics Indonesia considers a range of criteria, such as the share of population outside agriculture, the share with access to electricity and the presence of modern markets, high schools, health facilities and the like. The numbers are revised every 10 years when Indonesia undertakes its national population census, and re-estimated five years later when it undertakes its intercensal survey. The latest census was in 2000; the most recent intercensal survey was in 2005.
4   See especially Hugo (1997), Firman (1997) and Firman, Kombaitan and Pradono (2007). For a discussion of population and internal migration trends, see Muhidin (2002).
5   The reclassification of areas from rural to urban has also been a major source of urban population growth, probably accounting for at least another quarter of the total growth in the officially defined urban population in major cities. The balance is due to natural increase. See Gardiner (1997: 125) for an analysis of the period 1980–90.
6   There are no published data on the urban versus rural origins of migrants. In 2005, 67 per cent of lifetime migrants residing in urban areas were born in rural areas. By comparison, 61 per cent of recent migrants residing in towns and cities in 2005 had moved from rural areas to urban locations in the five years from 2000 to 2005. The census definition of rural residence differs from that adopted in this study, which is based on a 'socialization' concept of rural origins (see Chapter 11 for details).
7   See Chapter 8 for more details on patterns of circular migration in Indonesia.
8   Particularly in manufacturing, modern-sector employment growth has not recovered since the 1997–98 crisis. Hence, in the post-crisis period fewer jobs have been available for younger job seekers from rural areas (Manning 2008).
9   When Indonesia proclaimed its independence from the Dutch in 1945, its largest city, Jakarta, supported a population of less than 1 million (Abeyasekere 1987: 141). Other major cities were much smaller. Medan, the largest Outer Island city to be included in our survey, is now home to 2 million people, but in 1945 it is estimated to have had a population of just 80,000 (Widodo, n.d.).
10 Greater Surabaya, the second-largest urban conurbation in Indonesia, has some similarities with Jakarta. It embraces several neighbouring cities in addition to the core city of Surabaya and had a total population of around 5 million in 2005.
11 For a discussion of these procedures, see especially Hugo (1978) and Abeyasekere (1987).
12 The best known case was the dismal failure of the popular (and otherwise very successful) governor Ali Sadikin to limit the movement of migrants into Jakarta in the early 1970s by declaring it a closed city.
13 Part of this movement has been spontaneous in response to rising land prices and demand for space in the city centre, and part has occurred as a result of conscious public policy to clear the city centre of slums, especially in major cities like Jakarta. See, for example, Jellinek's (1991) study of the relocation of one urban community from Central Jakarta in the 1970s and 1980s.

PART I

CHINA

2 Why Don't More Chinese Migrate from the Countryside? Institutional Constraints and the Migration Decision

Leng Lee and Xin Meng

1 INTRODUCTION

Over the past 20 years or so, China has enjoyed unprecedented economic growth. Rural-to-urban migration has played an important role in this process. Currently, about 120–150 million rural migrant workers are employed in the cities, and it is widely accepted that an additional 150 million rural residents will join them over the next couple of decades. If China is the world's factory, then migrants have clearly been the factory hands manning the factory floor. As well as dominating manufacturing, migrants are heavily represented in the mining, retail and construction industries. The migration process has not only helped the Chinese economy develop quickly and cheaply, but has also benefited the migrants themselves. Our research indicates that, on average, migrants are able to make more money in the cities than they would be able to in the countryside. Anecdotal evidence suggests that many migrants return to their rural villages after working for a few years in the cities, well set up for the future.

Yet despite the scale and evident importance of rural–urban migration, our understanding of the migration process, and of the characteristics of China's 150 million migrants, is limited, primarily due to the lack of quality data. The Rural–Urban Migration in China and Indonesia (RUMiCI) project aims to remedy this. Analysis of the data collected through the first wave of the RUMiCI surveys in 2008 provides an opportunity to better understand this understudied demographic, and to help the government formulate sound policies to facilitate the migration process.

In this chapter, we examine two questions: what sort of people migrate from rural areas, and why many of their contemporaries choose not to migrate. If we accept that migration is good both for the Chinese economy and for migrant workers themselves, then the answers to these questions become both academically important and relevant to policy making. Understanding what prevents people from moving to the cities may guide policies to facilitate higher levels of migration if this is considered desirable.

The chapter is structured as follows. Section 2 provides some background on the institutional setting in which rural–urban migration occurs and reviews important aspects of the existing literature. Section 3 describes the data and section 4 outlines the summary statistics. Section 5 examines the determinants of migration and section 6 looks at the effect of institutional constraints. In the final section, we offer some concluding comments.

2   BACKGROUND AND LITERATURE

The sheer scale of rural–urban migration is not the only unusual feature of China's internal migration system; the country is also atypical in having adopted a 'guest worker' system for its own rural citizens working in urban areas (Roberts 1997; Solinger 1999; Meng 2000). There is a long history of rural and urban dwellers being treated differently in China, especially since the establishment of the People's Republic of China in 1949. Studies often explain this dichotomy in two ways. First, in the early 1950s China was unable to produce sufficient quantities of grain to feed the entire population, or to implement market policies to increase output. There was therefore an incentive for the government to prevent rural–urban migration, in order to increase production in the rural sector and reduce demand in the cities (Perkins and Yusuf 1984). Second, full employment, lifetime employment and a subsidized social welfare system were recognized as the basic elements of a socialist economy, but were too costly to be extended to the entire Chinese population (Meng 2000).

Despite the large numbers of migrants currently working in the cities, and the significant contribution they make to economic growth, rural–urban migrants must register as temporary residents in the cities and are denied access to many of the social benefits available to their urban counterparts. There is no social safety net for migrants, they do not have equal access to health care facilities and pension rights, and their children do not have the same access to schools as their urban peers. These institutional restrictions are likely to have a significant effect on the migration decisions of individuals. Because of the difficulty of gaining access to social services and welfare, for example, migrants often leave their families behind when they move to the cities to work. Consequently, women and other family members with greater family responsibilities may be less likely to migrate. Similarly, people with health problems and those who would have difficulty finding a job may choose either not to migrate or to return to the rural village, because they cannot obtain health services or unemployment benefits in the city.

One strand of the economic literature on migration takes a predominantly atomistic approach to the analysis of migration decision making. On the basis that migration is a form of investment in human capital, these works employ empirical methods and models centred on individual decision making.[1] Harris and Todaro (1970) and Fields (1982) find that the two most important factors in the decision to migrate are the income differential between the source and the destination region and the interaction of these income differences with age, gender and education. Kennan and Walker (2003) also approach the migration decision as an individual optimization problem in their research on the effect on migration of wage differentials in a range of destinations.

An alternative approach is to argue that migration should be considered a family decision. Such studies tend to find that a family's decision to relocate is related to the employment and earnings prospects of the parents and factors that affect their children's schooling. Within the United States, for example, Mincer (1978) finds that families with school-aged children are less likely to migrate to another state. However, Zahniser (1999) finds that marriage and the presence of young children do not affect the decisions of Mexican families contemplating a move to the United States.

Another group of studies focuses on migration as a means to spread income risk. Stark and Levhari (1982), for instance, argue that risk aversion and a desire to diversify family income are strong drivers of migration for small farming families in less developed countries. Rosenzweig and Stark (1989) provide some empirical support for this thesis, showing that, in India, migration for the purpose of marriage significantly reduces the variability of household food consumption—that is, that migration successfully mitigates risk.

Existing studies of migration decision making in China largely follow the path of explaining rural–urban migration in terms of economic factors at the individual level. Hare (1999), Zhao (1999a) and Zhu (2002) find that stronger demand for labour in the agricultural sector reduces the probability of migration, while a widening of the rural–urban wage gap increases it. In general, the authors find that young, single, male workers from families with a higher number of working-aged members and a lower per capita land endowment are more likely to migrate. On the whole education does not play a significant role, although Zhao (1999a) finds that junior high school graduates in Sichuan are marginally more likely to migrate than primary school graduates, and both groups are more likely to migrate than senior high school graduates.

A number of studies consider household and community characteristics when analysing the migration decision-making process in China. A model developed by Hare (1999) includes the following household characteristics: the ratio of female workers to total household members; the ratio of male workers to total household members; per capita production assets; and per capita land allocation. Community characteristics are captured by dummy variables for various townships. Zhao (1999a) looks at the number of preschool-aged children in the family but finds that it is not significant in the decision to migrate. She suggests that this may reflect the continuing Chinese tradition of grandparents helping to raise the children. Zhao (2003) examines the role of migration networks within the community in six Chinese provinces, finding that they have a positive and significant effect on the decision to migrate. In contrast to the individual approach to migration, Zhao (1999b) develops a model in which migration is a family decision to explain why more Chinese do not migrate.

While these findings are important, they do not examine the particular institutional settings that constrain the migration decisions of families in China. One exception is a study by Giles and Mu (2007), which finds that the unavailability of health care, the lack of pension rights and the poor health of dependent parents all reduce the probability of rural residents migrating to the city.

In this chapter, we are interested in looking at the interaction between China's internal guest worker system and the migration decision. To this end, we focus on the extent to which age, marital status, health and the presence of young children or elderly parents affect the migration decision. By estimating the marginal effects such household characteristics have in tying people to the countryside, we seek to estimate how much greater the probability of migration would be if the current institutional constraints were lifted.

3   DATA

This study is based on data from surveys conducted across China in 2008 as part of the RUMiCI project. Here, we rely mainly on data from the Rural Household Survey, complemented at times by data from the Urban Migrant Survey.[2] The Rural Household Survey sample comprises 8,000 households (31,781 individuals) living in rural areas; the Urban Migrant Survey sample comprises 5,000 households (8,446 individuals) registered in a rural area but living in an urban area.

It is important to note that the two samples are completely independent, that is, that there is no direct link between the rural-to-urban migrants sampled for the Urban Migrant Survey and the rural residents sampled for the Rural Household Survey.[3] However, because anyone registered in a rural area under the household registration (*hukou*) system would be part of the Rural Household Survey's sampling frame, and because sampling is random, the Rural Household Survey includes households both with and without migrant members. For migrants and other household members not present at the time of survey, we accepted information provided by the household head or that person's spouse. This allowed us to gather valuable information on individuals who had migrated to the city, and to compare this group with those who had not.

The Urban Migrant Survey, on the other hand, was restricted to rural *hukou* holders who had migrated to the city, and their households. To gauge the effect of the decision to migrate, we also requested limited information on family members who were not living with the migrant at the time, including that person's spouse, children and parents. Pulling these different strands together should provide us with a more complete picture of rural–urban migration in China.

4 SUMMARY STATISTICS BY MIGRATION STATUS

In this section, we use Rural Household Survey data to examine the characteristics of rural residents who have migrated to the city. Table 2.1 summarizes the characteristics of rural households with and without migrants. Of the 8,000 rural households in the sample, 38 per cent had at least one member who had migrated to a city (including a county-level city) to work in 2007. To be counted as a migrant, a person had to have moved to a city for the purpose of work and stayed away for at least three months. Of the households with a migrant member, 38 per cent contain three or more generations, compared with 24 per cent for households without a migrant member. This may be related to the fact that migrants often move to the city alone, leaving their children in the countryside to be cared for by other household members. Thus, a possible precondition for migration among individuals with children is to have the right household composition, that is, to live with parents or other relatives who can look after the children.

As a consequence of having more generations in the household, migrant families are, on aggregate, larger than families without migrants (4.5 household members compared with 3.7) and have more members in the labour force (3.4 compared with 2.5). This suggests that these households have enough family members to both farm the land and export surplus labour to the city. Among households with migrants, the average number of household members living in the rural village is 2.8, compared with 3.7 for households without migrants. Of the 3,015 households with migrants, 52.4 per cent have one migrant member and 47.6 per cent have two or more.

Of the 4,221 households with children aged 0–16, 1,666 households (39.5 per cent) have at least one parent who has migrated. Both parents have migrated in 511 (about one-third) of these 1,666 households. Households with migrant members have a higher proportion of children aged 0–16 (55.3 per cent) than

Table 2.1   China: Summary Statistics of Rural Household Characteristics

	Total Sample	Households with Migrants	Households without Migrants
No. of households	8,000	3,015	4,985
% of households with and without migrants		37.7	62.3
No. of generations in the household (%)			
1	11.53	0.93	17.93
2	59.27	61.09	58.18
3+	29.03	37.91	23.67
Other combination household	0.16	0.07	0.22
No. of household members	3.98	4.49	3.67
No. of household members in labour force	2.85	3.42	2.51
No. of household members living in the rural village	3.22	2.79	3.67
No. of migrants in the household (%)			
0	62.3		100.0
1	19.8	52.4	
2	13.2	34.9	
3+	4.7	12.7	
No. of households with children aged 0–16	4,221	1,666	2,555
No. of households with two migrant parents		511	
% of households with two migrant parents		30.7	
No. of children in household aged 0–16 (%)			
0	47.2	44.7	48.8
1	35.4	38.3	33.6
2	14.9	14.7	15.0
3+	2.5	2.3	2.6
% of households with elderly persons aged 70+			
No elderly persons aged 70+	88.5	89.8	87.7
At least one elderly person aged 70+	11.5	10.2	12.3
Annual household income per capita of rural household members (yuan)	8,876	10,013	8,189
Annual household expenditure per capita of rural household members (yuan)	7,535	8,314	7,064
Housing area per capita of households (m^2)	49.5	57.6	44.6

Source: Rural Household Survey, 2008.

Table 2.2   China: Characteristics of Individuals in Rural Households

	Total Sample	Total Labour Force	Migrated in 2007	Migrated but Not in 2007	Never Migrated
Age	35.98	41.02	28.95	37.40	45.49
% male	51.87	51.51	62.98	64.64	44.99
% married	62.02	81.69	55.60	80.05	89.01
No. of children ever born	1.60	1.59	0.76	1.36	1.90
Years of schooling	7.05	7.29	8.63	7.94	6.73
% sat university entry exam	3.72	4.84	7.05	5.98	3.91
% never had any training	61.11	77.94	64.66	73.19	83.03
% self-reported as healthy or very healthy	78.49	78.19	89.68	82.21	73.80
% sick in previous three months	8.90	8.50	3.15	8.77	10.06
No. of years since first migration					
1–5			50.42	36.17	
6–9			31.75	25.46	
10–14			9.78	12.97	
15+			6.44	23.18	
Other			1.61	2.22	
No. of observations	31,781	21,628	4,283	3,193	14,152
% of total labour force		100.00	19.81	14.76	65.43

Source: Rural Household Survey, 2008.

households without migrant members (51.2 per cent). However, they have a slightly lower proportion of elderly members aged 70 or above.

Finally, Table 2.1 indicates that, per capita, households with migrant members have higher annual incomes, higher annual expenditures and more living space than non-migrant households. This suggests that they are better off, possibly because they are receiving remittances from relatives who are working in the cities.

Table 2.2 summarizes the characteristics of individuals in five samples: the total sample; those defined as being in the labour force; and three subsamples of the labour force (individuals who were migrants in 2007, those who had been migrants but were not migrants in 2007, and those who had never migrated). Of the 31,781 individuals in the total sample, 21,628 (72 per cent) were defined as being in the labour force, that is, aged 16–65 and not currently at school or disabled. Of those, 19.8 per cent had migrated in 2007, 14.8 per cent had migrated previously and the remaining 65.4 per cent had never migrated. In other words, a high proportion of the rural population has never migrated.

The average age of the 2007 migrants is 29.0 years—much younger than that of previous migrants (37.4 years) and those who have never migrated (45.5 years). Over 60 per cent of migrants (both current and previous) are male, compared with just 45 per cent of those who have never migrated.

Figure 2.1 shows the distribution of males and females in each of the three subsamples by age. It indicates that more than 50 per cent of the 2007 male migrants migrated to the city between the ages of 20 and 31, with the highest proportion (66 per cent) migrating at age 23. After age 31, the proportion declines significantly and those who have never migrated become the dominant group. By age 43, less than 15 per cent of the 2007 male migrants are still working in the cities. Female migrants in 2007 move to the city at much younger ages. The proportion peaks at ages 18–20 and drops below 50 per cent at age 21. By age 26, the proportion of those who have never migrated overtakes those who have migrated to become the dominant group.

These patterns are closely related to family formation and childbearing. Without access to publicly assisted childcare services, migrant women simply cannot afford to have their children cared for in the cities. It is therefore mainly young single women who migrate to the cities to make money before returning to their rural hometowns to marry. After marrying and having children, most do not leave home again. Men, on the other hand, are not as constrained by family responsibilities and tend to stay in the cities for longer.

The types of jobs available to migrants in the cities may also contribute to the age and gender patters of migration. Because city labour markets discriminate against migrants, only a limited range of jobs is available to them. Migrant women work mainly in manufacturing, particularly textiles and electronics, where young, energetic women are in demand. Older migrant women are restricted to domestic and other service industries where there is limited demand. Men, on the other hand, can continue to work in construction and other physically demanding industries until their productivity begins to decline, usually in their late thirties.

Turning to marriage and fertility, we find that the 2007 migrants are far less likely to be married than either previous migrants or those who have never migrated, and that they have fewer children (Table 2.2). On average, 55.6 per cent of current migrants are married, and they have 0.8 children. In contrast, nearly all (89.0 per cent) of those who have never migrated are married, and, on average, they have 1.9 children.

Figure 2.2 plots the number of children ever born to females aged 20–60 (and a subgroup aged 20–35) by age and migration status. It shows that, at every age, non-migrants have given birth to slightly more children than their migrant counterparts. Looking at the female demographic most likely to migrate, those

Figure 2.1   China: Proportion of Male and Female Rural Residents by Age and Migration Status

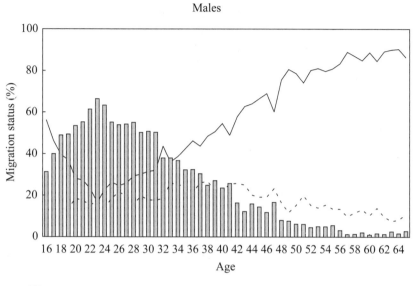

Males

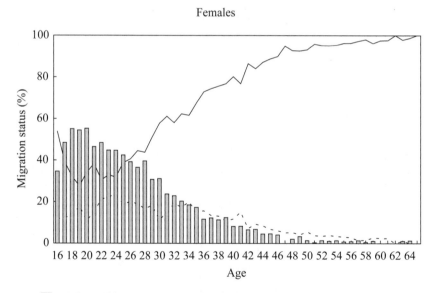

Females

Source: Rural Household Survey, 2008.

*Figure 2.2   China: Mean Number of Children Ever Born to Rural Women
          by Age and Migration Status*

Women aged 20–60

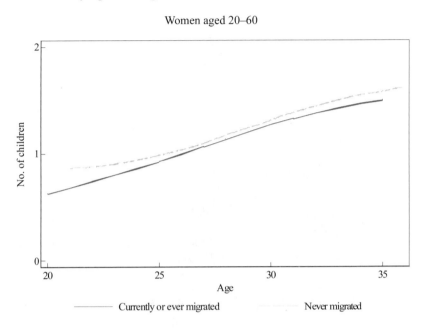

Women aged 20–35

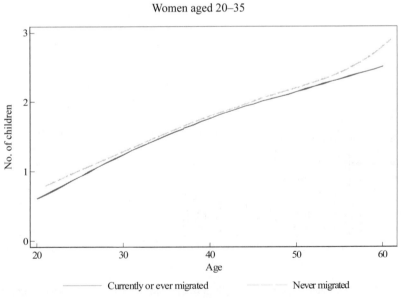

Source: Rural Household Survey, 2008.

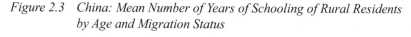

Figure 2.3   China: Mean Number of Years of Schooling of Rural Residents by Age and Migration Status

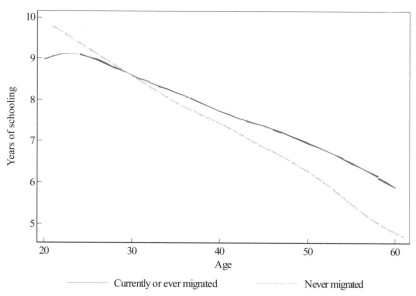

Source: Rural Household Survey, 2008.

aged 20–35, we find that the average difference between the two groups is only 0.1. However, this unconditional correlation cannot tell us whether migration really has such a small effect on childbearing activity.

The best educated groups are current migrants, with an average of 8.6 years of schooling, and former migrants, with an average of 7.9 years (Table 2.2). Those who have never migrated have the least education, 6.7 years, or almost two years less than the current migrants. The former two groups also have a higher proportion of post-school training.

The finding that migrants have higher levels of education than non-migrants is consistent with the migration decision literature for China.[4] However, if we examine years of schooling by age and migration status (Figure 2.3), we find that, up until age 30, those who have never migrated actually have more years of schooling than those who have migrated. Moreover, the younger the age group, the greater the gap. The average gap in schooling between migrants and non-migrants aged 27 years and below is 0.27 years. This difference is statistically significant—and worrying. It indicates that migration may prevent families from investing in their children's high school education, or that it raises the children's opportunity cost of schooling.[5] This finding is consistent with that of de Brauw and Giles (2006).

Table 2.2 also shows that both groups of migrants are healthier than those who have never migrated, based on their own assessments of their health, and have a lower proportion of members who have been sick in the previous three months.

Finally, Table 2.2 presents data on the year in which current and previous migrants first migrated. Around half of the former group first migrated between one and five years ago, and another 30 per cent between six and nine years ago. The data collected for the Rural Household Survey do not tell us anything about the duration of the first or subsequent migrations, but the Urban Migrant Survey does shed some light on this. Respondents to the Urban Migrant Survey were asked to report the first year of migration and whether there had been any interruptions since then of three months or more. Of the 6,677 rural–urban migrants aged 16–65 currently in the labour force, 5,571 reported no interruptions. The average duration of migration was 7.3 years: eight years among men and 6.2 years among women.

To find out more about the 60 per cent of the rural labour force that has never migrated, in the Rural Household Survey we asked this group of individuals directly why they did not migrate. We gave them six choices, including 'too old to migrate', 'worried I may not be able to find a job' and 'need to look after elderly household members or young children'. As shown in Table 2.3, the main reason given by women is the need to look after elderly parents or young children (35.8 per cent), while the main reason among men is that they are too old to migrate (29.8 per cent). Many men are also worried that they will not be able to find a job (23.3 per cent), and many women think they are too old to migrate (24.1 per cent). While the average age of those who believe they are too old to migrate is relatively high (55 for women and 56 for men), when we look at the actual age distributions of those who say they are too old to migrate (Figure 2.4), we find that a significant proportion of the women were 45–55 years of age at the time of the survey, and would have been even younger (35–40) at the time the first large-scale migrations to the cities began 10 years earlier.

When those who had never migrated were asked whether they planned to migrate in the near future, more than 89.0 per cent of men and 92.0 per cent of women said that they did not (Table 2.3). We also asked migrants who had retuned home for a period of more than three months why they had done so. A majority of both males and females answered that they needed to look after the family farm or some other business. In addition, a sizeable proportion of women indicated that they had returned to look after children.

The above descriptive statistics reveal some of the associations between migration status and household or individual characteristics. These unconditional associations suggest that the patterns of rural-to-urban migration in China are driven not just by the usual factors, but by an additional set of factors

Table 2.3   China: Reasons for the Decision Not to Migrate or to Return Home

	Share (%)		Mean Age	
	Males	Females	Males	Females
Why did you decide not to migrate?				
Too old	29.76	24.13	56.25	54.71
Sick or disabled	2.84	3.21	47.64	48.39
Worried would not find job	23.28	17.69	39.81	38.85
Need to look after children or elderly	15.93	35.75	45.40	42.98
Need to look after business	12.74	7.31	43.01	42.13
Other	15.45	11.92	41.73	40.35
No. of observations	6,271	7,581	6,271	7,581
Do you plan to migrate in the near future?				
Within a month	0.88	0.41	36.40	33.57
In the next half-year	0.83	0.84	32.15	38.24
In the next year	0.75	0.74	35.86	36.63
Not sure	8.49	5.93	37.26	36.48
No	89.04	92.07	47.73	45.60
No. of observations	6,241	7,532	6,241	7,532
The last time you returned home for three months or more, why did you return?				
I was sick	2.69	2.81	41.98	34.07
Family member was sick	2.52	2.13	38.40	35.12
To look after children	5.07	15.31	35.48	32.66
To look after the family farm or another business	42.03	30.25	39.85	34.66
Did not like city life or work	5.34	5.31	34.73	29.64
Marriage related	5.45	6.63	30.98	27.49
Unemployed and could not find job	4.03	3.25	34.45	27.53
Other	32.87	34.32	33.15	28.20
No. of observations	2,900	1,600	2,900	1,600

Source: Rural Household Survey, 2008; Urban Migrant Survey, 2008.

Figure 2.4　China: Distribution of Rural Residents Who Indicated They Were Too Old to Migrate by Age and Gender

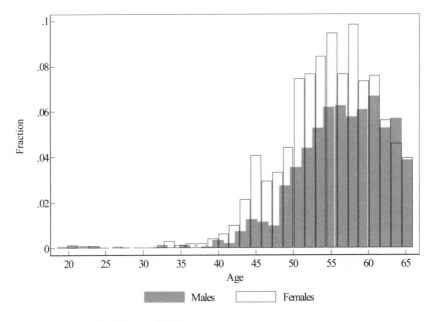

Source: Rural Household Survey, 2008.

related to the country's guest worker system. In particular, marriage, childbearing, the need to care for elderly household members and the need to look after the family agricultural business seem to have discouraged many people from migrating.

5　THE MIGRATION DECISION: REGRESSION ANALYSIS

The previous section examined the unconditional correlations between migration and individual or household characteristics. In this section, we pull all the pieces together and estimate a regression that can tell us something about the conditional correlations between the migration decision and individual or household characteristics.

We specify the estimation equation as follows:

$$M_i = \alpha + X'\beta + Z'\delta + \lambda(\ln W_i^M - \ln W_i^R) + v_j + \varepsilon_i \qquad (2.1)$$

where M_i is a binary variable indicating whether an individual migrated in 2007; X is a vector of individual characteristics including age, marital status, gender, self-assessed health and education; and Z is a vector of household characteristics.

To capture, to some extent, individuals' family responsibilities, we included the following variables: the number of household members in the labour force; household type (dummy for the number of generations in a household); the number of children ever born to an individual; the presence of children in different age groups (0–4, 5–9 and 10–15); the presence of elderly household members aged 70 or above; and the birth order of the individual. To capture the net effect of economic push and pull factors, $\ln W_i^M - \ln W_i^R$ is the difference in earnings between being a migrant and staying in a rural village, where W_i^M is an individual's actual or potential earnings as a migrant in the city and W_i^R is an individual's actual or potential earnings in the countryside. To capture the level of economic development in the village, the distance of the village from the nearest city and any other village-level fixed effect that might affect an individual's migration decision, we included a village-level fixed effects variable, v_j.[6]

There are some problems with the earnings variables, W_i^M and W_i^R. We can only observe one of the variables for a particular individual: for a migrant, the only available variable is W_i^M, and for a non-migrant, the only available variable is W_i^R. In addition, because most rural jobs are on the family farm, it is not straightforward to observe the earnings of rural households. In this study, therefore, we use per capita household income for non-migrant families as a proxy for rural earnings, W_i^R.

To solve the problem of unobserved earnings/per capita income, we first estimate the following earnings/per capita income equations:

$$\ln W_i^M = \theta X_i + P_j + \varepsilon_i \tag{2.2}$$

$$\ln W_i^R = \eta X_i + v_j + u_i \tag{2.3}$$

where P is the regional dummy variable for the province of origin and the other variables are the same as indicated previously. Equation (2.2) is estimated using wage and salary earners in the Urban Migrant Survey sample, and equation (2.3) is estimated using non-migrants in the Rural Household Survey sample. Both equations are estimated for the total sample as well as for males and females separately. The results are quite reasonable: age has an inverse-U-shaped relationship with the dependent variable; rates of return to education are higher for the migrant sample; and tall people earn more (see Table A2.1 in the appendix). The estimated coefficients are then used to predict $\widehat{W_i^M}$ or $\widehat{W_i^R}$ for individuals for whom we do not observe either of the two income variables. These variables are then substituted into equation (2.1).

Equation (2.1) is estimated using a linear probability model and the results are reported in Table 2.4. As expected, the earnings differential is positively related to the probability of migration; that is, any individual who can earn more in the city than they could in the countryside is more likely to migrate. Age has a negative effect on the probability of migration for both men and women. For females, however, the quadratic term is positive and significant. Using these estimated coefficients, we predict the effect of age on the probability of migration for both males and females, holding other variables constant (see Figure 2.5). For women, the probability drops below 20 per cent after age 26; for men, it does not fall below 20 per cent until they turn 40. In the pooled equation, this differential effect is represented by the positive coefficient for the male dummy variable, which suggests that men are more likely to migrate than women.

We find that better-educated people are more likely to migrate. This effect is stronger for females than for males, perhaps because women need to be particularly motivated to leave their families and children and migrate. We conjecture that the education variable may, to some extent, capture the unobserved drive and ambition of individuals.

Health is positively associated with migration. As discussed earlier, migrants do not have access to public health care in the cities, so unhealthy people are less likely to migrate and those who fall ill while working in the cities are more likely to return to their rural villages. Indeed, the summary statistics presented in Table 2.2 indicate that the proportion of migrants (ever migrated) that had been sick in the three months before the survey is two and a half times greater than the proportion for current migrants (8.8 per cent versus 3.2 per cent). The separate regressions for males and females indicate that the health effect is stronger for men than for women. This may be related to the different types of jobs that men and women perform in the cities, with men more likely to take up jobs that require greater physical strength.

Turning to household characteristics, we find that individuals from large households with more members in the labour force are more likely to migrate. This may be related to the landholding system in China. Until recently land trading was not allowed in China; also, rural households still have to pay land taxes even if they migrate. This system induces rural households to keep some household members at home to look after the family farm, so that it is only large families with spare labour over and above their agricultural requirements that can afford to allow family members to migrate.

Marriage is negatively and significantly related to migration, especially for women. However, the causality may go both ways: married individuals are less likely to migrate, but migration may also prevent or delay marriage. Fertility (the number of children ever born) is negatively related to migration, with the magnitude of the effect similar for men and women. More importantly, women

Table 2.4   China: Regression Results for the Migration Decisions of Rural Residents by Gender

	Total	Males	Females
Earnings differential (ln W^M – ln W^R)	0.017	0.014	0.012
	(0.004)***	(0.006)**	(0.005)**
Age	–0.017	–0.013	–0.024
	(0.002)***	(0.002)***	(0.002)***
Age^2/100	0.008	0.001	0.018
	(0.002)***	(0.003)	(0.002)***
Years of schooling	0.002	0.002	0.003
	(0.001)**	(0.001)*	(0.001)***
Being healthy	0.023	0.034	0.013
	(0.006)***	(0.009)***	(0.008)*
Dummy for male	0.080		
	(0.005)***		
No. of household members in labour force	0.027	0.021	0.032
	(0.003)***	(0.004)***	(0.004)***
Married	–0.068	–0.026	–0.099
	(0.009)***	(0.014)*	(0.012)***
No. of children ever born	–0.019	–0.020	–0.020
	(0.003)***	(0.005)***	(0.004)***
No. of children aged 0–4	–0.032	–0.015	–0.047
	(0.006)***	(0.010)	(0.008)***
No. of children aged 5–9	0.002	0.003	0.004
	(0.006)	(0.009)	(0.008)
No. of children aged 10–16	–0.001	–0.001	–0.001
	(0.004)	(0.007)	(0.005)
Birth order	–0.003	–0.006	0.000
	(0.002)*	(0.003)**	(0.002)
No. of elderly aged 70+	–0.036	–0.045	–0.021
	(0.008)***	(0.012)***	(0.011)**
Two-generation household	–0.091	–0.079	–0.092
	(0.011)***	(0.016)***	(0.014)***
Three-generation household	–0.036	–0.024	–0.045
	(0.013)***	(0.020)	(0.016)***
Four-generation household	–0.010	0.023	–0.047
	(0.024)	(0.036)	(0.031)
Other household type	–0.081	–0.106	0.008
	(0.062)	(0.090)	(0.084)
Village dummy variables	Yes	Yes	Yes
No. of observations	21,628	11,142	10,486
R^2	0.36	0.37	0.37

* = significant at 10 per cent; ** = significant at 5 per cent; *** = significant at 1 per cent. Standard errors are in parentheses.

Source: Rural Household Survey, 2008; Urban Migrant Survey, 2008.

Figure 2.5　China: Predicted Probability of Migration by Age and Gender

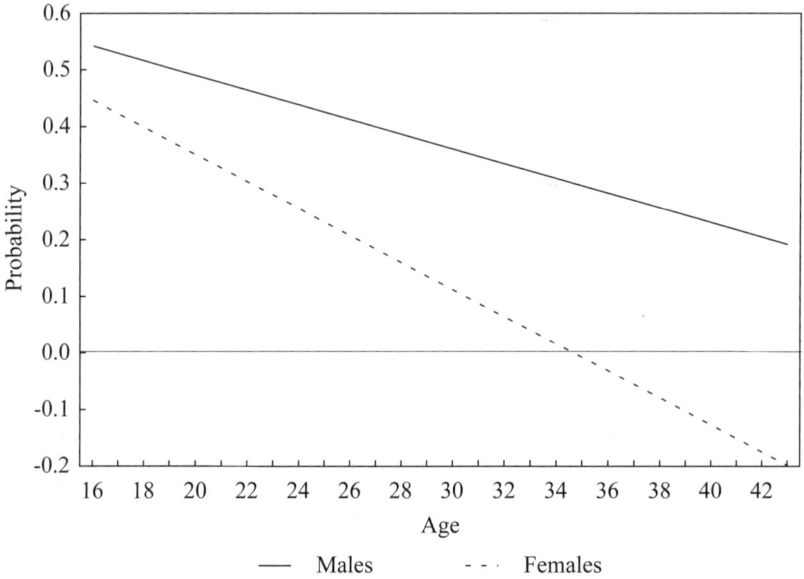

Source: Rural Household Survey, 2008.

with children aged 0–4 are less likely to migrate, with every additional child aged 0–4 years reducing the probability of a woman migrating by 5 per cent, over and above the effect of the total number of children on the probability of migration. This downward effect on the probability of female migration is nearly four times that of a 1 per cent change in the wage differential. Moreover, such an effect is not found for men: men with children aged 0–4 years are *not* less likely to migrate.

If we were estimating a labour force participation equation, this finding would not be regarded as significant, because women (but not men) with young children are less likely to participate in the labour market anywhere in the world. The difference here is that we are modelling a migration decision. In this context the finding *is* significant, because it indicates that the temporary nature of rural–urban migration and the lack of access to public services in the cities are splitting families, with many rural children aged 0–4 years growing up without the presence of a father.

Another interesting finding is that individuals from households that include an elderly person aged 70 or above are less likely to migrate. The effect is larger for men than for women, perhaps because, in rural China, it is sons rather than daughters that normally shoulder the responsibility for the care of ageing parents.

Finally, relative to a single-generation family, individuals from two-generation households have the lowest probability of migrating. Once again this suggests the importance of childcare responsibilities. Single-generation households do not have children to care for or other family responsibilities, and households with three or more generations have grandparents or other relatives who can look after the children while the parents are working in the cities. But workers from two-generation households have either children to look after with no assistance from grandparents or an ageing parent to care for. This makes it more difficult for them to migrate.

6 THE EFFECT OF INSTITUTIONAL CONSTRAINTS

The above analysis indicates that many of the variables affecting the migration decision may be policy induced. If migrant workers were given equal access to public services in the city, factors such as gender, marriage, age and the presence of young children or elderly household members might well exhibit a very different effect on the migration decision. In the United States, for example, Mincer (1978) finds that marriage has no effect on interstate migration; nor does the presence of school-aged children. On the other hand, he finds that family ties decrease the probability of migration, while we find that, in China, the presence of three or more generations in a household *increases* the migration probability. Stark (1991: 156) shows that age has a positive effect on both interstate migration within the United States and migration from Mexico to the United States, although the squared term has a small negative effect. This is very different from the situation in China, again suggesting the existence of institutional differences between countries.

Some might argue that many of the findings that we tie to institutional differences are similar to those obtained for other developing countries,[7] even though these countries place very few official restrictions on migrants' access to social services. This does not necessarily detract from our argument, however. Although most developing countries do not discriminate against rural–urban migrants by denying them access to social services and welfare, the level of such services and welfare for workers in the urban informal sector, where most migrants work, are often very low or nonexistent (ILO 2000; Fraser 2008). Thus, in effect, they face virtually the same restrictions as Chinese migrant workers.

Roberts (1997) finds that the migration decisions of Mexican illegal immigrants to the United States (who do not receive social services and welfare) are similar to those of rural–urban migrants in China. This lends further support to the idea that institutional restrictions on access to social services are reflected in the pattern of migration decision making.

To gauge the extent to which restrictions on access to social services act as a deterrent to migration, we consider two extreme scenarios. In the first scenario, we assume a change in official policy on migrants' access to social welfare such that there is no longer any effect of marriage status, the presence of young children or elderly, and household type on the migration decision. That is, we predict the probability of migration assuming the effect of these variables to be zero. Although this is undoubtedly based on a very strong assumption, it is nevertheless a valuable exercise, as the predicted probability gives us a theoretical upper bound for the effect of restrictions on the probability of migration.

In the second scenario, we assume that anyone who lives within one hour of the nearest county town and is currently working in that town is not constrained by restrictions on access to social services.[8] This group should represent people who have migrated in order to work but face low barriers in accessing essential social services. To compare this group with a base group of individuals who live in the same village but have not migrated, we estimate equation (2.1) with the dependent variable being whether the individual works in a nearby town. The results from this regression should tell us the extent to which the individual and household characteristics included in equation (2.1) affect individuals' migration decisions in a situation where there are minimum barriers to accessing social services. We find that the family-related variables that were formerly statistically significant determinants of migration, such as age, marriage and the presence of young children and elderly (see Table 2.4), are no longer statistically significant for this group.[9] We then use the estimated coefficients from this regression to predict the probability of migration for everyone in the sample. This may serve as another measure of the effect restrictions on access to social services has on the probability of migration.

Table 2.5 presents the actual and predicted probabilities for both scenarios, for the total sample and for the male and female samples. For the total sample, we observe that the actual probability of migration is 20 per cent. If we make the strong assumption from scenario 1 that the above-mentioned family-related variables have no effect, the predicted probability of migration increases to 36 per cent, a 45 per cent increase. The results from scenario 2 show that if we assume that everyone lives within one hour of the nearest town (and so is not subject to social service constraints), the predicted probability of migration rises from 20 per cent to 31 per cent, a 36 per cent increase. The effect of removing the barriers to social services is much stronger for females than males under the first scenario (a 56.5 per cent increase in the migration probability for women compared with a 31.7 per cent increase for men). The effect of removing the barriers under the second scenario does not differ much between men and women (a 31.3 per cent increase in the migration probability

Table 2.5 China: Predicted Effect of Policy Change on Migration Probability by Age Group

	Total Sample		Aged 16–25		Aged 26–35		Aged 36–45		Aged 46+	
	Migration Probability	Increase in Probability (%)	Migration Probability	Increase in Probability (%)	Migration Probability	Increase in Probability (%)	Migration Probability	Increase in Probability (%)	Migration Probability	Increase in Probability (%)
Scenario 1										
Total (actual)	0.20		0.51		0.35		0.15		0.03	
Total (predicted)	0.36	44.69	0.61	16.47	0.50	30.12	0.33	54.29	0.21	83.33
Males (actual)	0.24		0.55		0.42		0.22		0.05	
Males (predicted)	0.35	31.72	0.63	12.48	0.52	17.92	0.35	36.78	0.18	69.61
Females (actual)	0.15		0.48		0.26		0.09		0.01	
Females (predicted)	0.35	56.59	0.60	19.97	0.45	43.76	0.30	71.91	0.23	93.68
Scenario 2										
Total (actual)	0.20		0.51		0.35		0.15		0.03	
Total (predicted)	0.31	36.01	0.38	–33.20	0.39	11.01	0.32	52.40	0.24	85.23
Males (actual)	0.24		0.55		0.42		0.22		0.05	
Males (predicted)	0.39	38.05	0.38	–45.45	0.43	2.18	0.42	47.26	0.36	84.84
Females (actual)	0.15		0.48		0.26		0.09		0.01	
Females (predicted)	0.22	31.34	0.44	–8.38	0.37	31.07	0.19	55.06	0.08	81.92

Source: Rural Household Survey, 2008.

for women compared with a 38.0 per cent increase for men). This is mainly because females shoulder a higher share of family responsibilities. To induce a similar level of increase in the migration probability for women, the monetary difference between urban and rural earnings would have to be 15 times larger than it is currently.

When we split the sample into age groups, we find that the effect is larger among the older age groups. For example, for females aged 26–35, a change in family migration policy increases the migration rate by 31 per cent (to 44 per cent), but the same policy change increases the migration rate for females aged 36–45 by 55 per cent (to 72 per cent). Of course, as indicated above, these predicted effects are based on a strong assumption, so it is possible that they overstate the gains from a change in policy.

7   CONCLUSION

In this chapter, we have looked at the characteristics of those who migrate from the countryside to the city and why more rural people do not migrate. Our data show that, in 2007, about 19.8 per cent of the total rural labour force was working in the city. Most of these workers were young women aged 18–25 and relatively young men aged 18–35. On average, the migrants were better educated than those who did not migrate, but among those aged 30 and under, the reverse was the case. Migrants were less likely to be married and they were less likely to have children.

While monetary factors are part of the reason for rural people to consider migrating, these are far less important than family-related factors such as marriage, childbearing and the need to look after elderly household members. Our results suggest that the lack of social services and welfare for migrants in the cities interacts with family characteristics (especially the number and age of dependants) to play an important role in discouraging migration among certain groups of rural residents.

ACKNOWLEDGMENTS

We would like to thank the Australian Research Council, the Australian Agency for International Development (AusAID) and the Ford Foundation for their financial support.

NOTES

1   For a review, see Lucas (1997) and Yap (1977).
2   Chapter 7 of this book gives an overview of the three surveys conducted in China for the RUMiCI project: the Rural Household Survey, the Urban Household Survey and the Urban Migrant Survey. It also describes, in detail, the design and methodology underpinning the last of these. A range of background material, including the questionnaire for the Urban Migrant Survey, can be found at http://rumici.anu.edu.au.
3   Ideally, we would have linked Urban Migrant Survey respondents to their rural household of origin, but this would have been prohibitively expensive. As a compromise, we included households both with and without migrants in the Rural Household Survey, and collected some information on household members living in the countryside from Urban Migrant Survey respondents.
4   See, for example, Zhao (1999a), Hare (1999), Zhu (2002) and Giles and Mu (2007).
5   An alternative possibility is that those who are more highly educated migrate later. However, when we examine the data, we find that those who migrate at younger ages have higher levels of schooling (see Figure A2.1 in the appendix).
6   We acknowledge that many of the variables in equation (2.1), such as health, marriage and fertility, may be endogenous. However, in this study we do not claim that any estimated relationship is causal.
7   See, for example, Garip's (2006) study of the migration decision in Thailand.
8   Note that the choice of one hour is arbitrary. The reason for choosing this cut-off point is that one hour seems a reasonable time to allow for the daily trip to and from work, and at the same time gives us a large enough sample to estimate the equation.
9   Due to space constraints, we are not able to present the results here, but they are available from the authors upon request.

Table A2.1   China: Results of the Earnings/per Capita Income Equations

	Rural Income		Migrant Urban Earnings	
	Males	Females	Males	Females
Age	0.016	0.024	0.078	0.038
	(0.004)***	(0.004)***	(0.004)***	(0.006)***
Age^2/100	−0.015	−0.023	−0.107	−0.056
	(0.005)***	(0.005)***	(0.006)***	(0.009)***
Years of schooling	0.024	0.019	0.027	0.037
	(0.003)***	(0.003)***	(0.003)***	(0.004)***
Being healthy	0.036	0.011	−0.02	−0.001
	(0.021)*	(0.021)	(0.021)	(0.023)
Height	0.005	0.005	0.001	0.007
	(0.001)***	(0.002)***	(0.000)	(0.002)***
Regional dummies	Yes	Yes	Yes	Yes
No. of observations	6,213	5,964	3,051	1,968
R^2	0.34	0.33	0.18	0.17

* = significant at 10 per cent; ** = significant at 5 per cent; *** = significant at 1 per cent. Standard errors are in parentheses.

Source: Rural Household Survey, 2008; Urban Migrant Survey, 2008.

Figure A2.1   China: Years of Schooling by Age at First Migration

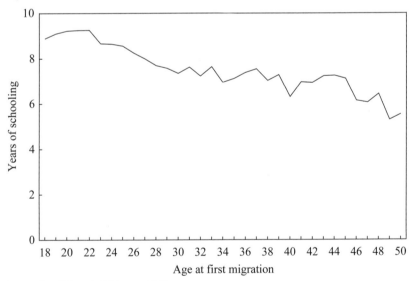

Source: Rural Household Survey, 2008.

3 Jobs, Working Hours and Remuneration Packages for Migrant and Urban Workers

Paul Frijters, Leng Lee and Xin Meng

1 INTRODUCTION

China is currently undergoing a transformation from an agricultural society to a modern society dominated by industry and services. By 2006, roughly 130 million of China's 900 million rural workers had shifted from the countryside to the city (NBS 2007). In some cities, rural-to-urban migrant workers already account for half, or even two-thirds, of the total labour force. How do these migrant workers fare in city labour markets relative to their urban counterparts? Are they competing in the same labour market? These are important policy issues, as well as being of academic interest.

In the past, migrant workers faced discrimination with regard to the types of jobs they were allowed to take and the compensation packages they received (Meng and Zhang 2001). The Chinese government has moved to eliminate such discrimination but is facing resistance from local governments and employers. Local governments are expected to protect the employment and earnings of local people—not migrants. To achieve this goal, they may introduce measures that make it more difficult for migrant workers to compete with the local workforce, or at least put migrants in a position where they have limited power to bargain for better conditions. The main priority of employers, meanwhile, is to minimize labour costs. As long as they are able to avoid serious scrutiny from the local government, they may underpay migrants, fail to make mandatory contributions on their behalf or force them to work long hours.

This chapter documents labour market characteristics and remuneration packages in China, with particular attention to labour market outcomes for migrants compared with urban *hukou* holders (those with official permission to live in the city). The main distinguishing feature of this analysis is that it attempts to systematically capture the importance of non-wage components in

total remuneration, by measuring and pricing the value of pensions, unemployment insurance, health insurance and other forms of in-kind income. The focus
on cross-city differences is another new aspect of this study, made possible by
the exceptionally wide coverage of the data.

The next section provides background information on Chinese labour
market regulations and the official welfare schemes for workers. Section 3
describes the most important aspects of the data and presents descriptive statistics on the labour market performance of migrant versus urban workers. The
fourth section looks in more depth at how migrants perform in the urban labour
market. Our conclusions are presented in section 5.

2   BACKGROUND

The historical segregation of the rural and urban labour markets in China has
had long-lasting effects on rural-to-urban migration. Because rural dwellers
were officially prohibited from moving to the city, and were denied social
welfare if they did, it was 'natural' to treat them as guest workers. As long
as the constituency of city governments was restricted to urban *hukou* holders, local governments saw their chief mandate as being to promote local economic growth and protect the jobs and earnings of locals. As a result, rural
migrants often faced restrictions on the types of jobs they were allowed to take,
with little central or local government scrutiny of their working conditions.
Public service positions and jobs in state-owned enterprises were—and often
still are—restricted to urban *hukou* holders. This forced migrant workers into
lower-paid jobs with harsher conditions and longer working hours.

China has made huge strides towards eliminating open discrimination
against rural–urban migrants. In 1995 the National People's Congress approved
a comprehensive set of labour market reforms, including a host of regulations
on job discrimination, working hours, wages, social insurance, worker safety,
labour disputes and labour contracts. In 2007 it passed the Labour Contract
Law, to be implemented in January 2008. While similar in scope to the 1995
law, the new law expanded the types of allowable labour contracts from one to
three, mandated written contracts for full-time workers and included additional
stipulations regarding the content of a contract. Importantly, the 2008 Labour
Contract Law required information on social insurance to be included in all
written contracts.

Officially, all workers now have equal access to jobs, welfare and an array
of basic labour market protections. Employers are required to pay a minimum
wage and are prohibited from making employees work unreasonably long
hours. They are also required to make welfare payments on behalf of all their
workers.

Despite the obvious importance of such legislation, however, China's welfare system is still embryonic, and local authorities retain considerable power. In 2004, for example, the Ministry of Labour and Social Security (now the Ministry of Human Resources and Social Security) announced China's first minimum wage,[1] but it proved to be more akin to an outline of the criteria provinces, municipalities and autonomous regions should consider when determining minimum wages rather than an actual minimum wage pronouncement as such. China is no different to many nations in allowing regional variations in work standards, wages and benefits to operate within a national framework. However, unlike the national governments of most of these nations, the Chinese government has not been able to enforce the basic labour market protections it provides for the benefit of all employees. In particular, our data indicate that many migrants are not receiving the centrally mandated insurance contributions from their employers.

Under the Chinese welfare system, both employers and employees are supposed to make contributions to unemployment, pension, health and work injury insurance, and to a housing fund. Known as 'Five Insurances, One Fund', these contributions are placed in the individual accounts of employees. The level of the contribution differs from region to region but would account for a large proportion of labour costs in any region. The extent to which employers comply with labour-protective laws and regulations, however, depends to a large extent on the level of scrutiny imposed on them by city governments. Given the high cost of these contributions to employers and the importance of economic growth to cities, very often city governments choose not to enforce the central government's labour market regulations.[2] Our chapter provides recent information on this subject.

Migrants, too, have little incentive to care about benefits they are unlikely ever to be in a position to claim—because they will simply not be allowed to stay in a city long enough to enjoy any pension or unemployment benefit connected to their working life. The Ministry of Human Resources and Social Security has considered reforming the system to allow itinerant workers to transfer their pension rights, but nothing concrete has eventuated so far.[3] At present, it can be assumed that migrants mainly care about their cash earnings and take-home pay.

In addition to cash and insurance payments, in-kind benefits are included in the compensation packages of both urban and migrant workers. The types of in-kind benefits received, however, differ between the two groups. For migrant workers, in-kind benefits usually take the form of meals and accommodation. For urban workers, the most common in-kind payments are foodstuffs (eggs, rice, tea) and shopping gift vouchers. Clearly meals and accommodation are more attractive to temporary residents, although urban single workers would find them useful as well.

3 DATA AND SUMMARY STATISTICS

We use data from the 2008 Urban Household Survey and Urban Migrant Survey to examine differences in types of jobs, working hours and remuneration packages between migrant workers and urban *hukou* holders.[4]

Table 3.1 presents summary statistics on the total labour force aged 16–65 (not currently at school or disabled) and wage and salary earners aged 16–50 reporting non-zero earnings.[5] The data for the total labour force show that, on average, urban workers are 11.5 years older than their migrant counterparts. The urban labour force contains fewer male workers and more married workers. In addition, urban workers have 1–1.5 more years of education and are 18 per cent more likely to have taken a university entrance exam. Among those who have taken such an exam, urban workers receive a 30–60 per cent higher average score than migrant workers.

There are big differences in the employment rates of the two groups. On average, 69 per cent of urban workers, but 91 per cent of migrant workers, are currently employed. More migrants are self-employed: 22 per cent compared with 5 per cent for urban workers. The determining factor here may be the lack of welfare benefits for migrant workers, which increases the urgency to work. In this sense, migrants are a self-selecting group: if they cannot support themselves through work, they will not migrate.

If we turn our attention to wage and salary earners aged 16–50, we find that the age gap between migrant and urban workers falls from 12 to eight years and the difference in the probability of having taken a university entrance exam increases from 18 to 30 per cent. In other respects, the differences between the two samples remain much the same.

Table 3.1 also describes wage and salary earners' working hours, occupations and job tenures. On average, migrant wage and salary earners work 35 per cent more hours per week than their urban counterparts. They mainly work in either trade/services or manual labouring jobs. The majority of urban workers, meanwhile, are professionals or clerks. Migrants have shorter job tenures than urban workers: most have worked in their current job for only three years, compared with 11 years for urban workers.

Table 3.2 reports summary statistics related to the three components of a remuneration package: insurance payments; wages/salary; and in-kind payments. The first panel shows that roughly 20 per cent of migrant workers have unemployment, pension, health, injury or maternity insurance, compared with 50–70 per cent for urban workers. This stark contrast indicates that many migrants are not receiving their correct welfare entitlements.

It is important to note, however, that these differences do not hold for all cities. In Wuxi, for instance, unemployment, pension and health insurance contributions are made on behalf of 60, 61 and 58 per cent of migrants

Table 3.1   China: Summary Statistics for Total Labour Force and Wage/Salary Earners

	Urban Workers			Migrant Workers		
	Total	Males	Females	Total	Males	Females
Total labour force						
Age	43.14	43.23	43.06	31.49	31.79	31.08
Dummy for male	0.49			0.57		
Dummy for married	0.85	0.84	0.86	0.64	0.61	0.67
Dummy for never married	0.11	0.14	0.09	0.34	0.37	0.31
Years of schooling	10.10	10.27	9.95	9.05	9.22	8.81
Dummy for sat university entrance exam	0.29	0.32	0.27	0.11	0.12	0.09
Exam scores	315.21	326.42	302.81	221.84	245.99	188.94
Dummy for healthy	0.69	0.71	0.66	0.84	0.85	0.83
Height (cm)	166.08	172.03	160.45	165.91	170.10	160.32
Dummy for employed	0.69	0.80	0.58	0.91	0.97	0.84
Dummy for self-employed	0.05	0.07	0.04	0.22	0.23	0.20
No. of observations	9,628	4,678	4,950	7,279	4,164	3,115
Wage/salary earners						
Age	36.49	36.75	36.21	28.73	29.09	28.20
Dummy for male	0.51			0.60		
Dummy for married	0.80	0.78	0.82	0.52	0.51	0.54
Dummy for never married	0.17	0.20	0.14	0.46	0.48	0.44
Years of schooling	10.63	10.69	10.57	9.45	9.53	9.32
Dummy for sat university entrance exam	0.42	0.44	0.40	0.13	0.13	0.11
Exam scores	354.19	366.09	340.47	267.95	279.18	250.18
Dummy for healthy	0.78	0.80	0.77	0.86	0.86	0.85
Height (cm)	166.62	172.36	160.58	166.38	170.51	160.27
Hours worked per week	43.40	44.11	42.66	58.38	59.15	57.22
Current job experience	10.96	11.83	10.04	3.01	3.46	2.56
Occupation						
Manager	6.16	8.21	4.01	1.82	2.05	1.49
Professional	24.28	26.67	21.75	1.06	0.59	1.75
Clerk	25.62	23.53	27.82	5.92	4.26	8.38
Wholesale/retail trade & services	20.38	15.11	25.93	52.59	46.15	62.13
Production worker	15.95	19.08	12.66	38.3	46.64	25.95
Other	7.61	7.39	7.84	0.31	0.31	0.31
No. of observations	4,776	2,451	2,325	4,841	2,890	1,951

Source: Urban Household Survey, 2008; Urban Migrant Survey, 2008.

Table 3.2   China: Summary Statistics for Workers' Remuneration Packages

	Urban Workers			Migrant Workers		
	Total	Males	Females	Total	Males	Females
Insurance						
% of workers receiving insurance						
Unemployment insurance	60.43	61.89	58.88	14.63	14.57	14.71
Pension insurance	72.99	73.40	72.56	21.65	23.25	19.27
Health insurance	71.57	72.95	70.11	11.26	12.08	10.05
Work injury insurance	54.29	56.87	51.57	21.83	24.01	18.61
Maternity insurance	19.07		39.18	2.40		5.95
Housing fund	51.42	55.57	47.05	8.68	9.03	8.15
Value of insurance (yuan)						
Unemployment insurance	333	381	284	54	56	51
Pension insurance	4,283	4,840	3,696	807	912	653
Health insurance	1,754	1,988	1,508	198	225	158
Work injury insurance	101	119	82	44	52	33
Maternity insurance	32	0	65	4	0	9
Housing fund	1,029	1,209	838	127	140	107
Total per year	**7,532**	**8,537**	**6,473**	**1,235**	**1,385**	**1,012**
Wages & total compensation						
Wages (yuan)						
Annual earnings	27,309	31,315	23,086	17,198	18,671	15,015
Hourly earnings	13.23	15.21	11.14	6.06	6.50	5.41
Total compensation (yuan)						
Total annual compensation	34,841	39,852	29,558	18,432	20,056	16,027
Total hourly compensation	16.87	19.31	14.29	6.56	7.05	5.83
In-kind compensation or subsidy						
% of workers receiving meals						
1 meal				16.63	15.99	17.58
2 meals				27.51	29.24	24.96
3 meals				20.53	19.17	22.55
No meals but meal subsidy				6.24	7.06	5.02
Nothing				29.08	28.55	29.88
Total per year (yuan)	**728**	**817**	**635**	**1,847**	**1,877**	**1,802**
% of workers receiving housing						
Housing in-kind				57.45	63.36	48.69
Housing subsidy				6.01	5.22	7.18
Nothing				36.54	31.42	44.13
Total per year (yuan)	**108**	**122**	**93**	**774**	**866**	**637**

Source: Urban Household Survey, 2008; Urban Migrant Survey, 2008.

respectively—not so different from the incidence for urban *hukou* holders of 72, 78 and 81 per cent respectively. But in Shanghai, a mere 120 kilometres away, the situation is completely different: only 4, 6 and 7 per cent of migrants receive unemployment, pension and health insurance contributions respectively, compared with 85, 90 and 71 per cent of urban workers. This suggests that there are big differences between cities in enforcement practices.

To compute the value of welfare contributions, we combined information self-reported by respondents on employer contributions to each of the six funds with information disseminated by each city on the level of compulsory employer contributions. Employers are supposed to contribute a base amount for each employee plus a percentage of the employee's wages. Both the base amount and the percentage are determined independently by each city government. Most governments stipulate an upper and lower limit for the base amount, thereby creating a minimum and maximum amount that firms must contribute.

Although the rules for calculating employer contributions differ between cities, most city governments adopt one of two approaches. The first is to require firms to pay a mandated proportion of their total wage bill for a particular type of insurance, with each worker 'receiving' the total amount divided by the number of workers in the firm. The overwhelming majority of cities adopt this method for all five insurance schemes. The alternative model is for each firm to pay a percentage of each worker's wage from the previous year into the various funds. Nearly every city uses this method to determine employer contributions to the housing fund, and Dongguan, Ningbo and Shanghai favour this approach for all five insurance schemes.[6]

As a rule of thumb, employers are required to contribute, as a percentage of a worker's wages, 20 per cent for pensions, 1 per cent for injury insurance, 8 per cent for medical insurance, 2 per cent for unemployment insurance, less than 1 per cent for maternity insurance and 5 per cent for the housing fund. Hence, the average worker who is fully insured would obtain non-wage monetary rights worth around 35 per cent of his or her wages, mainly in the form of a pension.

For each city we collected information on the mandatory level of employer contributions. Where there were a range of rates and no means of determining which rate an employer would use, we assumed that the employer contributed at the minimum rate. In the case of workplace injury insurance, however, we *were* able to determine the appropriate rate despite the range of possible contribution rates, because the rates were industry-specific and we knew the industry in which each worker in the sample worked. The basic wage upon which the value of insurance was calculated was bounded between 1,000 and 10,000 yuan per month.

We valued employer contributions equally with actual wages on the assumption that the cost of insurance to employers translates into an equivalent expected benefit to employees. We did not count employees' own contributions, because we regard this as simply a shift between take-home wages and future drawing rights when an employee retires, becomes unemployed or falls ill. Overall, our calculation method provides a conservative estimate of the amount of additional remuneration each Chinese worker receives in the form of welfare benefits.

As Table 3.2 shows, urban workers receive substantially more welfare benefits than migrant workers: on average, 7,532 yuan annually, compared with just 1,235 yuan for migrant workers. In other words, migrant workers receive only 16 per cent of the benefits received by their urban counterparts.

The second panel of Table 3.2 shows annual and hourly earnings for urban and migrant workers.[7] On average, urban workers earn 27,309 yuan annually, while migrant workers earn 17,198 yuan per year, or 40 per cent less. If we look at hourly earnings, the pay differential actually increases, with migrant workers earning just 45 per cent of the hourly pay of urban workers. This differential is almost the same as that observed 12 years ago in Shanghai, where the hourly earnings of migrants were 48 per cent those of their urban counterparts (Meng and Zhang 2001).

The second measure shown in this panel is total compensation, that is, wages plus non-wage remuneration. We regard this as a better measure of remuneration than wages alone. On this measure, the difference between the two groups of workers becomes even more marked. Per hour, migrant workers receive about 38 per cent less than urban *hukou* holders, with male migrants receiving 36 per cent less than urban males and female migrants receiving 45 per cent less than urban females.

The third panel of Table 3.2 examines the monetary subsidy implied by in-kind payments. Unlike insurance contributions, these are reported as part of wages. The data show that around 70 per cent of migrants receive an in-kind payment or subsidy for meals and 64 per cent receive an in-kind payment or subsidy for accommodation. The meal subsidy is on average worth 1,847 yuan for migrant workers and 728 yuan for urban workers, representing 11 per cent and 2.5 per cent of their respective annual wages. The housing subsidy is much lower, accounting for 4.5 and 0.3 per cent respectively of migrant and urban workers' annual earnings.

As can be seen in Figure 3.1, there is an almost linear relationship between annual earnings and insurance payments. Surprisingly, despite the big difference in the incidence of insurance contributions for migrant and urban workers, the relationship between earnings and insurance payments is almost the same for both groups of workers.

The unconditional relationship between total hourly compensation and various human capital-related variables is shown in Figures 3.2–3.4. The figures differentiate between male and female urban and migrant workers. Figure 3.2

*Figure 3.1   China: Relationship between Annual Earnings and Total
         Insurance Payments*

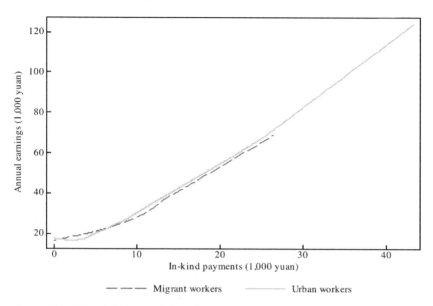

Source: Urban Household Survey, 2008; Urban Migrant Survey, 2008.

shows the relation between age and total hourly compensation. The profiles
for urban and rural workers differ markedly, but the differences in gender profiles are small. The age profiles for urban workers are sharper, with earnings
peaking at around 35 for women and 40 for men. This is in line with what one
would expect from human capital theory—that experience in a particular field
makes individuals more productive and gives them time to show the value of
their education. For migrant workers, however, the relationship between age
and compensation is very flat. It is also interesting to note that the starting
wage of 15–18-year-olds is only marginally higher for urban workers. This is
probably because the few urban workers who do start work at such a young
age are school dropouts.

Figure 3.3 shows the relation between job tenure and total hourly compensation. The tenure–earnings profiles of urban workers are similar to their
age–earnings profiles, except that the benefits of longer tenure tail off after 10
years. For migrants, the tenure–earnings profiles are again very flat.

Figure 3.4 shows the relation between education and total hourly compensation. There are positive returns to education for both urban and migrant
workers, but the bigger gains are made by urban workers. Urban workers also
have a higher level of educational attainment than migrant workers: most have

*Figure 3.2   China: Relationship between Age and Total Hourly
              Compensation*

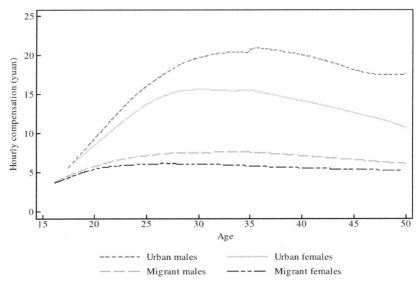

Source: Urban Household Survey, 2008; Urban Migrant Survey, 2008.

*Figure 3.3   China: Relationship between Current Job Tenure and Total
              Hourly Compensation*

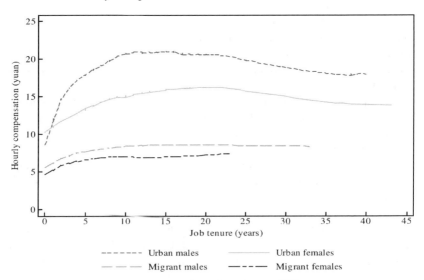

Source: Urban Household Survey, 2008; Urban Migrant Survey, 2008.

*Figure 3.4   China: Relationship between Level of Education and Total
            Hourly Compensation*

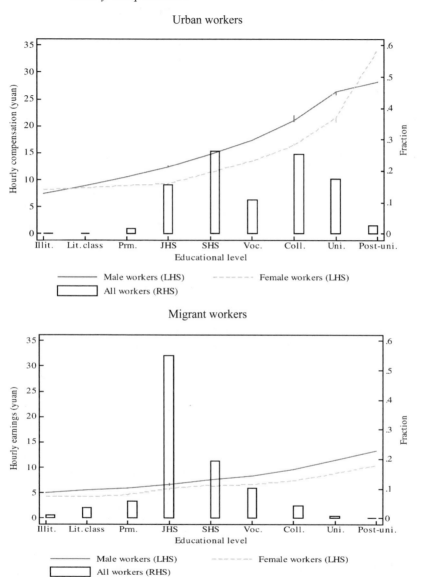

Illit. = illiterate; Lit. class = literacy class; Prm. = primary; JHS = junior high school; SHS = senior high school; Voc. = vocational school; Coll. = three-year college; Uni. = university; Post-uni. = postgraduate.

Source: Urban Household Survey, 2008; Urban Migrant Survey, 2008.

at least a senior high school qualification, whereas most migrant workers have only a junior high school qualification. If the returns to higher education are increasing (which they are), then the rates of return to education will be higher for urban than for migrant workers.

The above summary statistics lead to the following general findings. Migrant workers are more likely to work in blue-collar jobs. They work around 35 per cent more hours per week than urban workers yet are paid 50 per cent less per hour. In addition, they are likely to miss out on 70–80 per cent of their welfare entitlements from employers.

4   A CLOSER LOOK AT REMUNERATION

To gain a more in-depth understanding of the relationship between the observed differences in education, tenure, age and other characteristics, and the differences in wages and total compensation, we estimated a standard Mincerian compensation regression for migrant and urban workers, as follows:

$$Y_i^M = X_i^M \beta^M + u_i$$
$$Y_i^U = X_i^U \beta^U + v_i \qquad (3.1)$$

where the superscripts M and U indicate migrant and urban workers respectively, and the subscript i represents individuals. The outcome variable, Y, takes the form of either the log of hourly earnings or the log of total hourly compensation. X is a vector of observable individual and firm characteristics, including age and its square; current job tenure and its squared term; gender; marital status; health; height; years of education; university entrance exam score (the score is set to 0 if the individual did not take such an exam); a group of city dummy variables; and firm size.[8] u_i and v_i are error terms.

The main criterion for a variable to be included in this type of regression is that it can reasonably be argued to measure a productive characteristic; if all productive characteristics are included and are equally rewarded across groups, one would expect to find the same coefficients on all variables in (3.1). Education and experience are obviously important human capital characteristics that are quite likely to influence productivity. Similar productivity arguments can be made for all the other variables included in the model. The firm size and city dummy variables need more careful interpretation, however. Larger firms that enjoy economies of scale tend to pay higher wages and attract better workers, but they also train their workforces better and are more likely to implement minimum labour standards. Hence, coefficients on firm size partly reflect unobserved individual differences in productivity and rent sharing (that is, selectivity), but also pick up the true productivity-increasing effect of workers being in large firms.

Table 3.3 presents the results of the estimation of equation (3.1) for migrant and urban workers, and Table 3.4 shows the results for separate regressions of the male and female samples. Columns 1 to 3 of Table 3.3 show the results for the migrant sample and columns 4 to 6 the results for the urban sample. The first column for each sample (columns 1 and 4) reports the results from using log(total compensation) as the dependent variable; the other columns report the results from using log(hourly earnings). The specification for columns 2 and 3 is the same, except that column 3 includes additional variables (whether an individual has received a housing subsidy as well as various welfare insurance dummy variables). These additional variables are included to examine the conditional correlation between the non-monetary and monetary components of the remuneration package. In the same way, the inclusion of additional variables explains the difference between columns 5 and 6. When separately estimating the earnings equation for men and women in Table 3.4, however, we did not include regressions for these extra variables.

For simplicity, we focus in particular on the log(total compensation) results (columns 1 and 4 of Table 3.3), unless significant differences in the findings are observed. We find that most of the variables that proxy human capital are statistically significant and have the right sign for both samples. In particular, age and current job tenure have a non-linear relationship with the log of hourly earnings for both samples. While urban workers have a much higher age–earnings profile than migrant workers, the two groups have a very similar profile for current job tenure. The difference in age–earnings profile is driven mainly by the differences between male urban and migrant workers, with the latter having the steeper profile. The small difference in tenure–earnings profile is driven by the differences between female urban and migrant workers, with the latter again having the steeper profile. Compared with migrant workers, urban workers have more than double the return to years of schooling (Table 3.3). If we use dummy variables to indicate the different educational levels, we find that the return to education is slightly higher for migrants at the junior and senior high school levels, but higher for urban workers at the senior high school level and above (see Figure 3.5).[9] Over 70 per cent of migrant workers have a junior high school qualification or less, whereas 53 per cent of urban workers have a senior high school qualification or better (see Figure 3.4). This means that urban workers are in a far better position than migrant workers to get the returns to higher levels of education.

Ability sorting does, of course, slightly bias these findings. If the majority of urban workers have at least a senior high school qualification, this would suggest that those who have only a junior (or even senior) high school qualification may be relatively lacking in ability. On the other hand, if only a tiny

Table 3.3   China: Earnings Regression Results for Migrant and Urban Wage/Salary Earners

	Migrant Wage/Salary Earners			Urban Wage/Salary Earners		
	ln(total-comp)	ln(Wage)	ln(Wage)	ln(total-comp)	ln(Wage)	ln(Wage)
Age	0.08 (0.007)***	0.07 (0.007)***	0.07 (0.007)***	0.04 (0.012)***	0.05 (0.012)***	0.05 (0.012)***
Age^2/100	-0.12	-0.11	-0.10	-0.06	-0.07	-0.08
Current job tenure	0.04 (0.010)***	0.04 (0.010)***	0.03 (0.010)***	0.04 (0.017)***	0.03 (0.016)***	0.02 (0.016)***
Current job tenure^2/100	-0.11 (0.004)***	-0.08 (0.004)***	-0.06 (0.004)***	-0.09 (0.004)***	-0.07 (0.004)***	-0.05 (0.004)***
Years of schooling	0.04 (0.023)***	0.04 (0.022)***	0.03 (0.021)***	0.07 (0.013)***	0.07 (0.013)***	0.06 (0.012)***
University entry exam score/100	0.01 (0.003)***	0.01 (0.003)***	0.01 (0.003)***	0.03 (0.004)***	0.02 (0.004)***	0.02 (0.004)***
Dummy for healthy	0.04 (0.019)**	0.04 (0.018)**	0.04 (0.018)*	0.06 (0.022)***	0.05 (0.022)**	0.05 (0.021)**
Height	0.01 (0.001)***	0.01 (0.001)***	0.01 (0.001)***	0.00 (0.002)	0.00 (0.002)	0.00 (0.002)
Dummy for male	0.04 (0.019)**	0.05 (0.018)***	0.06 (0.018)***	0.17 (0.027)***	0.18 (0.029)***	0.18 (0.030)***
Dummy for married	-0.02 (0.020)	-0.02 (0.019)	-0.02 (0.019)	0.08 (0.030)***	0.09 (0.028)***	0.09 (0.028)***
Dummy for divorced	-0.16 (0.073)**	-0.15 (0.067)**	-0.14 (0.065)**	0.05 (0.072)	0.08 (0.069)	0.09 (0.068)
Divorced male	0.29 (0.111)***	0.27 (0.101)***	0.25 (0.097)**	-0.17 (0.133)	-0.33 (0.239)	-0.33 (0.232)
Firm size 21–49	0.11 (0.020)***	0.10 (0.019)***	0.09 (0.019)***	0.16 (0.029)***	0.13 (0.030)***	0.11 (0.029)***
Firm size 50–99	0.11 (0.020)***	0.08 (0.020)***	0.06 (0.020)***	0.26 (0.030)***	0.24 (0.030)***	0.19 (0.029)***
Firm size 100–999	0.23 (0.017)***	0.18 (0.016)***	0.13 (0.016)***	0.28 (0.024)***	0.23 (0.024)***	0.17 (0.024)***
Firm size 1,000+	0.31 (0.023)***	0.21 (0.022)***	0.13 (0.022)***	0.32 (0.029)***	0.24 (0.030)***	0.14 (0.031)***
Dongguan	-0.38 (0.031)***	-0.35 (0.029)***	-0.34 (0.022)***	-0.22 (0.049)***	-0.17 (0.048)***	-0.14 (0.048)***
Shenzhen	-0.01 (0.029)	0.02 (0.027)	0.03 (0.028)	-0.01 (0.048)	0.06 (0.047)	0.16 (0.047)***
Zhengzhou	-0.56 (0.032)***	-0.49 (0.031)***	-0.44 (0.031)***	-0.69 (0.048)***	-0.69 (0.047)***	-0.68 (0.045)***

	(1)	(2)	(3)	(4)	(5)	(6)
Luoyang	-0.73 (0.035)***	-0.67 (0.034)***	-0.63 (0.034)***	-0.85 (0.052)***	-0.86 (0.052)***	-0.87 (0.049)***
Hefei	-0.39 (0.037)***	-0.36 (0.037)***	-0.32 (0.037)***	-0.47 (0.040)***	-0.55 (0.039)***	-0.50 (0.038)***
Bengbu	-0.54 (0.046)***	-0.52 (0.045)***	-0.50 (0.045)***	-0.95 (0.052)***	-0.99 (0.051)***	-0.96 (0.049)***
Chongqing	-0.45 (0.026)***	-0.42 (0.024)***	-0.39 (0.024)***	-0.52 (0.040)***	-0.52 (0.039)***	-0.50 (0.037)***
Shanghai	-0.11 (0.028)**	-0.06 (0.026)**	-0.02 (0.026)	0.05 (0.038)	-0.05 (0.038)	-0.09 (0.037)**
Nanjing	-0.09 (0.029)***	-0.07 (0.027)***	-0.05 (0.027)**	-0.35 (0.042)***	-0.41 (0.046)***	-0.40 (0.046)***
Wuxi	0.19 (0.035)***	0.09 (0.031)***	-0.01 (0.035)	-0.46 (0.046)***	-0.51 (0.045)***	-0.50 (0.046)***
Hangzhou	-0.03 (0.030)	-0.03 (0.027)	-0.02 (0.027)	-0.23 (0.043)***	-0.29 (0.042)***	-0.31 (0.042)***
Ningbo	-0.08 (0.036)**	-0.07 (0.034)**	-0.07 (0.033)**	-0.04 (0.047)	-0.12 (0.045)**	-0.14 (0.045)***
Wuhan	-0.38 (0.028)***	-0.35 (0.026)***	-0.31 (0.026)***	-0.48 (0.048)***	-0.51 (0.050)***	-0.48 (0.049)***
Chengdu	-0.44 (0.029)***	-0.40 (0.027)***	-0.37 (0.027)***	-0.57 (0.049)***	-0.59 (0.049)***	-0.56 (0.049)***
With unemployment insurance			-0.01 (0.029)			-0.03 (0.028)
With pension insurance			0.07 (0.026)***			-0.01 (0.030)
With health insurance			0.02 (0.024)			0.02 (0.023)
With work injury insurance			0.09 (0.023)***			0.04 (0.025)
With maternity insurance			0.01 (0.043)**			-0.01 (0.031)
With housing fund			0.01 (0.028)***			0.28 (0.022)***
Constant	-1.21 (0.242)***	-1.00 (0.231)***	-0.85 (0.228)***	0.22 (0.358)	0.18 (0.352)	0.20 (0.348)
No. of observations	4,829	4,829	4,829	4,732	4,732	4,732
R²	0.39	0.35	0.37	0.41	0.37	0.39

* = significant at 10 per cent; ** = significant at 5 per cent; *** = significant at 1 per cent. Robust standard errors are in parentheses.

Source: Urban Household Survey, 2008; Urban Migrant Survey, 2008.

61

Table 3.4   China: Earnings Regression Results for Migrant and Urban Wage/Salary Earners by Gender

| | Migrant Wage/Salary Earners | | | |
| | Compensation | | Wages | |
	Males	Females	Males	Females
Age	0.09	0.06	0.08	0.06
	(0.009)***	(0.010)***	(0.009)***	(0.010)***
Age^2/100	−0.13	−0.09	−0.13	−0.09
	(0.014)***	(0.016)***	(0.013)***	(0.015)***
Current job tenure	0.04	0.05	0.04	0.04
	(0.005)***	(0.008)***	(0.005)***	(0.008)***
Current job tenure^2/100	−0.10	−0.21	−0.08	−0.16
	(0.026)***	(0.058)***	(0.024)***	(0.059)***
Years of schooling	0.03	0.05	0.03	0.04
	(0.004)***	(0.004)***	(0.004)***	(0.004)***
University entry exam score/100	0.02	0.01	0.01	0.01
	(0.008)*	(0.010)	(0.008)*	(0.009)
Dummy for healthy	0.04	0.04	0.04	0.04
	(0.026)	(0.028)	(0.025)*	(0.026)
Height	0.01	0.01	0.01	0.01
	(0.002)***	(0.002)***	(0.002)***	(0.002)***
Dummy for married	0.02	−0.08	0.02	−0.07
	(0.027)	(0.031)**	(0.026)	(0.030)**
Dummy for divorced	0.13	−0.18	0.12	−0.17
	(0.087)	(0.073)**	(0.079)	(0.068)**
Firm size 21–49	0.13	0.09	0.12	0.08
	(0.027)***	(0.029)***	(0.025)***	(0.028)***
Firm size 50–99	0.09	0.13	0.06	0.11
	(0.028)***	(0.029)***	(0.027)**	(0.028)***
Firm size 100–999	0.22	0.25	0.17	0.20
	(0.022)***	(0.025)***	(0.022)***	(0.024)***
Firm size 1,000+	0.32	0.29	0.23	0.19
	(0.030)***	(0.037)***	(0.028)***	(0.035)***
Dongguan	−0.46	−0.25	−0.42	−0.23
	(0.040)***	(0.048)***	(0.037)***	(0.046)***
Shenzhen	−0.04	0.02	−0.00	0.04
	(0.040)	(0.039)	(0.038)	(0.038)
Zhengzhou	−0.56	−0.59	−0.49	−0.54
	(0.043)***	(0.048)***	(0.041)***	(0.045)***
Luoyang	−0.74	−0.72	−0.68	−0.67
	(0.044)***	(0.060)***	(0.043)***	(0.059)***
Hefei	−0.41	−0.36	−0.37	−0.33
	(0.047)***	(0.058)***	(0.046)***	(0.057)***
Bengbu	−0.54	−0.56	−0.51	−0.56
	(0.060)***	(0.070)***	(0.059)***	(0.069)***
Chongqing	−0.44	−0.46	−0.41	−0.43
	(0.036)***	(0.038)***	(0.033)***	(0.035)***
Shanghai	−0.15	−0.04	−0.09	−0.01
	(0.038)***	(0.042)	(0.035)***	(0.039)
Nanjing	−0.12	−0.05	−0.11	−0.03
	(0.039)***	(0.045)	(0.036)***	(0.041)
Wuxi	0.06	0.29	−0.03	0.18
	(0.051)	(0.045)***	(0.045)	(0.040)***
Hangzhou	−0.02	−0.07	−0.02	−0.06
	(0.041)	(0.041)*	(0.038)	(0.038)
Ningbo	−0.10	−0.06	−0.09	−0.06
	(0.051)**	(0.051)	(0.047)*	(0.048)
Wuhan	−0.39	−0.39	−0.36	−0.35
	(0.040)***	(0.039)***	(0.037)***	(0.036)***
Chengdu	−0.46	−0.42	0.41	−0.38
	(0.039)***	(0.041)***	(0.037)***	(0.040)***
Constant	−1.41	−1.07	−1.15	−0.98
	(0.328)***	(0.387)***	(0.314)***	(0.365)***
No. of observations	2,884	1,945	2,884	1,945
R^2	0.37	0.42	0.33	0.38

* = significant at 10 per cent; ** = significant at 5 per cent; *** = significant at 1 per cent. Robust standard errors are in parentheses.

Table 3.4 (continued)

	Urban Wage/Salary Earners			
	Compensation		Wages	
	Males	Females	Males	Females
Age	0.03	0.06	0.04	0.06
	(0.018)*	(0.017)***	(0.018)**	(0.016)***
Age^2/100	−0.05	−0.08	−0.06	−0.09
	(0.024)**	(0.023)***	(0.024)**	(0.022)***
Current job tenure	0.04	0.04	0.04	0.03
	(0.006)***	(0.005)***	(0.006)***	(0.005)***
Current job tenure^2/100	−0.09	−0.09	−0.08	−0.07
	(0.018)***	(0.019)***	(0.018)***	(0.018)***
Years of schooling	0.07	0.08	0.06	0.07
	(0.005)***	(0.006)***	(0.005)***	(0.006)***
University entry exam score/100	0.03	0.02	0.03	0.01
	(0.007)***	(0.007)***	(0.007)***	(0.007)**
Dummy for healthy	0.05	0.06	0.03	0.07
	(0.033)	(0.029)**	(0.033)	(0.029)**
Height	0.00	0.00	0.00	0.00
	(0.002)	(0.003)	(0.002)	(0.002)
Dummy for married	0.15	−0.01	0.15	0.01
	(0.044)***	(0.040)	(0.042)***	(0.039)
Dummy for divorced	−0.04	−0.04	−0.19	0.00
	(0.121)	(0.077)	(0.232)	(0.074)
Firm size 21–49	0.18	0.13	0.15	0.12
	(0.044)***	(0.039)***	(0.047)***	(0.037)***
Firm size 50–99	0.26	0.26	0.23	0.25
	(0.048)***	(0.039)***	(0.047)***	(0.038)***
Firm size 100–999	0.29	0.27	0.24	0.22
	(0.036)***	(0.032)***	(0.036)***	(0.032)***
Firm size 1,000+	0.33	0.31	0.25	0.25
	(0.041)***	(0.042)***	(0.042)***	(0.045)***
Dongguan	−0.21	−0.22	−0.14	−0.20
	(0.068)***	(0.070)***	(0.067)**	(0.070)***
Shenzhen	−0.04	0.01	0.03	0.07
	(0.068)	(0.068)	(0.067)	(0.066)
Zhengzhou	−0.75	−0.63	−0.74	−0.63
	(0.068)***	(0.069)***	(0.067)***	(0.066)***
Luoyang	−0.89	−0.80	−0.90	−0.82
	(0.066)***	(0.081)***	(0.065)***	(0.082)***
Hefei	−0.49	−0.44	−0.56	−0.53
	(0.053)***	(0.062)***	(0.051)***	(0.060)***
Bengbu	−0.98	−0.91	−0.99	−1.00
	(0.070)***	(0.080)***	(0.068)***	(0.078)***
Chongqing	−0.57	−0.47	−0.57	−0.48
	(0.056)***	(0.059)***	(0.053)***	(0.056)***
Shanghai	0.05	0.05	−0.04	−0.05
	(0.053)	(0.055)	(0.053)	(0.053)
Nanjing	−0.36	−0.33	−0.42	−0.40
	(0.061)***	(0.059)***	(0.067)***	(0.064)***
Wuxi	−0.53	−0.37	−0.57	−0.43
	(0.067)***	(0.064)***	(0.066)***	(0.062)***
Hangzhou	−0.22	−0.23	−0.28	−0.28
	(0.061)***	(0.060)***	(0.061)***	(0.057)***
Ningbo	−0.03	−0.04	−0.11	−0.12
	(0.066)	(0.066)	(0.065)*	(0.064)*
Wuhan	−0.49	−0.45	−0.53	−0.48
	(0.069)***	(0.068)***	(0.076)***	(0.066)***
Chengdu	−0.62	−0.50	−0.64	−0.54
	(0.067)***	(0.072)***	(0.067)***	(0.072)***
Constant	0.88	−0.38	0.79	−0.38
	(0.534)*	(0.504)	(0.525)	(0.498)
No. of observations	2,429	2,303	2,429	2,303
R^2	0.40	0.40	0.35	0.36

Source: Urban Household Survey, 2008; Urban Migrant Survey, 2008.

*Figure 3.5   China: Conditional Rate of Return to Education by Level of
                Education*

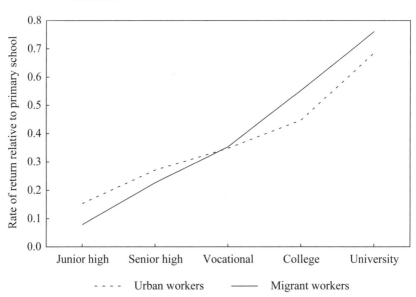

Source: Urban Household Survey, 2008; Urban Migrant Survey, 2008.

proportion of migrant workers have any post-senior high school qualifications,
this would suggest that some of those with low levels of education may be high
on the ability distribution for migrant workers. The existence of such workers
would bias upward the estimated returns for low levels of education.

Note that while the results for years of schooling reflect the average incre-
ments in wages across the various levels of education for each group, the
estimated return to each level of education is relative to the omitted category
(primary) within the group. Thus, for our purposes, the estimated return to
years of schooling is more relevant, because it reflects the average difference
in returns to education between the two groups.

Another interesting finding is that university entrance scores have a positive
and significant effect on earnings for both migrant and urban workers, suggesting that it may, to a certain extent, capture individuals' ability. However, the
return for urban workers is more than double that for migrant workers. The
separate regressions for the male and female samples show that this effect is
strongest for male migrant workers and female urban workers.

The other two human capital variables, health and height, both have a positive and significant effect on the earnings of migrant and urban workers. While
the effect of health is larger for the urban sample, the effect of height is much

larger for the migrant sample. Perhaps this is because the majority of migrants are engaged in manual labour, where physical strength is well rewarded.

There is a large premium for marriage among the urban sample (8.3 per cent), as has been observed for Western labour markets. The usual explanation is that marriage selects the more productive individuals; that is, unproductive men do not marry. Another common interpretation is that married people are better looked after, and thus healthier, than unmarried people (see, for example, Chun and Lee 2001). Interestingly, though, there is no marriage premium for migrants, perhaps because there are no such selectivity or 'caring' effects of marriage in China. While divorced female migrants suffer a wage penalty (the dummy variable for being divorced is negative), divorced male migrants do not (the interaction between the dummy variables for being male and being divorced is positive). Females earn less than males, but the gender differential in earnings is much greater among urban workers (17 per cent) than among migrant workers (4 per cent). This may also, to some extent, indicate the degree of marketization of the two labour markets. Migrant females seem to be treated more fairly in the marketplace than urban females, though one might read this result the other way round, that is, that urban females face some form of discrimination relative to urban males, whereas there is no such distinction between male and female migrants.

Firm size has a strong impact on earnings for both migrant and urban workers, though there is no unambiguous theoretical interpretation of firm size. Because we have so far interpreted wage differences as productivity differences, we implicitly interpret the firm size effect as picking up unobserved heterogeneity of workers (that is, bigger firms are more selective). However, the effect is stronger for urban workers than for migrant workers. Particularly in medium-sized firms (those with 55–99 employees), urban workers receive a big premium relative to migrants. Interestingly, we can see that the compensation premium is about 10 per cent higher than the wage premium for migrants working in the largest firms (those with 1,000 or more employees). This suggests that very large firms enforce labour laws and regulations more strongly.

Finally, we find that there are significant variations in earnings between cities for both migrant and urban workers. These partly reflect differences in the cost of living, but they may also reflect variations in labour demand. The city that pays migrants the least is Luoyang; it pays migrant workers about 57 per cent $(=100\%*(1-e^{-0.845}))$ less than the default city, Guangzhou, all else remaining constant. For urban individuals, the lowest-paying city is Bengbu; it pays urban workers about 61 per cent $(=100\%*(1-e^{-0.952}))$ less than Guangzhou, all else remaining constant. Interestingly, a ranking of cities by pay reveals considerable differences between the migrant and urban samples, suggesting that there are factors over and above the cost of living that affect cross-city earnings. For instance, even though the hourly earnings of urban *hukou* holders in Shanghai are almost the same as in Guangzhou (the city dummy is small and insignificant for urban workers), migrant workers are paid 10 per cent less in Shanghai than in Guangzhou.

We now turn briefly to the results presented in columns 3 and 6 of Table 3.3, to investigate whether the non-monetary components of the remuneration package play a compensating differential, entitlement or efficiency wage role. We find that, for migrant workers, the conditional relationship between wages and receiving unemployment insurance is negative, but positive for all other types of insurance. Given the fact that the conditional relationship 'should be neutral' (entitlements are proportional to wages), these findings can be interpreted to mean that migrants are more likely to be given their entitlements, except unemployment benefit, when paid higher wages. For urban workers, however, none of the coefficients are statistically significant, confirming that wages and entitlements are proportionally (and hence constantly) related. For both groups, the housing fund has a positive relationship with log-earnings, suggesting that it mainly benefits higher wage earners. For migrants, most insurance payments, including the housing fund, are positively related to earnings.

What are the reasons for the differences in the remuneration of urban and migrant workers? To answer this question, we adopt a Blinder–Oaxaca-type decomposition methodology. This essentially allows us to decompose remuneration into the parts that can be captured by differences between two groups in observed characteristics (say, different levels of education) and the parts that can be captured by differences in the coefficients of these characteristics (say, differences in the coefficient on education). Specifically:

$$
\exp\{\overline{Y}_i^U\} - \exp\{\overline{Y}_i^M\} = [\exp\{\overline{X}^U \beta^U\} - \exp\{\overline{X}^U \beta^U\}]
$$
$$
+ [\exp\{\overline{X}^M \beta^U\} - \exp\{\overline{X}^M \beta^M\}] \qquad (3.2)
$$

where the first term on the right-hand side of equation (3.2) denotes the contribution of observable characteristics to differences in hourly earnings, and the second term denotes the difference due to differential returns to characteristics. The latter is the part that is due to 'constraints', by which we mean constraints on the equal market valuation of the same characteristics between the two groups. We will interpret the first part as arising from characteristics and the second part as arising from the various constraints on migrant workers, including impediments to their ability to choose jobs. To handle the index number problem, we weight the decomposition by both urban and migrant coefficients and take the average of the two decomposition results.

Table 3.5 presents the results of a decomposition exercise for mean anti-log hourly earnings and compensation, based on the regression results for the total sample, the male sample and the female sample.[10] The regression results for the total sample indicate that mean anti-log hourly earnings are 9.42 yuan for

Table 3.5   China: Decomposition of Mean Anti-log Earnings and Compensation (yuan)

	Total Sample		Male Sample		Female Sample	
	Earn-ings	Compen-sation	Earn-ings	Compen-sation	Earn-ings	Compen-sation
Urban predicted	10.90	14.00	12.32	15.81	9.42	12.08
Migrant predicted	5.55	5.95	5.92	6.35	5.02	5.36
Migrant counterfactual	7.02	8.33	7.57	9.04	6.07	7.13
Urban counterfactual	7.45	8.23	8.11	9.02	6.12	6.68
Total differential	5.35	8.05	6.39	9.46	4.40	6.72
Urban weighted unexplained	1.46	2.38	1.64	2.69	1.05	1.77
Migrant weighted unexplained	3.45	5.76	4.20	6.79	3.29	5.39
Mean unexplained	2.46	4.07	2.92	4.74	2.17	3.58
Mean unexplained as % of total differential	45.94	50.58	45.72	50.11	49.37	53.29

Source: Urban Household Survey, 2008; Urban Migrant Survey, 2008.

urban workers and 5.02 for migrant workers. Around half of this difference is explained by observable characteristics; that is, migrant workers would earn 7.02 yuan per hour if they were paid according to the returns enjoyed by urban workers, and urban workers would earn 7.45 yuan if they were paid according to the returns obtained by migrant workers. The other 46 per cent of the difference is 'unexplained' in terms of the characteristics and is driven by differential returns. The unexplained portion is generally higher for female than male workers.

The decomposition results for total hourly compensation show the same basic pattern as those for hourly earnings. However, the size of the unexplained component is higher, at 51 per cent of the compensation differential between the two groups.

If we look at the earnings differential between urban and migrant workers by city (Table 3.6), we find some interesting differences. Here, we will focus mainly on total compensation. In some cities, migrants are paid much less than would be predicted by urban pay scales. In Dongguan, for instance, migrant workers are paid only 5.13 yuan per hour, even though the equivalent urban individual would have been paid 8.85 yuan per hour—or about 80 per cent more. Similar large differences that cannot be explained by the endowment differentials are seen for Guangzhou, Shenzhen, Chongqing, Shanghai, Wuhan and Chengdu.

Table 3.6 Decomposition of Hourly Earnings/Total Compensation Differentials between Urban and Migrant Workers by City

	Urban Predicted	Migrant Predicted	Migrant Counter-factual	Urban Counter-factual	Total Differential	Urban-weighted Unexplained	Migrant-weighted Unexplained	Mean Unexplained
Hourly earnings								
Guangzhou	16.07	6.69	9.43	9.35	9.37	2.73	6.72	50.43
Dongguan	11.53	5.13	8.85	5.88	6.40	3.72	5.65	73.23
Shenzhen	16.63	6.80	10.20	9.39	9.83	3.41	7.24	54.17
Zhengzhou	7.72	4.24	4.81	5.92	3.48	0.57	1.80	33.98
Luoyang	7.53	3.31	4.03	5.24	4.22	0.72	2.29	35.71
Hefei	9.76	4.55	5.32	6.93	5.21	0.77	2.83	34.56
Bangbu	5.04	3.57	3.03	5.13	1.47	-0.54	-0.09	-21.17
Chongqing	8.33	4.27	5.36	5.75	4.06	1.09	2.57	45.14
Shanghai	14.34	6.33	8.91	8.51	8.01	2.58	5.83	52.51
Nanjing	10.65	6.31	6.26	8.82	4.34	-0.05	1.83	20.52
Wuxi	9.27	7.76	5.94	10.08	1.50	-1.82	-0.81	-87.72
Hangzhou	11.44	6.72	7.46	8.76	4.72	0.75	2.67	36.25
Ningbo	13.65	5.61	7.48	8.48	8.04	1.87	5.16	43.74
Wuhan	8.83	4.97	6.10	6.22	3.86	1.13	2.61	48.41
Chengdu	7.84	4.29	5.01	5.63	3.55	0.81	2.21	42.50
Total	**10.89**	**5.55**	**6.95**	**7.45**	**5.33**	**1.40**	**3.43**	**45.28**

Total hourly compensation

Guangzhou	19.96	7.29	10.90	10.53	12.67	3.61	9.42	51.45
Dongguan	13.22	5.57	9.92	6.33	7.65	4.35	6.89	73.44
Shenzhen	19.20	7.22	11.01	10.30	11.98	3.79	8.90	52.96
Zhengzhou	9.63	4.33	5.56	6.26	5.30	1.23	3.37	43.37
Luoyang	9.65	3.36	4.65	5.64	6.30	1.29	4.01	42.13
Hefei	13.25	4.70	6.53	7.56	8.55	1.83	5.69	43.95
Bangbu	6.41	3.70	3.53	5.61	2.72	-0.17	0.81	11.72
Chongqing	10.27	4.48	6.18	6.28	5.79	1.71	3.99	49.19
Shanghai	19.55	6.52	11.25	9.17	13.03	4.73	10.37	57.96
Nanjing	14.29	6.73	7.76	9.77	7.56	1.03	4.52	36.66
Wuxi	12.01	9.56	7.34	12.70	2.45	-2.22	-0.69	-59.36
Hangzhou	15.07	7.37	9.22	9.81	7.71	1.85	5.26	46.17
Ningbo	18.19	5.95	9.13	9.54	12.24	3.18	8.64	48.29
Wuhan	11.23	5.24	7.30	6.71	5.99	2.05	4.53	54.91
Chengdu	9.86	4.39	5.99	6.01	5.46	1.59	3.84	49.75
Total	**13.97**	**5.94**	**8.23**	**8.23**	**8.02**	**2.29**	**5.74**	**50.00**

Source: Urban Household Survey, 2008; Urban Migrant Survey, 2008.

Perhaps most interesting of all, though, is that there are two cities where migrant workers are paid almost the same as, or even more than, their urban equivalents: Bengbu and Wuxi. In Bengbu, migrants are paid 3.57 yuan per hour, whereas their urban equivalents would have been paid 3.03 yuan per hour. Similarly, urban workers are paid 5.04 yuan per hour, whereas their migrant equivalents would have been paid 5.13 yuan per hour. Taking the average of the two differences, we find that around 20 per cent of the total earnings differential in Bengbu is unexplained; in other words, migrant workers are treated 20 per cent better than their urban equivalents in the Bengbu labour market. If we consider total hourly compensation, however, the wage advantage observed for migrant workers in Bengbu disappears.

In Wuxi, migrant workers are paid 1.5 yuan less per hour than urban workers (7.76 yuan versus 9.27 yuan). However, if migrant workers received the same rates of return to their endowments as their urban counterparts, their average hourly earnings would have been 5.94 yuan, or 1.82 yuan less than what they actually earned. The opposite is the case for urban workers: had they been treated as migrant workers, their earnings would have been 10.08 yuan per hour, or 0.81 yuan more than what they actually earned. On average, therefore, migrant workers in Wuxi are doing better than urban workers with the same endowments, although the inclusion of insurance payments slightly reduces this advantage.

The above decomposition results reveal big differences between cities in how migrants fare in the urban labour market. The majority of cities in the sample pay migrants much less than their urban equivalents, but Wuxi and Bengbu seem to be different. It is perhaps important to point out here that it is not the case that all 'equal pay' cities are poor. Wuxi ranks fifth among the 15 cities in term of average compensation for urban residents, yet migrants are still paid more than urban workers. What does appear to be true is that pay in all the largest cities is very unequal.

5   CONCLUSION

To summarize, we found that:

1   The starting salaries of migrant wage and salary earners are much lower than those of urban workers. Migrants work some 58 hours per week on average, compared with 43 hours per week for urban wage and salary earners. They mainly occupy the lower end of the labour market: over 90 per cent work in trades and services or manual labouring jobs, compared with just 36 per cent for urban workers.

2   Not only do migrant workers receive lower wages than their urban coun-
    terparts, but they also receive less non-monetary compensation in the form
    of employer insurance contributions. They do, however, receive higher
    in-kind payments in the form of meals and accommodation. The inclu-
    sion of non-wage remuneration increases the gap between migrant and
    urban workers. The average migrant earns 6.06 yuan per hour in wages
    and the average urban worker 13.23 yuan, but when welfare contributions
    are included, the migrant still receives only 6.56 yuan per hour, while the
    urban resident's hourly wage rises to 16.87 yuan. To put it another way, the
    hourly pay of a migrant worker is 45 per cent that of an urban resident, but
    the total hourly compensation of a migrant worker is just 37 per cent that of
    an urban resident.

3   The rates of return to job tenure are similar for migrant and urban work-
    ers, but the rates of return to ability, captured by university entrance exam
    scores, are markedly lower for migrants. Returns to education are also
    lower for migrants, though this may have something to do with the dif-
    ferential returns at different points along the education distribution: urban
    returns are on the steep part of the education production function (between
    senior high school and university), while migrant returns are on the flat part
    (between junior and senior high school).

4   Decomposition analysis reveals that the observable characteristics of
    migrant workers (age, education, gender, marital status) explain over 50
    per cent of the basic hourly remuneration difference between migrant and
    urban workers, mainly due to the much lower levels of experience and
    education of migrants. The difference in experience may be caused by the
    restrictions on migrants staying in the cities; the difference in education
    may be related to a lack of investment in education in rural areas.

5   The wage differences between cities are enormous, for both migrant and
    urban workers. In Bengbu and Wuxi, migrant workers receive roughly
    the same level of total compensation as an equivalent urban city dweller
    with the same characteristics. Yet in Shenzhen, Guangzhou, Shanghai
    and Dongguan, they are paid less than half the total compensation of an
    equivalent urban city dweller. These patterns indicate large policy differ-
    ences between cities, with some cities actively competing for migrants and
    others trying to keep them out of the higher-paid professions and denying
    them insurance contributions. The wage differences between cities extend
    beyond the urban–migrant divide and are found within the urban labour
    force as well: for urban workers with the same observable characteristics,
    wages in Guangzhou are about 100 per cent higher than those in Bengbu.
    The wage differences between migrants working in different cities are less
    pronounced, suggesting perhaps that there is greater mobility across cities
    among migrants than among urban workers.

One conclusion that can be drawn from these findings is that young migrants are being used as cheap labour in the cities. On average, migrants stay in the same job for six years,[11] working around 60 hours per week. They are still often housed and fed at the workplace. They are paid less than urban workers, partly because they receive lower returns to education, but also because they have lower levels of accumulated experience due to the temporary nature of migration. The potential productivity gain that would be possible if migrant workers achieved the same returns to their investments as urban *hukou* holders is in the order of a 50 per cent remuneration increase for the migrants.

However, the system under which migrants are treated as second-class citizens in the cities appears to be creaking at the seams. In cities where workers are in high demand, migrant workers are relatively well paid and receive their full welfare and insurance entitlements from employers.

It also appears that it is not only migrants whose position is maintained (constrained?) by means of strong restrictions on labour mobility. In some cities, urban workers earn so much less than they would in a richer city that they actually earn less than an equivalent migrant with the same characteristics and would surely migrate themselves if given the chance. Although the focus is usually on the ways in which the *hukou* system prevents rural *hukou* holders from gaining access to jobs and benefits in the cities, it is equally true that an urban *hukou* holder who moves to another city would not be eligible for city-specific benefits such as education and childcare. Our results suggest that a relaxation of the constraints on movement between cities would lead to large flows of urban residents moving from low-wage to high-wage cities.

In short, the Chinese labour market is hiding major strains that would be difficult to maintain in a more laissez-faire system. In a laissez-faire system, the wage differences between migrant and urban workers would quickly disappear as employers favoured the cheaper labourers. In addition, migration would quickly even out the large differences between cities in the wages received by urban workers.

NOTES

1   Provisions on Minimum Wages, Order 21, Ministry of Labour and Social Services, 20 January 2004, available at http://www.fdi.gov.cn/pub/FDI_EN/Laws/labourmanagement/ P020060620378448281759.pdf, accessed 31 March 2009.
2   The exceptions to this general rule are large firms and firms that treat welfare payments as part of an efficiency wage package. Although we do not examine this issue in detail in this chapter, we can confirm that our data show that large firms do indeed offer better total compensation packages.
3   'Renli ziyuan shehui baozhang bu fuzeren jiu nongmingong canjia jiben yanglaobaoxian deng liang ge ban fa dawen' [A spokesperson for the Human Resources and Social Security Department replies to questions about two models put forward to allow migrant workers to

gain access to the pension insurance], *Xinhua News*, 5 February 2009, available at http://news.xinhuanet.com/politics/2009-02/05/content_10769408.htm, accessed 31 March 2009.

4 See Chapter 7 for an overview of the surveys conducted for the Chinese component of the Rural–Urban Migration in China and Indonesia (RUMiCI) project and a detailed description of the design and methodology underpinning the Urban Migrant Survey. The questionnaire for the Urban Migrant Survey and other background material can be found at http://rumici.anu.edu.au.

5 The sample is restricted to those aged 16–50 for two reasons. First, migrant workers aged 50 and above account for just 4.3 per cent of the total sample, compared with 20 per cent for urban workers. Second, the retirement age for urban workers ranges from 50 to 65, so those still working after age 50 may be a select group. The exclusion of workers aged 50 and over reduces the possible selection bias for urban workers and increases the comparability of the two groups.

6 Detailed information on the rules for each of the 15 cities is available from the authors upon request.

7 The relevant question asks workers to state their monthly earnings from all paid jobs, including wages, bonuses, subsidies and the monetary equivalent of employers' in-kind contributions (that is, housing and food). However, estimating the monetary value of these contributions is a complicated process, particularly if they are paid annually or irregularly, and we suspect that most respondents did not include them. For this reason, it seemed sensible to consider the responses to this question to apply to cash payments only. This question will be modified in the next wave of the survey.

8 Usually in wage regressions, the problem of selectivity arises: not all who can work do work, and those who do work have some unobserved characteristics that are not the same as the unobserved characteristics of those who do not work. For the migrants in our sample, this issue does not seem to be serious, as more than 90 per cent are employed, although the decision to migrate in itself poses an important selection issue. However, it seems reasonable to assume that the unobserved characteristics determining who works (migrates), and who does not, are the same for both migrants and city dwellers. The rationale for this is that whatever reasons we can think of for selection among urban workers also seem likely to apply to migrant workers: those who are currently at school, the elderly, the sick or those looking after children are not in a position to work/migrate, whether they live in the city or in the countryside. In the case of this analysis, neither the instrumental variable approach nor the inclusion of preference variables would be realistic given the cross-sectional nature of the data. Hence, we will rely on the plausibility argument that whatever selectivity applies to the migrant community would also apply to the urban community.

9 The full results are not reported here but are available from the authors upon request.

10 Since log-wages are virtually symmetrically distributed, we interpret the decomposition as a decomposition in median wages. Mean hourly wages are of course higher than the exponent of the average log wage by a factor equal to $e^{0.5*s*s}$, where s is the standard deviation of log compensation. Mean wages are roughly 30 per cent higher than median wages. Focusing on median wages, however, means that we focus on the middle of the sample, so that the results are less affected by outliers.

11 This figure is derived by taking the average amount of time spent in the current job and assuming a constant exit rate. The average total duration then becomes double the average observed duration.

4 Wage Structures and Inequality among Local and Migrant Workers in Urban China

Deng Quheng and Li Shi

1 INTRODUCTION

China has been in transition from a planned to a market economy since the end of the 1970s when economic reform began. Although the labour market has been slower to change than other markets, such as commodity and capital markets, there can be no doubt that a labour market has gradually developed. Currently, the labour market plays an important role in labour allocation and wage determination. Governments, both central and local, are no longer responsible for assigning jobs to workers, and enterprises now possess complete autonomy over hiring, firing and wage determination. Governments may still have control over the quantity of labour hired by state-owned enterprises and the public sector, but not over who to hire and at what price.

Nevertheless, China's labour market is still far from competitive, and institutional barriers, both formal and informal, continue to exist. One of those barriers is the restrictions on rural migrants in the urban labour market implemented through the household registration (*hukou*) system. Under this system, only individuals who hold an urban *hukou* are eligible to obtain certain types of jobs in urban areas. This has led to a concentration of urban *hukou* holders in the professional and managerial sections of the workforce. In 1995, for instance, Meng and Zhang (2001) found that 36.7 per cent of urban *hukou* holders in Shanghai held white-collar jobs, whereas the proportion for rural migrant workers was only 3.4 per cent. The situation has not improved greatly since then. Based on data from the 2002 wave of the China Household Income Project survey, Démurger et al. (2009) found that 52.4 per cent of urban workers, but just 6.7 per cent of rural migrant workers, were professionals, technicians or office workers.

As a result of these job restrictions, the earnings of migrant workers are much lower than they would be otherwise, and far below those of urban workers. Based on surveys conducted in Shanghai in late 1995 and early 1996, for instance, Meng and Zhang (2001) estimated that the hourly earnings of migrant workers were less than 50 per cent those of urban workers. Deng (2007) showed that this ratio remained low in 2002, at 62 per cent. This chapter finds a ratio of 48 per cent in 2007 based on data from the 2008 Rural–Urban Migration in China and Indonesia (RUMiCI) surveys.

The question naturally arises as to how the wage structures for urban and migrant workers differ, and to what extent the significant increase in rural-to-urban migration and the existence of job restrictions on migrants affect earnings inequality in the urban labour market.

Most of the studies mentioned above focus on the mean, rather than dispersion, of wages and no study has explicitly examined the effect of migration on urban wage inequality. This chapter aims to shed light on the role of migration in wage inequality in urban China based on the large quantity of representative data collected through the RUMiCI surveys.

The chapter is structured as follows. The next section provides a preliminary description of the data and summary statistics related to the issues under study. As wage structures are the key to understanding wage inequality in the urban labour market, the third section concentrates on the wage functions for urban workers, migrant workers, and urban and migrant workers combined. The fourth section examines wage inequality and its constituent elements, and the final section presents our conclusions.

2   DATA AND DESCRIPTIVE STATISTICS

The data used for this study are derived from the first wave of the RUMiCI surveys, which were conducted in China between March and May 2008. Three independent surveys were conducted: the Rural Household Survey, the Urban Household Survey and the Urban Migrant Survey. The Urban Migrant Survey covered 5,000 households and 8,446 individuals in 15 cities: Shanghai, Nanjing, Wuxi, Hangzhou, Ningbo, Hefei, Bengbu, Zhengzhou, Luoyang, Wuhan, Guangzhou, Shenzhen, Dongguan, Chongqing and Chengdu. The Urban Household Survey covered 4,601 households in the same 15 cities in addition to 399 households in the cities of Anyang, Mianyang and Leshan, resulting in a total sample of 5,000 households and 14,697 individuals. This chapter focuses on the data from the 15 consistent cities.

In this study, urban workers are defined as urban *hukou* holders aged 16–60 who were working and had a positive wage income at the time of the survey. Similarly, migrant workers are defined as rural *hukou* holders aged 16–60 who were working in an urban area and had a positive wage income at the time of the survey. Since migrant workers are overrepresented in the sample, a simple combination of the figures for urban and migrant workers would lead to a biased picture of wage structures and inequality among urban workers as a whole. To correct for this bias, we weight each sample by weights computed from the 1% National Population Sample Survey. Details on how these weights are constructed are presented in Appendix A4.1.

Table 4.1 reports descriptive statistics for urban workers, migrant workers, and urban and migrant workers combined. On average, migrant workers are nine years younger than urban workers. They are also clustered in the younger age groups: around 55 per cent of migrant workers are aged 30 or below, whereas 60 per cent of urban workers are aged 31–50. The proportions for urban and migrant workers combined, meanwhile, are 44 per cent for those aged 30 or below and 48 per cent for those aged 31–50. There seems to be little difference in the gender composition of urban and migrant workers, with more men than women working in both groups. In line with the difference in age structure, the marriage rate for migrant workers (59 per cent) is much lower than that for urban workers (97 per cent).

The rural–urban divide in education in China has been the subject of much criticism (Knight and Li 1996; UNDP 2005: 47–8). In our data, it is reflected in huge differences in educational attainment between urban and migrant workers. Only 3 per cent of urban workers did not complete junior high school; among migrant workers, however, the figure is 12 per cent. A majority of migrant workers (57 per cent) are junior high school graduates and another 27 per cent have completed high school. Only 3.9 per cent have a tertiary education. In contrast, a majority of urban workers (36 per cent) have finished senior high school and another 44 per cent have a tertiary degree—25 per cent from a junior college and 19 per cent from a university. Among urban and migrant workers combined, the proportion of workers with at least a senior high school education is 48 per cent. Training is another way to invest in human capital. Once again, however, migrant workers are at a disadvantage. Only 26 per cent of migrant workers have received training, compared with 42 per cent of urban workers.

There are also significant differences in the employment characteristics of urban and migrant workers. Most obviously, urban workers are more likely to work in white-collar (managerial, professional or clerical) jobs: 56 per cent, compared with just 7 per cent of migrant workers. The distribution of workers by enterprise ownership also reveals striking differences. In workplaces where there are formidable barriers to entry, such as government departments, institutions and state-owned enterprises, there are fewer migrant workers. Around 51 per cent of urban workers, but just 9 per cent of migrant workers, work in these types of workplaces. On the other hand, private or individual enterprises absorb 79 per cent of migrant workers but only 32 per cent of urban workers. These differences extend to the distribution of workers by sector, with larger shares of migrant workers employed in manufacturing, construction, whole-sale and retail trade, and accommodation and catering.

Table 4.1 also provides information on the potential work experience and monthly and hourly earnings of workers.[1] The mean potential work experience of urban workers is six years more than that of migrant workers. The monthly wage of migrant workers is 1,648 yuan, or 46 per cent less than that of urban workers.[2] The difference in hourly wages is even greater. Migrant workers earn 7 yuan per hour, or 62 per cent less than urban workers, but work 62 hours per week, or 42 per cent more hours than urban workers.

Figure 4.1 shows the education–wage profiles of urban and migrant work-ers, and Figure 4.2 their age–wage profiles. As can be seen from Figure 4.1, monthly and hourly wages increase monotonically with educational level, but the slope is much steeper for urban than for migrant workers, especially in the case of hourly earnings. Figure 4.2 indicates that there is an inverse-U-shaped relationship between age and earnings for both urban and migrant workers, although the profile for the latter is flatter than that for the former. Depending on whether hourly or monthly earnings are used, the profile peaks at age 30 or 36 for urban workers, and at age 27 or 34 for migrant workers.

3 WAGE STRUCTURES

In this section we estimate logarithmic monthly and hourly wage functions for urban workers, migrant workers, and urban and migrant workers combined. The independent variables are potential work experience and its squared term, gender, marital status, education, training, whether or not an individual is self-employed, occupation, enterprise ownership, industry of employment and city dummies. To test the extent to which employment-related factors such as occu-pation, ownership and industry of employment affect earnings, in a separate model we exclude these variables from the specification.

Selected regression results are reported in Table 4.2. The first four columns report the results for urban and migrant workers combined; the last four col-umns show the results of the separate regressions for the two groups.[3]

In the combined sample estimation, an additional dummy variable indicat-ing whether or not a person is a migrant is included. We find that migrant workers earn less than urban workers, and that the level of the difference is much higher in the log of hourly earnings equation than in the log of monthly earnings equation. The discrepancy between the two results can be reconciled by the longer hours worked by migrant workers.

Columns 1 and 3 report the results from the models that include the occupa-tion, ownership and industry dummy variables, and columns 2 and 4 show the results excluding these variables. If we compare the coefficients for the migrant

Table 4.1   China: Descriptive Statistics for the Urban Labour Force

	Urban Workers	Migrant Workers	All Urban Workers
Age group (%)			
16–20	0.52	14.26	9.45
21–25	7.67	23.57	18.01
26–30	15.16	17.25	16.52
31–35	13.98	13.55	13.70
36–40	17.93	14.08	15.42
41–45	15.58	9.48	11.61
46–50	13.39	4.54	7.63
51–55	10.99	2.23	5.29
56–60	4.78	1.04	2.35
Mean age (years)	39.32	30.74	33.74
Gender (%)			
Male	58.39	60.10	59.50
Female	41.61	39.90	40.50
Marital status (%)			
Married	97.08	59.30	72.51
Not married	2.92	40.70	27.49
Education (%)			
Primary or below	3.02	12.29	9.06
Junior high school	17.02	56.85	42.98
Senior high school	36.38	26.94	30.23
Junior college	24.83	3.32	10.81
University or above	18.75	0.60	6.92
Training (%)			
Received	41.57	26.30	31.62
Not received	58.43	73.70	68.38
Occupation (%)			
Manager	6.43	1.72	3.36
Professional	21.05	0.83	7.86
Clerk	28.60	4.76	13.05
Service worker or peddler	17.66	53.25	40.87
Production worker	11.62	27.23	21.80
Owner of private or individual enterprise	7.25	11.93	10.30
Other	7.39	0.28	2.75

Table 4.1 (continued)

	Urban Workers	Migrant Workers	All Urban Workers
Enterprise ownership type (%)			
Government departments	32.20	2.31	12.90
Non-public enterprises or institutions	4.61	2.11	3.00
State-owned enterprises	14.43	4.96	8.32
Collective enterprises	6.38	4.33	5.05
Foreign enterprises	6.25	7.02	6.75
Private or individual enterprises	32.25	79.15	62.53
Other	3.88	0.12	1.45
Sector (%)			
Primary	1.45	0.03	0.53
Manufacturing	16.64	24.38	21.68
Electricity, gas & water	3.59	0.15	1.35
Construction	3.28	8.38	6.60
Transport, warehousing & posts	8.81	2.68	4.83
Information transmission & computer services	5.11	0.77	2.28
Wholesale & retail trade	12.74	24.75	20.55
Accommodation & catering	2.86	17.37	12.30
Finance & real estate	6.07	3.95	4.69
Leasing & business services	4.66	0.11	1.70
Scientific research & technical services	1.33	0.76	0.96
Water supply, environmental services & public utilities	1.34	2.80	2.28
Residential & other services	12.87	1.55	5.51
Education	4.01	8.36	6.84
Health, social security & social welfare	3.68	2.52	2.92
Culture, sport & entertainment	2.18	0.36	0.99
Public administration & social organizations	9.38	1.09	3.99
Experience, wages & hours			
Potential work experience (years)	21.04	15.30	17.32
Monthly wage (yuan)	3,075.21	1,648.38	2,147.21
Hourly wage (yuan)	18.40	7.09	11.04
No. of hours worked per week	43.45	61.53	55.20
No. of observations	5,628	6,554	12,182

Source: Urban Household Survey, 2008; Urban Migrant Survey, 2008.

*Figure 4.1   China: Monthly and Hourly Wages of Urban and Migrant
            Workers by Educational Level*

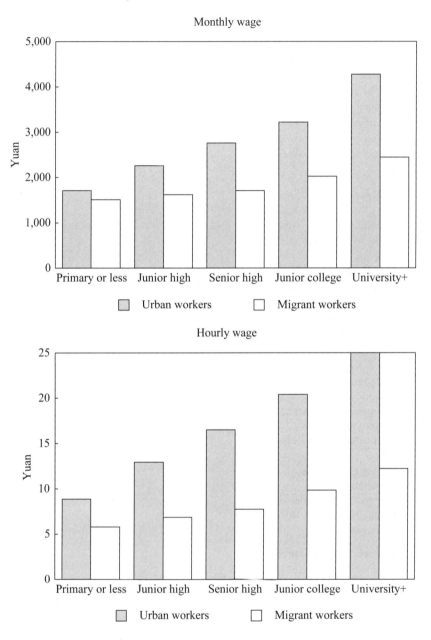

Source: Urban Household Survey, 2008; Urban Migrant Survey, 2008.

Figure 4.2   China: Monthly and Hourly Wages of Urban and Migrant Workers by Age

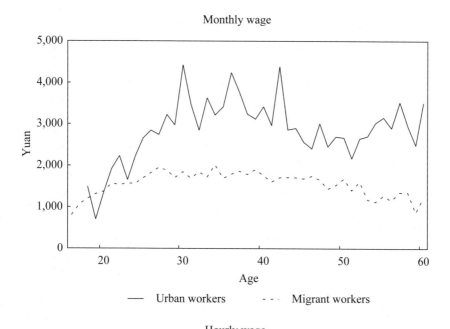

Monthly wage

Hourly wage

Source: Urban Household Survey, 2008; Urban Migrant Survey, 2008.

Table 4.2   China: Wage Functions for Urban, Migrant and All Urban
Workers

	Combined Regression			
	Log Monthly Earnings		Log Hourly Earnings	
	With Controls[a] (1)	Without Controls[a] (2)	With Controls[a] (3)	Without Controls[a] (4)
Migrant	−0.061	−0.118	−0.283	−0.386
	(0.015)***	(0.014)***	(0.017)***	(0.015)***
Experience	0.019	0.022	0.019	0.023
	(0.002)***	(0.002)***	(0.002)***	(0.002)***
Experience^2	−0.000	−0.001	−0.000	−0.001
	(0.000)***	(0.000)***	(0.000)***	(0.000)***
Junior high school	0.064	0.069	0.123	0.133
	(0.019)***	(0.019)***	(0.021)***	(0.022)***
Senior high school	0.147	0.177	0.243	0.287
	(0.020)***	(0.021)***	(0.023)***	(0.024)***
Junior college	0.314	0.425	0.431	0.573
	(0.025)***	(0.026)***	(0.029)***	(0.029)***
University or above	0.518	0.692	0.615	0.830
	(0.029)***	(0.028)***	(0.032)***	(0.032)***
Received training	0.065	0.077	0.059	0.074
	(0.010)***	(0.010)***	(0.011)***	(0.012)***
Male	0.184	0.220	0.156	0.192
	(0.010)***	(0.010)***	(0.011)***	(0.011)***
Married	0.032	0.039	0.016	0.023
	(0.014)**	(0.015)***	(0.016)	(0.017)
Han nationality	0.061	0.072	0.101	0.113
	(0.038)	(0.040)*	(0.043)**	(0.045)**
Self-employed	0.368	0.354	0.130	0.089
	(0.022)***	(0.014)***	(0.025)***	(0.016)***
Occupation	Yes	No	Yes	No
Ownership	Yes	No	Yes	No
Industry	Yes	No	Yes	No
City	Yes	Yes	Yes	Yes
No. of observations	11,832	11,832	11,758	11,758
R^2	0.36	0.31	0.44	0.39

*** = significant at 1 per cent; ** = significant at 5 per cent; * = significant at 10 per cent. Standard errors are in parentheses.
a   The control variables are occupation, enterprise ownership type and industry of employment.

Table 4.2 (continued)

	Separate Regressions			
	Migrant Workers		Urban Workers	
	Log Monthly Earnings (5)	Log Hourly Earnings (6)	Log Monthly Earnings (7)	Log Hourly Earnings (8)
Migrant				
Experience	0.018	0.019	0.022	0.021
	(0.002)***	(0.003)***	(0.003)***	(0.003)***
Experience^2	−0.001	−0.001	−0.000	−0.000
	(0.000)***	(0.000)***	(0.000)***	(0.000)***
Junior high school	0.068	0.114	−0.044	0.009
	(0.019)***	(0.022)***	(0.048)	(0.054)
Senior high school	0.160	0.246	0.051	0.132
	(0.022)***	(0.025)***	(0.048)	(0.054)**
Junior college	0.267	0.391	0.238	0.344
	(0.037)***	(0.042)***	(0.051)***	(0.057)***
University or above	0.349	0.474	0.429	0.519
	(0.075)***	(0.086)***	(0.053)***	(0.059)***
Received training	0.076	0.093	0.064	0.047
	(0.014)***	(0.015)***	(0.015)***	(0.017)***
Male	0.155	0.134	0.214	0.185
	(0.012)***	(0.014)***	(0.015)***	(0.017)***
Married	0.056	0.048	0.035	0.027
	(0.017)***	(0.020)**	(0.035)	(0.039)
Han nationality	−0.013	0.036	0.082	0.097
	(0.043)	(0.049)	(0.069)	(0.076)
Self-employed	0.338	0.106	0.465	0.231
	(0.021)***	(0.024)***	(0.120)***	(0.137)*
Occupation	Yes	Yes	Yes	Yes
Ownership	Yes	Yes	Yes	Yes
Industry	Yes	Yes	Yes	Yes
City	Yes	Yes	Yes	Yes
No. of observations	6,308	6,274	5,524	5,484
R^2	0.29	0.26	0.40	0.38

Source: Urban Household Survey, 2008; Urban Migrant Survey, 2008.

dummy variable with and without these variables, we observe that the negative earnings premium for migrants increases from 6 per cent to 12 per cent in the case of monthly earnings (see columns 1 and 2) and from 28 per cent to 39 per cent in the case of hourly earnings (see columns 3 and 4). This suggests that, conditional on other control variables, around half (six percentage points) of the monthly earnings gap and slightly more than one-quarter (11 percentage points) of the hourly earnings gap can be explained by employment-related factors.

Recognizing that the wage determination process for urban and migrant workers may not be the same, we also estimate the wage equation for the two groups of workers separately (see columns 5–8 of Table 4.2). After controlling for all independent variables, we find that wages rise with experience for both samples, then peak and finally decline. The inverted-U-shaped relationship between experience and wages suggests the existence of a learning process up to a certain number of working years. The profile peaks earlier for migrant workers than for urban workers but the difference in the profiles for the two groups is not statistically significant.[4]

Compared with the reference group (workers with a primary school education or less), urban workers with a junior college education receive a 24 per cent premium in monthly wages and a 34 per cent premium in hourly wages, while those with a university degree earn a premium of 43 per cent in monthly wages and 52 per cent in hourly wages. Migrant workers with more than a primary school education receive both a monthly and an hourly wage premium. Training is another strong predictor of monthly and hourly wages for both groups, in line with Knight, Song and Jia (1999). The coefficients suggest that training is more important for migrant workers than it is for urban workers.

Self-employment provides a significant monthly and hourly earnings premium, for both migrant and urban workers. This may be related to the fact that we are only able to observe the net income of self-employed individuals rather than their labour earnings; the contribution of unpaid family labour is another part of the explanation (Strauss and Thomas 1995: 1,960).

Men earn more than women, but the wage gap between males and females is greater among urban workers.[5] Unlike urban workers, migrant workers are rewarded for marriage. This may indicate a greater increase in the work aspirations of migrant workers after marriage or self-selection into marriage by individuals with a greater earning capability.[6]

We find that occupation is a significant indicator of earnings for both migrant and urban workers. Among both groups, managers receive the highest monthly and hourly wages, and service workers the lowest.[7] In the case of urban workers, foreign enterprises pay higher wages than the reference group (governments and public institutions); all other types of enterprises offer lower wages. For migrant workers, most ownership categories provide the same level of pay as the reference group.[8] Employment in different industries does not affect the earnings of migrant workers. Among urban workers, however, those working in electricity, gas and water, information and computer services, and finance and real estate earn more than their counterparts in the manufacturing sector (the reference group), while those working in wholesale and retail trade, accommodation and catering, and residential services earn less.

4 WAGE INEQUALITY AND ITS COMPONENTS

Although wage functions reveal useful information about the conditional mean of wages, a more interesting issue in understanding wage structures is to study the distribution and dispersion of wages within and between migrant and urban workers. In this section, we examine wage inequality and decompose the factors that contribute to it.

Figure 4.3 plots monthly and hourly wage distributions for urban workers, migrant workers, and urban and migrant workers combined. It is apparent that the distributions of both monthly and hourly wages are more concentrated for migrant workers than for urban workers. However, the effect of migration on the distribution of monthly and hourly wages in urban areas is not so easy to detect. To shed light on this, we provide summary measures of wage inequality in Table 4.3. To increase understanding of the monthly and hourly wage distributions, in Figure 4.4 we also plot the Kernel density distribution curves for the weekly working hours of urban and migrant workers. As Figure 4.4 suggests, the distribution of hours worked per week is more equal for urban workers than for migrant workers.[9]

The measures selected for presentation in Table 4.3 are the Gini coefficient, the Theil index and the mean logarithmic deviation (MLD). Urban workers have a Gini coefficient of 0.38, a Theil index of 0.28 and an MLD of 0.24 for monthly wages, and a Gini coefficient of 0.39, a Theil index of 0.26 and an MLD of 0.26 for hourly wages. It seems that wages are more equally distributed among migrant workers: they have a Gini coefficient, Theil index and MLD of 0.29, 0.17 and 0.14 respectively for monthly wages, and 0.31, 0.17 and 0.16 respectively for hourly wages.

The inclusion of migrant workers in the urban labour market alters the pattern of the urban wage distribution. When we compare wage inequality among urban *hukou* holders with that among all urban workers, we find that the Gini coefficient for monthly wages falls from 0.38 to 0.37 with the presence of migrants in urban areas. However, migration slightly widens the distribution of hourly wages: the Gini coefficient for hourly wages rises from 0.39 for urban *hukou* holders to 0.43 for all urban workers.

Figure 4.3   China: Kernel Density of Monthly and Hourly Wages for Urban,
Migrant and All Urban Workers

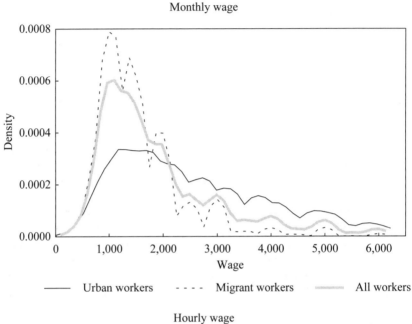

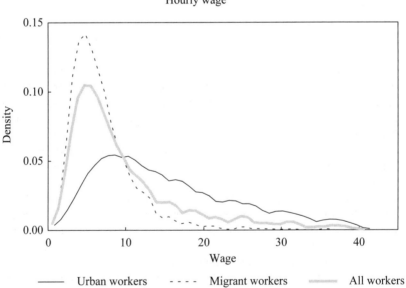

Source: Urban Household Survey, 2008; Urban Migrant Survey, 2008.

Table 4.3   China: Inequality Indices for the Monthly and Hourly Wages of Urban, Migrant and All Urban Workers

	Urban Workers		Migrant Workers		All Urban Workers	
	Monthly Wage	Hourly Wage	Monthly Wage	Hourly Wage	Monthly Wage	Hourly Wage
Gini	0.38	0.39	0.29	0.31	0.37	0.43
Theil	0.28	0.26	0.17	0.17	0.27	0.34
MLD	0.24	0.26	0.14	0.16	0.22	0.30

MLD = mean logarithmic deviation.
Source: Urban Household Survey, 2008; Urban Migrant Survey, 2008.

Figure 4.4   China: Kernel Density of Working Hours per Week for Urban, Migrant and All Urban Workers

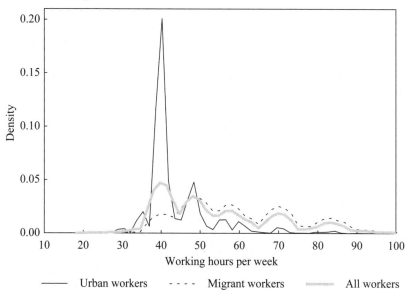

Source: Urban Household Survey, 2008; Urban Migrant Survey, 2008.

To explore the underlying factors contributing to wage inequality in the urban labour market, we decompose the inequality measures presented above by various contributing factors. Decompositions of wage inequality by wage source and population group have been implemented in the past (see, for instance, Gustafsson and Li 2001). However, as Fields (1998), Morduch and

Sicular (2002), Wan (2004) and others have pointed out, decomposition by wage source cannot reveal the effect of factors such as gender, education and occupation on the wage distribution, although it does shed light on the contribution of wage components to wage inequality. Decomposition by population group is not immune to this flaw either; the grouping variables tend to become confounded with other factors that contribute to wage inequality, with the result that the decompositions convey little information. Moreover, when decomposing inequality by population group, the grouping variables are dichotomous while the continuous variables have to be grouped artificially. Also, when multiple grouping variables are used, the decompositions become increasingly difficult, because the number of observations within each cell decreases multiplicatively.

To overcome the drawbacks of traditional decompositions, researchers have developed several regression-based decomposition approaches.[10] This chapter adopts the approach used by Shorrocks (1999) to disentangle the contribution of constituent elements to earnings inequality. The basic idea is to estimate the income flows associated with certain characteristics, compute the marginal contribution of each income flow to total inequality in consideration of all possible decomposition sequences and, finally, derive the contribution of each income flow by taking the average of its marginal contributions in all possible sequences.[11]

To implement the Shapley-value decomposition approach proposed by Shorrocks (1999), the first step would be to generate the predicted wage attributable to each independent variable. It is well known that the choice of reference groups of dummy variables will affect the estimate of the constant term, which eventually influences the decomposition results. To get around this problem, we obtain predicted wages from the estimates of the log of monthly and hourly wages, shown in Table 4.2. After anti-log, the constant term becomes a multiplier of predicted income, which has no effect on wage inequality.

Table 4.4 reports the Shapley-value decomposition results for wage inequality, measured by Gini coefficients. It is noteworthy that a significant proportion of wage inequality remains unexplained, reflecting the inability to control for the exhaustive list of factors that might explain inequality.

City dummies play the most important role in explaining inequality of monthly and hourly wages among migrant workers as well as inequality of monthly wages among urban workers, implying that unobserved factors at the city level are a vital driving force of wage inequality. There are several ways to explore, at least in part, unobserved factors at the city level. If spatial price deflators are taken into account, the contribution of city dummies to wage inequality would be expected to decrease.[12] The movement of workers across cities in response to spatial variations in living costs is another way of shedding light on this 'black box' (Moretti 2008), but this is beyond the scope of this chapter.

Table 4.4   China: Shapley-value Decomposition of the Gini Coefficient for Wages (%)

	Urban Workers		Migrant Workers		All Urban Workers	
	Monthly Wage	Hourly Wage	Monthly Wage	Hourly Wage	Monthly Wage	Hourly Wage
Migrant					2.13	14.57
Experience	2.29	1.97	3.51	3.21	2.67	2.31
Gender	5.41	4.13	5.64	3.93	4.58	3.09
Marital status	0.06	0.07	1.51	0.79	0.83	0.45
Education	13.99	16.25	3.28	6.33	12.01	17.22
Training	1.10	0.78	1.33	1.70	1.22	1.26
Occupation	8.69	10.39	5.44	6.02	9.27	11.83
Ownership	4.62	6.33	1.02	3.22	3.38	7.14
Sector	6.73	6.64	3.74	4.38	3.35	3.49
City	14.70	13.84	12.88	18.24	13.44	16.35
Han	0.01	0.01	0.02	0.04	0.04	0.12
Self-employed	3.40	0.43	11.77	1.13	4.96	0.07
Residual	39.00	39.15	49.87	51.01	42.11	38.26
Constant	0	0	0	0	0	0
Total	**100.00**	**100.00**	**100.00**	**100.00**	**100.00**	**100.00**

Source: Urban Household Survey, 2008; Urban Migrant Survey, 2008.

While education plays a vital role in explaining wage inequality among urban workers, it explains only a small share of the wage inequality among migrant workers. Possibly this is because education is more equally distributed across migrant than urban workers. The combined contribution of occupation, enterprise ownership and industry of employment to wage inequality is large in magnitude, and bigger for urban workers than for migrant workers. The reason may be that migrants are more concentrated in certain employment categories, as reflected in the summary statistics.

Among urban and migrant workers combined, the decomposition results suggest that the presence of migrants tends to increase the Gini coefficient for hourly wages—that is, increases inequality. In the case of monthly wages, however, migrants help to mitigate inequality by working longer hours, which lends further support to the findings in Table 4.3.[13] Education and city are the two most important factors explaining inequality of wages among urban and migrant workers combined. Occupation, ownership and industry sector together account for 16 per cent of monthly wage inequality and 22 per cent of hourly wage inequality.

5   CONCLUSIONS

Based on large-scale data from two surveys conducted in 2008, this chapter has investigated wage structures and wage inequality among urban and migrant workers. We estimated the wage functions for urban workers, migrant workers, and urban and migrant workers combined, and compared the wage determination processes for each group. We then quantified the extent of wage inequality and conducted a Shapley-value decomposition to explore the constituent elements of wage inequality. The results support the following conclusions.

First, there are significant differences between urban and migrant workers, in terms of both demography and employment structure. Migrant workers are younger, less well educated and less likely to have received training; they are more concentrated in the private sector and in service industries.

Second, there are unconditional monthly and hourly wage gaps between urban and migrant workers, which persist even when certain factors are controlled for. The hourly wage gap is greater than the monthly wage gap, both unconditionally and conditionally.

Third, wage inequality is greater among urban workers than among migrant workers. Our results show that the inclusion of migrant workers in the urban labour force decreases monthly wage inequality but increases hourly wage inequality.

Fourth, the regression-based decomposition results suggest that location and education play an important role in explaining wage inequality among urban workers. However, education is much less important in explaining wage inequality among migrant workers.

Finally, for urban and migrant workers combined, education and city are the most significant factors in explaining wage inequality. Occupation, enterprise ownership and industry of employment also account for a significant proportion of wage inequality.

NOTES

1   Potential work experience is measured as age minus years of schooling minus six.
2   The monthly wage comprises the worker's basic wage and any subsidies and bonuses, but not the contributions an employer makes to various insurance schemes on the employee's behalf. The hourly wage is the ratio of monthly wages to hours worked per month.
3   The results reported in Table 4.2 are unweighted. The weighted results are available from the authors upon request.
4   To test for statistically significant differences between the urban and migrant wage structures, in a separate specification we included the interaction terms for the migrant dummy and each independent variable in the wage functions. The results are not reported here but can be obtained from the authors upon request.
5   The gender wage differential is revealed by a large body of literature. On the wage differences between male and female urban workers, see, for instance, Gustafsson and Li (2000)

and Démurger, Fournier and Chen (2005); on the gender wage differential among migrant workers, see Knight, Song and Jia (1999).

6   There is no consensus among researchers on the explanation for the marriage wage premium. See Krashinsky (2004) for a review.

7   Knight, Song and Jia (1999) and Démurger et al. (2009) also find that the occupation dummies in the wage functions are statistically significant for migrant workers. Although they do not report the results, Meng and Zhang (2001) estimate the earnings functions separately for each occupation, on the implicit assumption that wage determination processes differ across occupations.

8   Chen, Démurger and Fournier (2005) find that, for urban workers, foreign enterprises provide the highest wages, followed by state-owned enterprises, private or individual enterprises and collective enterprises. In the case of migrant workers, Knight, Song and Jia (1999) find that collective enterprises provide the highest wages, followed by foreign enterprises, private enterprises and state-owned enterprises. In this study, we find that the interaction terms for the migrant dummy and ownership are jointly significant in both the monthly and hourly wage functions.

9   The Gini coefficients for hours worked per week are 0.11 and 0.15 respectively for urban and migrant workers.

10 Knight and Song (2001) use the approach proposed by Fields (1998) to decompose urban earnings, and Meng (2004) uses it to decompose income inequality. Deng and Li (2009) employ the regression-based decomposition approaches developed by Fields (1998), Morduch and Sicular (2002) and Shorrocks (1999) to decompose earnings inequality in urban China in 1988, 1995 and 2002.

11 The marginal contributions of an income flow are calculated as the change in inequality after isolating the effect of this income flow from inequality. Morduch and Sicular (2002) provide two alternatives to isolation of factors: deleting the factors, and replacing the means of the factors with the factors themselves. The marginal contributions of each income flow always vary with the decomposition sequence.

12 Démurger, Fournier and Li (2006) find that income inequality in urban China is overstated if spatial price deflators are not used.

13 The decomposition results for total urban workers should be interpreted with care, since the decompositions of wage inequality for this group of workers are based on the wage functions in Table 4.3, which implicitly assumes that the wage determination processes for urban and migrant workers are the same.

APPENDIX A4.1 SURVEY WEIGHTS

The weights used in this study are designed to make the urban and migrant samples in each province representative of the respective populations in those provinces. To this end, we use the figures from the 2005 1% National Population Sample Survey for the total number of urban, and migrant, workers aged 16–60 who are working in cities to calculate the inverse probability of the urban and migrant workers in our sample being selected within each province. These weights are presented in Table A4.1.

Table A4.1 China: Weights for Urban and Migrant Workers by Province

	1% Population Survey		RUMiCI Survey		Weights	
	Migrant Workers	Urban Workers	Migrant Workers	Urban Workers	Migrant Workers	Urban Workers
Shanghai	10,898	20,540	772	677	14.12	30.34
Jiangsu	4,126	12,431	714	804	5.78	15.46
Zhejiang	6,120	6,133	696	833	8.79	7.36
Anhui	889	6,890	738	665	1.20	10.36
Henan	449	6,678	579	732	0.78	9.12
Hubei	1,254	8,837	419	495	2.99	17.85
Guangdong	38,971	45,468	904	1,267	43.11	35.89
Chongqing	965	5,893	499	565	1.93	10.43
Sichuan	1,078	6,995	326	516	3.31	13.56

Source: 2005 1% National Population Sample Survey; Urban Household Survey, 2008; Urban Migrant Survey, 2008.

5 The Educational and Health Outcomes of the Children of Migrants

Sherry Tao Kong and Xin Meng

1 INTRODUCTION

In 2005, at least 126 million migrants from rural areas were working in Chinese cities (NBS 2006a). In addition to its immediate—and sizeable—economic effects, migration on such a scale has important implications for the welfare of the next generation. The children of migrants either move to the cities with their parents or stay behind in the countryside to be cared for by other family members. While reliable statistics on the number of children left behind in the countryside are hard to come by, a figure of 20 million is commonly cited in the literature (Ye, Murray and Huan 2005; State Council Research Group 2006: 229).[1] Similarly, only rough estimates of the numbers of children who have migrated to the city with their parents are available. It has been suggested that this floating population comprises about 15 million children (State Council Research Group 2006: 229; Shi 2005).

The well-being of children is important not just to their parents but to society as a whole. If the development of migrants' children is compromised, not only may they fail to reach their potential, but they may become an economic and social drag on society. Like other children, the children of migrants will play an important role in China's future social, economic and political development. They will help shape the society of tomorrow.

This chapter studies the educational and health outcomes of the children of migrants against the backdrop of the huge flows of rural migrants to the cities over the past two decades. Migration may affect children's educational and health outcomes in a number of ways. Collectively, the higher rates of return to education and health in the cities are likely to encourage migrant parents to increase their investment in their children's education and health. At an individual level, however, the effect of migration is less clear-cut. For the children left behind in the countryside, migration leads to a trade-off between an increased level of family income through the remittances sent home by

93

parents and a reduced level of parental care invested in their education and health. For those who travel to the city with their parents, on the other hand, the act of migration itself inevitably disrupts the continuity of the children's education and their daily life. In addition, in many Chinese cities migrants and their children are given only limited access to urban services, compromising the quality of education and health care they receive. Thus, while the quality of education and health care in the cities is generally higher than in rural areas, the net impact of migration is unclear for children who move to the cities with their migrant parents.

Empirically, the economic literature generally finds that migration has a positive effect on children's educational and health outcomes (Edwards and Ureta 2003; Hanson and Woodruff 2003; Mansuri 2006), but has adverse effects on family life and the continuity of education (Long 1975; Pribesh and Downey 1999) and on the opportunity cost of study (de Brauw and Giles 2006). Studies focusing on the effect of migration on Chinese children's education and health are scarce, and often rely on a small sample of data collected within a limited geographic area (see, for example, Han 2003, Shi 2005 and Liang and Chen 2007).

Using large-scale data from three surveys conducted in China as part of the Rural–Urban Migration in China and Indonesia (RUMiCI) project, this chapter aims to provide a general picture of how the children of migrants are faring relative to the children of non-migrants in terms of both education and health. The chapter is structured as follows. The next section briefly introduces some background information on the institutional setting of rural–urban migration and how it may affect the educational and health outcomes of children. Section 3 describes the data and the basic characteristics of four groups of interest: rural children; left-behind children; migrated children; and urban children. Section 4 examines the effect of migration on the educational outcomes of migrants' children, and section 5 looks at the effect on health. Our main conclusions are summarized in section 6.

2 BACKGROUND

In most parts of the world, rural-to-urban migration is a household-level event in which children move to the destination city with their parents. During this process, the children's education and health may suffer from the disruption caused to their family life and schooling. In China, however, many migrants are unable to take their families with them to the cities. This is essentially a consequence of the household registration (*hukou*) system, which excludes rural migrant workers from the urban social welfare system. The deep rural–urban divide in social welfare provision means that migrant workers are largely denied access to the benefits enjoyed by urban *hukou* holders, such as unemployment benefits, pension payments and health care insurance. In addition, they and their children are given only limited access to education, health and other public services. Because of the precarious nature of migrant life in the cities, rural-to-urban migrants often choose to leave their children behind in the countryside where they can be cared for by other family members. In the literature, the children who move to the cities with their migrant parents are usually called 'migrated children', while those who remain behind in the countryside are called 'left-behind children'.

Left-behind children are generally looked after by a single parent or by other family members, usually grandparents. Our data show that 35 per cent of all left-behind children are living with a single parent, 59 per cent are living with grandparents and 4 per cent are living with other relatives. The remaining 2 per cent are at boarding school. The quality of the day-to-day supervision provided by grandparents and other family members is likely to differ considerably from that provided by the children's own parents; left-behind children in single-parent households may also suffer from a reduced level of parental care. This is likely to have consequences for the education and health of this group of children. A study on left-behind children in Central and West China by Ye, Murray and Huan (2005) suggests that they suffer from increased levels of mental pressure and insecurity, although the overall effect on school performance is limited.

Children who move to the cities with their migrant parents face a different, but equally challenging, set of conditions. For a start, they must adapt to a new and totally unfamiliar environment. This can be difficult, even for adults. The children of migrants also face discrimination in gaining access to public education in urban areas, because they do not have the requisite *hukou* status. Liang and Chen (2007) find not only that migrated children have lower enrolment rates than urban children, but that they have lower enrolment rates than the non-migrant children in the rural communities from whence they came.

Perhaps out of desperation, in the mid to late 1990s migrants began to establish their own schools in a number of cities. While a full account of these schools has yet to be written, Han (2003) reported that there were over 200 such schools in Beijing alone, most of them operating under very modest conditions. Many were not equipped with permanent classrooms and most of the teachers were not properly qualified. As a consequence, the quality of education they offered was relatively poor (Han 2003; Shi 2005). In the past few years, the central government has instructed urban schools to accept the children of migrants. Nevertheless, in some cities they still face discriminatory practices such as the imposition of prohibitively high charges or 'donations' in addition to the usual tuition fees. Such obstacles are expected to continue to adversely affect migrated children's educational outcomes for some time to come.

Rural-to-urban migrants and their families are yet to be included in the urban health care system, with obvious implications for their health. Chan et al. (2008), Lin et al. (2003) and Liang, Guo and Duan (2007) find a lower coverage rate of vaccination among migrated children and a general lack of knowledge among migrant parents about child health. However, to the best of our knowledge no study has systematically investigated the overall effect of migration on the health of migrated children. Our data indicate that less than 7 per cent of the 7,161 migrant workers surveyed had any type of urban health insurance, and 42 per cent were not covered by health insurance of any kind. Although 47 per cent participated in the rural cooperative medical insurance system, this was of little practical benefit to them as long as they remained in the cities. In short, migrants and their families enjoy less access to quality health care, and must pay more for it.

Against the institutional background described in this section, we attempt to gauge the effect of migration on the educational and health outcomes of migrants' children. To shed light on this subject, we compare rural children from non-migrant families with left-behind children; migrated children with left-behind children; and migrated children with urban children. We hope to identify the effect of migration on the children of migrants by using rural children and urban children as counterfactuals.

3   DATA AND SUMMARY STATISTICS

The data on which this study is based are taken from three surveys conducted in China in 2008 as part of the RUMiCI project. This gave us three independent samples: a sample of 8,000 rural households from the Rural Household Survey, one of 5,000 urban households from the Urban Household Survey and one of 5,000 rural-to-urban migrant households from the Urban Migrant Survey. It is important to note that, because the surveys were conducted independently, households from the rural sample cannot be linked to households in the migrant sample, even though both types of households contain children with migrant parents. However, as both the Rural Household and Urban Migrant surveys ask for information about children who have been left behind in the countryside and those who have moved to the cities with their parents, we are able to conduct consistent comparisons of the educational and health outcomes of the two groups of children within each survey.

Table 5.1 presents some summary statistics for the total sample of 8,781 children aged 15 or below covered by the three datasets. We distinguish four groups of interest: (1) rural children (those living with both parents in the countryside); (2) left-behind children (those living in rural areas who have at least one parent living in the city); (3) migrated children (those from rural

Table 5.1   China: Number and Share of Rural, Left-behind, Migrated and Urban Children and Their Living Arrangements

	Rural Household Survey (N = 4,717)			Urban Migrant Survey (N = 2,311)		Urban House-hold Survey (N = 1,753)
	Rural	Left-behind	Migrated	Left-behind	Migrated	Urban
No. of observations	2,462	2,027	228	1,298	1,013	1,604
(%)	(52)	(43)	(5)	(56)	(44)	(92)
% living with:						
Both parents	100		32		87	100
Single parent		44	18	35	6	
Not living with parents		56	50	65	7	

Source: Rural Household Survey, 2008; Urban Migrant Survey, 2008; Urban Household Survey, 2008.

households who are living in the city); and (4) urban children (those living with both parents in the city).[2] The Rural Household Survey sample is the only one to contain observations on rural children, and the Urban Household Survey sample is the only one to contain observations on urban children. Both the Rural Household and Urban Migrant samples, however, contain data on left-behind children, as well as observations on migrated children.[3]

According to the Rural Household Survey sample, 44 per cent of left-behind children live with a single parent and the other 56 per cent do not live with their parents. The Urban Migrant Survey data, meanwhile, indicate that about 35 per cent of left-behind children live with a single parent and 65 per cent do not live with their parents. Of the 2,311 children aged 15 or below in the Urban Migrant Survey sample, 56 per cent are children who have been left behind in the countryside and 44 per cent are children who are living in the cities, either with one or both parents or, in the case of 3 per cent of children, for other reasons (mainly to attend boarding school).

The Urban Migrant Survey data paint a more complete picture of migrated children's living arrangements than the Rural Household Survey data. When an entire family moves to the city, this household may no long exist in the countryside and hence would not be covered by the Rural Household Survey. In contrast, children who move to the city with their families would be covered by the Urban Migrant Survey. We therefore use the Urban Migrant Survey as our main source of information on migrated children. It indicates that the

Table 5.2   China: Age and Gender Composition of Rural, Left-behind,
*   Migrated and Urban Children*

	Rural Household Survey			Urban Migrant Survey		Urban Household Survey
	Rural	Left-behind	Migrated	Left-behind	Migrated	Urban
Age						
Mean age (years)	9.3	8.6	10.1	8.0	7.2	8.2
Standard deviation	4.3	4.4	4.1	4.5	4.5	4.3
Aged 0–5 (no.)	698	726	60	539	486	590
(%)	(28)	(36)	(26)	(42)	(48)	(37)
Aged 6–15 (no.)	1,764	1,301	168	759	527	1,014
(%)	(72)	(64)	(74)	(59)	(52)	(63)
Gender (%)						
Male	55	55	58	55	56	53
Female	45	45	42	45	44	47
School attendance (%)						
Below school age	30	37	26	41	47	39
Primary school	49	43	35	40	37	43
Junior high school	19	18	29	18	14	17
Senior high school	1	1	6	1	1	1
Dropped out	1	1	3	1	1	0
No. of observations	2,462	2,027	228	1,298	1,013	1,604

Source: Rural Household Survey, 2008; Urban Migrant Survey, 2008; Urban Household Survey, 2008.

majority of migrated children (87 per cent) are living with both parents in the city (see Table 5.1).

The age and gender structures of the four groups of children, as well as the proportions attending school, are described in Table 5.2. Gender structures are roughly uniform across all four groups. Migrated children have the youngest average age (7.2 years) and nearly half of them are under the age of six. Among school-aged children (those aged 6–15), a higher proportion of left-behind than migrated children are attending primary school or junior high school. Given the poor access to education in the cities, it is no surprise to observe that the proportion of migrated children of school age in the Urban Migrant Survey (52 per cent) is lower than that of left-behind children (59 per cent), indicating that school-aged children are the ones most likely to be left behind in the countryside.

It is also of interest to observe the difference in the relative mean ages of migrated and left-behind children in the Rural Household and Urban Migrant samples: in the Rural Household Survey migrated children are older, whereas in the Urban Migrant sample left-behind children are older. One explanation for this difference may be that households with young children are less likely to migrate, but if they do, they tend to take the younger children with them to the city and leave the older children behind in the countryside. An alternative explanation is that family migration is more likely among couples with younger children, with the result that these children are underrepresented in the Rural Household Survey sample.

Children's well-being has much to do with the characteristics of their parents and of the household as a whole. Table 5.3 depicts a number of key indicators for parents and households for each group of children. It is important to emphasize that the household-level information is strictly associated with the source of the data. In other words, where children do not live in the same household as the survey respondent (as would be the case, for example, with migrated children in the Rural Household Survey or left-behind children in the Urban Migrant Survey), the characteristics obtained for the household do not reflect the environment in which the children actually live.

Migrant parents are generally three to five years younger than rural children's parents. Youngest of all are the parents of left-behind children in the Rural Household Survey. To some extent, these age differentials probably reflect the different age profiles of migrant workers and non-migrant rural workers. Meanwhile, it is evident from Table 5.3 that there are a number of conflicts between the descriptions of the parents of left-behind versus migrated children in the Rural Household and Urban Migrant surveys. On the one hand, the Rural Household Survey data suggest that the parents of left-behind children have a slightly lower average level of education than the parents of non-migrant rural parents: around five to six years of schooling (a score of 1.5–1.8), compared with seven to eight years for the parents of non-migrant rural parents (a score of 1.6–1.9). On the other hand, the Urban Migrant Survey data indicate that the parents of both migrated children and left-behind children have higher average levels of education (scores of around 1.9–2.3, that is, junior high school or slightly above). Moreover, although there is only a slight difference in the average age and educational level of these two groups of parents in the Urban Migrant Survey sample, according to the Rural Household Survey the parents of left-behind children are around three years younger than the parents of migrated children, and have two to three more years of schooling.

The differences between the parents of left-behind children in the Rural Household and Urban Migrant surveys are somewhat puzzling. The explanation

The Great Migration

Table 5.3 China: Characteristics of Children's Parents and Households

	Rural Household Survey			Urban Migrant Survey		Urban Household Survey
	Rural	Left-behind	Migrated	Left-behind	Migrated	Urban
Parents' age (years)						
Mother	36.1	30.9	34.2	32.7	33.2	35.6
Father	37.9	32.9	36.5	34.2	34.7	38.1
Parents' education[a]						
Mother	1.62	1.51	1.72	1.93	1.95	3.1
Father	1.89	1.76	2.09	2.22	2.26	3.2
Parents' migration duration (years)[b]						
Mother	0–1.6	2–4	1.9–3.4	4.4–8.5	5.7–9.5	n.a.
Father	0.1–3.5	4.8–7.7	3.6–6.2	6.1–10.9	6.9–11.6	n.a.
Household size (no. of members)	4.7	5.0	4.8	1.5	3.4	3.5
Living area (m²)	30.9	28.2	30.6	10.4	11.7	–
Income per capita (yuan)						
Mean	4,661	3,799	4,393	19,632	12,331	20,218
SD	3,793	2,678	2,982	14,265	10,344	16,384
Consumption expenditure per capita (yuan)						
Mean	3,540	2,879	3,576	10,174	8,427	11,669
SD	3,378	2,708	3,024	6,932	12,089	8,762
Total expenditure per capita (yuan)						
Mean	5,160	4,045	5,337	16,874	11,654	15,535
SD	5,606	4,140	5,529	16,468	15,377	23,062
No. of observations	2,462	2,027	228	1,298	1,013	1,604

SD = standard deviation; n.a. = not applicable; – = no information available.
a   1 = primary; 2 = junior high; 3 = senior high; 4 = college; 5 = university or above.
b   The figures are lower and upper bounds. The lower bound is the number of years since beginning the current job; the upper bound is the number of years since first migrating to a city.

Source: Rural Household Survey, 2008; Urban Migrant Survey, 2008; Urban Household Survey, 2008.

may be that the two surveys capture different groups of such parents. It is sensible to expect that the Urban Migrant Survey would capture a greater number of migrants with longer durations of migration. It is also intuitively sound to expect that parents who take their children with them to the cities would have longer durations of migration than the parents who leave their children behind. In short, it seems likely that many migrant parents leave their children behind when they first move to the cities, but take them with them after a few years when they feel sufficiently established to do so.

Table 5.3 also provides some basic information on the households with which children are associated. Children residing in rural areas typically live in larger households consisting of around five members, compared with 3.5 for households residing in the cities. It is probably useful to reiterate here that the household-level information is only meaningful where children reside in the same place as the person from whom the data were collected. Thus, for instance, the average household size of 1.5 for left-behind children in the Urban Migrant Survey does not mean that these children live in small families, but rather—as one would intuitively expect—that their parents living in the cities have smaller households. This qualification also applies to the household income and expenditure data: without accounting for the vastly different cost of living between rural and urban areas, and across various regions and cities, the figures can only be interpreted as indicative of the fact that children who live in the city tend to have higher living standards than children who live in rural villages, as measured by per capita household income or expenditure.

We estimate a probit model to identify the factors that differentiate children who move to the cities from those who are left behind. The sample comprises children whose parent/s have migrated—that is, both left-behind and migrated children—from the Rural Household and Urban Migrant surveys. The dependent variable takes a value of 1 if a child has been left behind and a value of 0 if a child has moved to the city with his or her migrant parent/s. The independent variables are child's age and number of siblings. The dummy variables are gender, health and education: the gender variable takes a value of 1 if the child is a girl; the health variable takes a value of 1 if the child has above-average health; and the education variable takes a value of 1 if the child is currently attending school. Additional explanatory variables include the age of each parent, the migration duration of each parent in years and the household's per capita income. Three more dummy variables are included to indicate whether both parents are migrants, whether the mother/father has more than a junior high school education and whether at least one parent is self-employed.

Table 5.4 presents the results of the estimation using the combined Rural Household and Urban Migrant samples, as well as the Urban Migrant Survey sample alone. For the reasons mentioned earlier, we consider the Urban Migrant Survey data to provide better information on migrated children than

*Table 5.4   China: Probit Model for Left-behind versus Migrated Children:
           Prob(left-behind = 1)*

	Urban Migrant Survey (1)	Urban Migrant Survey + Rural Household Survey (2)
Child's age	0.051***	0.034***
	(0.013)	(0.011)
Child is female	−0.009	0.033
	(0.060)	(0.051)
No. of siblings of child	0.113**	0.128***
	(0.052)	(0.043)
Child has above-average health	−0.371***	−0.271***
	(0.097)	(0.085)
Child is attending school	−0.057	−0.013
	(0.112)	(0.096)
Father's age	−0.004	−0.008*
	(0.005)	(0.004)
Mother's age	−0.013***	−0.013***
	(0.005)	(0.004)
Father has more than a	−0.035	−0.098
junior high school education	(0.068)	(0.060)
Mother has more than a	−0.146*	−0.155**
junior high school education	(0.080)	(0.073)
No. of years of migration	−0.024***	−0.014***
	(0.005)	(0.005)
Both parents are migrants	−0.998***	−0.691***
	(0.083)	(0.064)
Household income per capita	0.414***	0.419***
	(0.030)	(0.030)
At least one parent is self-employed	−0.767***	−0.762***
	(0.082)	(0.074)
Constant	1.172***	2.427***
	(0.204)	(0.172)
No. of observations	2,238	3,757

*** = $p < 0.01$; ** = $p < 0.05$; * = $p < 0.1$. Standard errors are in parentheses.
Source: Rural Household Survey, 2008; Urban Migrant Survey, 2008.

the Rural Household Survey data. We find that most of the explanatory variables are significantly associated with the decision as to whether or not to take a child to the city. The results show that older children and less healthy children are more likely to be left behind. Older and better-educated parents, especially mothers, are less likely to leave their child behind. The longer the duration of the parents' migration, the more likely they are to take their children to the city. Both parents being migrants and one or both being self-employed decrease the probability that they will leave their children behind, but a higher per capita household income increases the chance that a child will be left behind.

These conditional correlations do not suggest a causal relationship. We do not know, for example, whether leaving children behind makes them unhealthy or, rather, whether parents are less likely to take an unhealthy child with them to the city because they are concerned about the high cost of urban health care. Again, we cannot tell if parents with higher incomes tend to leave their children in the home village or whether they receive higher incomes because they do not need to look after their children in the cities. Nevertheless, the results are informative in pointing out factors that are associated with the outcome of a child's migration status.

4   MIGRATION AND EDUCATIONAL OUTCOMES

In this section we examine the effect of rural–urban migration on the education of children as measured by parental ratings of their school performance. Table 5.5 presents a range of background information on the education of the four groups of children based on the Rural Household, Urban Migrant and Urban Household samples.

The first panel shows the distribution of children by school attendance. As our sample is restricted to children aged 15 or below, most of the children in the sample are either not yet at school or are in primary or junior high school. The drop-out rate is no higher than 1 per cent across all types of children.

The second panel shows the distribution of children by quality of school attended, based on the assessments of parents and guardians. It indicates that both urban children in the cities and left-behind children in the countryside are more likely to attend good schools than migrated children. It is important to point out, however, that these assessments of school quality are subjective and a product of perceptions. Parents' perceptions are very likely to be affected by unobserved factors that co-determine the assessment of a child's performance.

The third panel shows the distribution of children by school performance, again based on the subjective assessments of parents and guardians. While 62 per cent of urban children are rated as performing well or very well, only half

Table 5.5   China: Summary Statistics for Children's Education

	Rural Household Survey		Urban Migrant Survey		Urban Household Survey
	Rural	Left-behind	Left-behind	Migrated	Urban
School attendance (%)					
Below school age	30	37	41	47	39
Primary school	49	43	40	37	43
Junior high school	19	18	18	14	17
Senior high school	1	1	1	1	1
Dropped out	1	1	1	1	0
School quality (%)					
Very good	6	4	6	3	15
Above average	25	22	26	37	54
Average	67	72	64	58	31
Below average	2	2	4	3	0
School performance (%)					
Very good	8	6	13	8	13
Good	40	41	37	44	49
Average	49	49	46	46	37
Poor	3	4	4	2	1
Very poor	0	0	1	0	0
Concerns about children (%)					
No concerns	35	36	43	40	43
School performance	55	55	42	45	40
Excessive internet, computer or television use	6	4	6	9	10
Being bullied or bad friends	4	4	6	4	5
Other	1	1	4	2	3
Annual school fees in 2007 (yuan)					
Primary school	403	454	797	1,404	1,566
Junior high school	1,018	1,211	1,716	1,787	2,093
No. of observations	2,462	2,027	1,298	1,013	1,604

Source: Rural Household Survey, 2008; Urban Migrant Survey, 2008; Urban Household Survey, 2008.

of the migrated, left-behind and rural children are in the 'good' or 'very good' categories. It is important to note that the survey question on which the data are based asks about *within-class* performance, not about overall educational achievement. Thus, the results do not reflect differences in the quality of rural versus urban schools, or of normal urban schools versus those set up specifically for the children of migrants.

It is interesting to note that the main concern of parents and guardians living in the countryside is that their children are not performing well at school. On average, they registered concerns about the school performance of around 55 per cent of rural and left-behind children in the Rural Household Survey sample—well above the ratios for the children in the other samples.

The final panel of Table 5.5 concerns the total amount of school fees paid in 2007, that is, the minimum fee imposed by the school, not including voluntary sponsorships, donations or any other costs of attending a particular school.[4] Urban and migrated children pay more to attend primary school and junior high school than rural and left-behind children. Given that migrated children are often not admitted to urban schools because of their non-urban *hukou* status, the fees reported for migrated children are more likely to relate to schools specifically set up for them in the cities. The data from the Urban Migrant Survey indicate that urban migrant primary schools charge about 1,400 yuan and junior high schools 1,800 yuan. In both cases, this is equivalent to around 85–90 per cent of the average school fees paid by urban children.

Children's educational outcomes may be associated with a wide range of factors. We estimate the following regression to measure the conditional correlations between the parent-assessed school performance of children and parents' migration status:

$$Y_i^c = \beta X_i^c + \theta S_i^c + \delta Z_i^p + \gamma^{c,p} D_i^{c,p} + \varepsilon_i, \qquad (5.1)$$

where Y is parent-assessed school performance (as summarized in Table 5.5) as a proxy for educational outcome; X^c is a vector of child's characteristics (age, gender, health, number of siblings); S^c is a vector of school-related factors (distance to school, annual school fees in 2007, number of hours per week the child spends on homework); Z^p is a vector of parental and household information (parents' age, parents' education, whether the parents are concerned about a child's education, per capita household income, region of residence); and $D^{c,p}$ is a dummy variable indicating child's/parent's migration status. The latter variable differs according to the sample: for the Rural Household Survey sample, we use a dummy variable indicating whether one or both parents have migrated; for the Urban Migrant Survey sample, we use a dummy variable indicating whether the child has been left behind in the rural village or is in the city with the parents; and for the urban and migrated children in the combined Urban Household and Urban Migrant samples, we use a dummy variable indicating whether one or both parents are migrants, and hence the child is a migrated child.[5]

Table 5.6 reports the results for the three sets of regressions. The dependent variable is 1 if the child is rated as performing very well at school and 0 otherwise. The following results are consistent across regressions.

- The older a child is, the more likely he or she is to be rated as performing very well at school. However, the variable is statistically significant only for the rural sample.
- Girls and children with better health are more likely to be rated as performing very well at school.
- Mother's education is positively associated with the school performance of their sons.
- If a parent is concerned about a child's education, the child is more likely to be rated as not having performed very well at school. However, the conditional correlation between the two variables is less than 15 per cent in every equation, suggesting that there are considerable differences in the importance parents place on school performance.

The most important variable in Table 5.6 is child's/parent's migration status. Based on the Rural Household Survey sample, we find that children with one or two migrant parents, whether boys or girls, are more likely to be rated as not performing very well at school. The results for the Urban Migrant Survey sample do not reveal any statistically significant relationship between child's migration status and parent-rated school performance. If anything, children living with their parents in the cities are rated lower on school performance than those who are left behind in the rural villages, but none of the coefficients are statistically significant. Finally, the results for the combined Urban Household and Urban Migrant samples suggest that migrated children are performing less well than their urban counterparts, though the variable is statistically significant for the female sample only. This result could be interpreted as migrated children performing just as well as urban children, but in schools of very different quality.

At this point we would like to stress that the results reported in Table 5.6 are conditional correlations between children's educational performance and children's or parents' migration status. Thus, the negative correlation found in the Rural Household Survey sample between school performance and having migrant parents does not necessarily indicate that a parent's migration status adversely affects a child's school performance. The reasons for not being able to claim any causal relationship are twofold. First, there may be reverse causality between children's education and parental migration status: on the one hand, the children of migrants (both left-behind and migrated) may perform less well than other rural children; on the other hand, parents may decide to move to the cities because they think their children are doing well at school. Second, our measure of children's school performance is based on the assessments of parents and guardians. Unobserved characteristics among parents may affect whether or not they rate their children as doing well, whether or not they decide to migrate and whether or not they decide to take their children to the city. A similar problem exists with the results obtained from the Urban Migrant Survey sample. Resolving this endogeneity issue will require a legitimate instrumental variable that affects parents' decisions but not children's school performance. The results for urban and migrated children are not affected by reverse causality, although possible measurement errors associated with the subjective assessment of school performance remain.

In summary, we find some negative relationship between parental rating of a child's school performance and child's/parent's migration status. To examine the causal effect further, we would need to gather more objective information on children's school performance.

5 MIGRATION AND HEALTH OUTCOMES

In this section we examine the effect of migration on the health outcomes of children. Table 5.7 presents some summary statistics on health-related variables for the four groups of children. As assessed by their parents, the general health of the majority of children is better than average. Migrant workers are particularly positive about the health of their children, both those in the cities and those left behind in the countryside.

Height is a commonly used indicator of the long-term health of children. We collected information on the height of children as reported by their parents and collated it by age. The results are shown in Figure 5.1. It shows that left-behind children are shorter at almost every age than both rural children from non-migrant families and migrated children living with their parents in the cities. Relative to urban children, however, migrated children are shorter at almost every age.

Data on the incidence of illness during the three months preceding the survey suggest that children living in the countryside (both rural and left-behind) are healthier than children living in the cities. However, the interpretation of this result is conditional on parents' and physicians' ability to diagnose illness, which may differ between urban and rural areas, as well as differing perceptions among parents living in rural and urban areas about what constitutes an illness. Around 12–15 per cent of the children living in cities fell ill within the three-month period, compared with 5–7 per cent in rural areas. Although

Table 5.6 China: Correlation between Migration Status and Children's School Performance

	Rural Household Survey			Urban Migrant Survey			Rural Household Survey + Migrated Children in Urban Migrant Survey		
	Total	Males	Females	Total	Males	Females	Total	Males	Females
One or both parents migrated	-0.03 (0.010)**	-0.02 (0.013)*	-0.03 (0.016)*				-0.02 (0.024)	0.02 (0.031)	-0.09 (0.040)**
Dummy for being in city				-0.03 (0.020)	-0.02 (0.025)	-0.02 (0.044)			
Age of child	-0.00 (0.002)**	-0.00 (0.002)	-0.01 (0.003)**	-0.00 (0.003)	-0.00 (0.004)	-0.01 (0.006)	-0.00 (0.003)	-0.00 (0.004)	-0.00 (0.005)
Child is male	-0.02 (0.009)**			-0.01 (0.019)			-0.03 (0.016)**		
Child is healthy	0.03 (0.010)***	0.03 (0.013)**	0.03 (0.016)**	0.08 (0.018)***	0.08 (0.023)***	0.08 (0.033)**	0.07 (0.018)***	0.06 (0.023)**	0.08 (0.028)***
Hours of homework	0.01 (0.006)	0.00 (0.008)	0.01 (0.011)	0.00 (0.001)	0.00 (0.001)	0.00 (0.001)	0.00 (0.001)	0.00 (0.001)	0.00 (0.001)
Parent/guardian is concerned about education	-0.10 (0.010)***	-0.11 (0.013)***	-0.01 (0.015)***	-0.06 (0.017)***	-0.07 (0.021)***	-0.05 (0.029)*	-0.12 (0.014)***	-0.09 (0.019)***	-0.15 (0.022)***
School distance/100	0.02 (0.019)	-0.02 (0.013)	0.03 (0.024)	-0.00 (0.001)	-0.00 (0.001)	-0.00 (0.001)	-0.00 (0.001)	0.00 (0.008)	-0.00 (0.001)
School fee/10,000	0.07 (0.057)	0.00 (0.069)	0.17 (0.092)*	-0.02 (0.060)	-0.05 (0.073)	0.04 (0.109)	-0.03 (0.065)	-0.08 (0.063)	0.08 (0.134)

	(1)	(2)	(3)	(4)	(5)	(6)	(7)	(8)	(9)
No. of siblings	0.00	0.00	0.00	-0.00	0.00	-0.02	-0.02	-0.02	-0.01
	(0.006)	(0.008)	(0.010)	(0.014)	(0.018)	(0.025)	(0.015)	(0.017)	(0.026)
Mother's years of schooling	0.00	0.01	0.00	0.01	0.01	0.01	0.00	0.01	-0.01
	(0.002)*	(0.002)**	(0.004)	(0.006)	(0.006)	(0.009)	(0.005)	(0.005)**	(0.009)
Father's years of schooling	-0.00	-0.00	0.00	0.01	0.01	-0.00	0.00	0.01	0.00
	(0.002)	(0.003)	(0.004)	(0.004)	(0.004)	(0.008)	(0.003)	(0.004)*	(0.005)
Mother's age	-0.00	-0.00	0.00	0.00	0.00	0.01	0.00	-0.00	0.01
	(0.001)	(0.001)*	(0.001)	(0.002)**	(0.002)	(0.003)*	(0.001)	(0.001)	(0.003)*
Father's age	0.00	0.00	-0.00	0.00	0.00	0.01	0.00	-0.00	0.00
	(0.001)	(0.001)	(0.001)	(0.002)**	(0.002)	(0.003)**	(0.001)	(0.001)	(0.002)
Household income per capita	-0.02	-0.02	-0.01	2.63	3.14	0.03	0.08	0.10	0.01
	(0.067)	(0.090)	(0.100)	(1.107)**	(1.226)**	(2.261)	(0.074)	(0.098)	(0.103)
Regional dummies	Yes	Yes	Yes	Yes	Yes	Yes	Yes	Yes	Yes
Constant	0.16	0.12	0.19	-0.01	-0.07	-0.10	0.12	0.01	0.10
	(0.040)***	(0.049)**	(0.063)***	(0.074)	(0.092)	(0.123)	(0.056)**	(0.071)	(0.087)
No. of observations	3,017	1,679	1,338	1,305	894	411	1,656	896	760
R²	0.06	0.07	0.07	0.07	0.08	0.11	0.07	0.09	0.10

* = significant at 10 per cent; ** = significant at 5 per cent; *** = significant at 1 per cent. Robust standard errors are in parentheses.

Source: Rural Household Survey, 2008; Urban Migrant Survey, 2008; Urban Household Survey, 2008.

Table 5.7   China: Summary Statistics on Children's Health

	Rural Household Survey		Urban Migrant Survey		Urban Household Survey
	Rural	Left-behind	Left-behind	Migrated	Urban
Parental assessment of child's health (%)					
Excellent	39	38	45	45	27
Good	52	52	43	46	61
Average	8	10	11	8	12
Poor	0	0	1	1	0
Very poor	0	0	0	0	0
Mean height (cm)	124.2	114.7	117.2	117.5	126.8
Sick during previous three months (%)					
Yes	5	7	n.a.	15	12
No	95	91	n.a.	85	88
Total health expenditure in previous three months (yuan)	178	138	n.a.	34	671
Out-of-pocket health expenditure (% of total health expenditure)	89.4	87.7	n.a.	95.2	15.0
Health subsidy or insurance (%)					
Rural cooperative system	89.1	88.4	53.8	38.6	18.5
Public system	0.1	0.3	8.4	3.5	15.2
Commercial health insurance	0.3	0.1	2.4	3.8	4.0
Other health insurance	0.8	0.1	1.6	3.6	8.5
None	8.6	8.5	33.8	50.6	52.5
No. of observations	2,462	2,027	1,298	1,013	1,604

n.a. = not available.

Source: Rural Household Survey, 2008; Urban Migrant Survey, 2008; Urban Household Survey, 2008.

Figure 5.1   China: Children's Height by Age

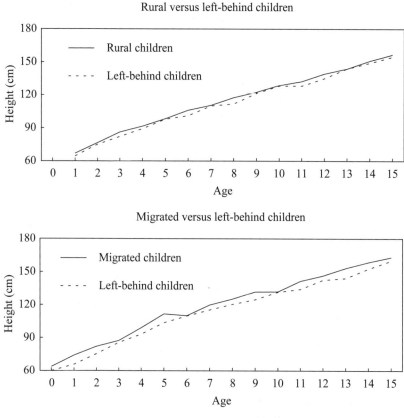

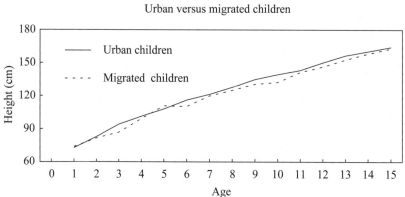

Source: Rural Household Survey, 2008; Urban Migrant Survey, 2008; Urban Household Survey, 2008.

a higher proportion of migrated children than urban children fell ill, nearly 20 times as much was spent on the medical treatment of urban children. Indeed, health expenditure on migrated children was lowest among all four groups of children, and spending on urban children by far the highest. Moreover, only 15 per cent of the health expenditures on urban children were out-of-pocket payments, compared with a minimum of 88 per cent for the other three groups. Although children living in rural areas seem to be able to claim a small part of the cost of their medical treatment, the children of migrants must bear almost the entire cost themselves.

This is again evident when we look at the health insurance situation of the four groups of children. Most children living in rural areas are covered by the rural cooperative health care system, while around 28 per cent of urban children either have access to public medical care or are covered by commercial or other kinds of health insurance. In stark contrast, only 11 per cent of migrated children are covered by any kind of health insurance.

To investigate the factors that potentially contribute to the differing health outcomes of children from different types of families, we re-estimate equation (5.1), where Y_i^c indicates the health outcome of child i: either the height of the child or whether the child is rated as having excellent health. The regression specification is similar to that used for the education analysis: X^c is a vector of child's characteristics (age, gender, number of siblings); H^c is the birth weight of a child;[6] Z^p contains information about parents and households (parents' age, parents' education, per capita household income, whether a parent is concerned about any aspect of the child's development); and $D^{c,p}$ is a dummy variable indicating child's/parent's migration status.

Selected results for the equations on health outcomes are presented in Table 5.8. The top panel shows the results for the height equation. Controlling for age in linear form[7] and gender, birth weight is associated with taller stature for all samples. The effect of the number of siblings is generally negative for the rural and migrant samples, but positive and not significant for the urban sample.

The most important findings, though, relate to the effect of the migration indicators. We find that left-behind children are on average 1.2 centimetres shorter than rural children whose parents are not migrants, and 3.9 centimetres shorter than children who have migrated to the cities with their parents. Children who have migrated to the cities are themselves 3.7 centimetres shorter than other urban children. However, since the information on height is obtained from parents, it seems possible that migrant parents may systematically underestimate the height of the children they have left behind in the countryside. If this is true, then the results may be affected by a measurement error.

The results for both the Rural Household and Urban Migrant samples indicate that children's long-term health is negatively associated with an absence of parental care, despite the higher income of migrant parents. While these results may not be causal, so that the decision to migrate or to take a child to the city may or may not be correlated with the health of children, it is hard to believe that parents choose to migrate because their children are shorter. Further investigation is warranted to pin down the nature and extent of any causal relationship. The main cause of the large difference in height between urban and migrated children should be long-term nutritional differences between rural and urban dwellers, as most migrated children have spent only a short time in the city. A thorough investigation of the underlying reasons for the height differentials between the different groups of children would require a complete migration history of the children. Unfortunately, this is not yet available.

The bottom panel of Table 5.8 shows selected results for the equation in which parents' subjective assessments of their children's health is the dependent variable. As before, the sign for children's birth weight is generally positive and significant for the Rural Household and Urban Migrant samples. However, for reasons that are not entirely clear to us, it is negative and insignificant for the combined Urban Household and Urban Migrant samples. The results for the Rural Household Survey sample indicate that parents and guardians are less likely to rate left-behind children as having excellent health, with the effect being more profound for girls than for boys. The results for the Urban Migrant Survey sample indicate that parents are more likely to rate migrated children as having excellent health, but this is true only for boys and the effect is not precisely estimated. The results for the combined sample of urban and migrated children show that the parents of migrated children are more likely than those of urban children to rate their children's health as excellent. The rating of a child's health status is subject to the same caveat described in the previous section for parental assessments of children's school performance. Due to the subjective nature of the dependent variable, it is very hard to gauge why the results are inconsistent across the samples and largely insignificant in the regressions.

6   CONCLUSIONS

In this chapter we have examined the educational and health outcomes of the children of migrants (both left-behind and migrated) by comparing them with non-migrant rural children and urban children. We found some evidence that left-behind children are less likely than non-migrant rural children—and migrated children less likely than urban children—to be rated as having very good school performance. Similarly, we found that, as measured by their height, the long-term health of left-behind children is not as good as that of rural children, and the long-term health of migrated children is not as good as

Table 5.8   China: Correlation between Migration Status and Children's Health

	Rural Household Survey			Urban Migrant Survey			Rural Household Survey + Migrated Children in Urban Migrant Survey		
	Total	Males	Females	Total	Males	Females	Total	Males	Females
Dependent variable: height									
One or both parents migrated	-1.17	-0.76	-1.66				-3.66	-4.03	-2.87
	(0.528)**	(0.713)	(0.778)**				(0.725)***	(0.955)***	(1.003)***
Dummy for being in city				3.93	4.15	2.94			
				(0.662)***	(0.880)***	(1.322)**			
Birth weight (kg)	2.09	2.59	1.46	1.73	1.76	1.59	0.73	0.83	0.62
	(0.487)***	(0.676)***	(0.698)**	(0.631)***	(0.818)**	(1.032)	(0.277)***	(0.381)**	(0.399)
Age of child	6.11	6.11	6.12	6.35	6.37	6.30	6.31	6.45	6.17
	(0.067)***	(0.091)***	(0.102)***	(0.083)***	(0.111)***	(0.127)***	(0.062)***	(0.082)***	(0.096)***
Child is male	0.45	0.00	0.00	0.01	0.00	0.00	1.34	0.00	0.00
	(0.472)	(0.000)	(0.000)	(0.684)	(0.000)	(0.000)	(0.456)***	(0.000)	(0.000)
No. of siblings	-0.21	-0.38	-0.06	-1.19	-1.40	-0.59	0.09	0.19	0.01
	(0.320)	(0.430)	(0.491)	(0.616)*	(0.840)*	(0.824)	(0.488)	(0.669)	(0.710)
Parental & household-level controls	Yes	Yes	Yes	Yes	Yes	Yes	Yes	Yes	Yes
Regional controls	Yes	Yes	Yes	Yes	Yes	Yes	Yes	Yes	Yes
No. of observations	4,443	2,468	1,975	2,202	1,446	756	2,788	1,514	1,274
R^2	0.75	0.75	0.76	0.80	0.79	0.83	0.85	0.85	0.85

Dependent variable: excellent health

	(1)	(2)	(3)	(4)	(5)	(6)	(7)	(8)	(9)
One or both parents migrated	-0.03 (0.016)**	-0.02 (0.021)	-0.04 (0.023)*				0.18 (0.026)***	0.21 (0.035)***	0.14 (0.039)***
Dummy for being in city				0.03 (0.022)	0.04 (0.029)	-0.01 (0.046)			
Birth weight (kg)	0.05 (0.015)***	0.06 (0.020)***	0.03 (0.022)	0.05 (0.021)**	0.06 (0.026)**	0.03 (0.035)	-0.01 (0.010)	-0.01 (0.014)	-0.02 (0.016)
Age of child	0.00 (0.002)	0.00 (0.003)	0.00 (0.003)	-0.00 (0.003)	-0.01 (0.003)*	-0.00 (0.005)	0.01 (0.002)**	0.00 (0.003)	0.01 (0.003)**
Child is male	0.05 (0.014)***	0.00 (0.000)	0.00 (0.000)	0.00 (0.025)	0.00 (0.000)	0.00 (0.000)	0.02 (0.018)	0.00 (0.000)	0.00 (0.000)
No. of siblings	0.01 (0.010)	-0.01 (0.013)	0.05 (0.015)***	-0.02 (0.019)	-0.05 (0.023)**	0.03 (0.032)	0.01 (0.019)	-0.01 (0.026)	0.04 (0.028)
Parental & household-level controls	Yes	Yes	Yes	Yes	Yes	Yes	Yes	Yes	Yes
Regional controls	Yes	Yes	Yes	Yes	Yes	Yes	Yes	Yes	Yes
No. of observations	4,448	2,471	1,977	2,312	1,526	786	2,814	1,527	1,287
R^2	0.05	0.06	0.05	0.08	0.10	0.09	0.05	0.06	0.06

* = significant at 10 per cent; ** = significant at 5 per cent; *** = significant at 1 per cent. Robust standard errors are in parentheses.

Source: Rural Household Survey, 2008; Urban Migrant Survey, 2008; Urban Household Survey, 2008.

that of urban children. No obvious difference was found between the children of migrants and non-migrants with regard to parental-rated health.

These findings, however, are not causal. Part of the problem is the subjective nature of the outcome measures, which makes it very hard to disentangle the attitudes and assessments of parents and guardians from reality. To push the research agenda forward, researchers will need to collect more objective information on children's educational and health outcomes. Because of the endogenous behaviour of migration, future studies in this area would benefit significantly if a valid instrument for the parental migration decision could be found.

NOTES

1   Some estimates put the figure much higher. In an in-depth study based on the 2005 1% National Population Sample Survey, for example, the All-China Women's Federation (2006) estimated that there were about 58 million children below the age of 18, and 40 million below the age of 15, left behind in the countryside, accounting for 28 per cent of all rural-dwelling children. However, to the best of the authors' knowledge, the sampling methods employed in these studies have not been made publicly available, so it is not possible for us to assess how well they represent the populations of interest.

2   We excluded 149 urban children (8 per cent of the total sample of children in the Urban Household Survey) from the analysis because they had non-standard living arrangements (that is, they were living with a single parent, with grandparents or the like). This allowed us to focus on urban children with standard living arrangements—those living with both parents—as the benchmark for our comparison of urban and migrated children.

3   Although the Urban Migrant Survey sample contains no ambiguities on the status of left-behind children—they are the children of rural–urban migrants, strictly defined—this is not the case with the Rural Household Survey. Of the left-behind children in the latter survey, 77 per cent are the children of parents who have moved to the city and the other 23 per cent are the children of parents have moved to another rural area. At this stage we do not differentiate between these two groups of children. However, in the next stage of the research, we will discuss them separately and take into account the differing conditions facing their parents.

4   As very few of the school-aged children in the sample had attended senior high school or above, and even fewer had dropped out of school, in Table 5.5 we confine our attention to children attending primary or junior high school.

5   There were a sizeable number of missing values for some variables, such as hours spent on homework, distance from school and school fees. Although we includes these variables, to ensure a consistent sample size we added dummy variables to address the problem of missing values in many observations.

6   The birth weight of children is well known to be correlated with health outcomes later in life (see, for example, Gamborg et al. 2009).

7   Including age as a group of dummy variables does not change the results.

6   Rural–Urban Migration and Poverty in China

Chuliang Luo and Ximing Yue

1   INTRODUCTION

Two of the most striking features of the Chinese economy over the past three decades have been the substantial decline in poverty in rural areas and the sharp increase in migration from rural to urban areas. According to official statistics, the rural poverty rate fell from 30.7 per cent in 1978 to 3.4 per cent in 2000 and 2.3 per cent in 2006. China's official poverty statistics are often criticized for their use of a very low poverty line, but even if stricter standards are applied to the cut-off line for poverty, it is still clear that China has made remarkable achievements in reducing the extent of rural poverty (Chen and Ravallion 2008).

Rural-to-urban migration is a common phenomenon in the process of economic development, affecting both the rural societies that send migrants and the urban societies that receive them. In countries with a widening gap between the rural and urban economies, such as China, the effect of migration on income and poverty will depend on whether the marginal product of labour is negative or positive, and whether there is surplus labour.[1] If the marginal product of labour in a rural area is negative, then the migration of rural workers to the cities will improve the welfare of the household members remaining behind in the countryside, not only through the remittances that the migrant members send home, but also through the increase in productivity of the family members left behind in the rural village. If the marginal product of labour in a rural area is positive, then the effect of migration on the economic situation of rural households will depend on the relative size of the remittances that migrants send home and the reduction in household income caused by the loss of family members to migration. In this study we investigate the effect of migration on poverty in rural China by linking poverty indices directly to their determinants, including a set of migration variables, without identifying the routes through which migration exerts an influence on poverty.

Figure 6.1 *China: No. of Rural–Urban Migrants, Share of Migrants in the*
Rural Labour Force, and Poverty Incidence in Rural Regions,
1985–2006

- - -   LHS: Poverty incidence in rural China

———   LHS: Share of migrants in rural labour force

▢   RHS: No. of rural–urban migrants

Source: Sheng (2008: 72–3); NBS (2006b: 110).

Since the Chinese government initiated its first economic reform policies in
1978, surplus rural labour has continually been released as a result of increases
in agricultural productivity. The consequence has been a rapid increase in the
number of rural–urban migrants, especially since the late 1990s (Figure 6.1).
About 130 million migrant workers from rural areas—or almost 26 per cent
of the total rural population—were working in cities in 2006. This increase in
migration has coincided with a marked fall in poverty.

Despite the potential link between the decline in rural poverty and the
increase in rural-to-urban migration, very few studies have analysed the effect
of migration on rural poverty. Taylor, Rozelle and de Brauw (2003) examined
the effect of migration on the income sources of rural households with migrants
in two provinces, Hebei and Liaoning. They concluded that migration affects
different sources of income in different ways, but the net result is to reduce
the total income of the rural households of origin. However, when they looked
at per capita income, they found that the reverse was the case: that migration
increases income and reduces poverty among the families that are left behind

in the rural villages. The source of the positive contribution of migration to rural household income is the smaller size of migrant households, because migrants themselves are not counted as members of their rural households of origin. This suggests that the way in which a household member is defined is important. This issue will be discussed in more detail below.

A study by Du, Park and Wang (2005) is the only one to focus entirely on the effect of migration on rural poverty in China. The authors first estimate the effect of migration on the per capita income of rural households. They then use these estimates to gauge the extent to which migration contributes to a fall in rural poverty. They find that having a migrant in the household can increase a household's per capita income by 8.5–13.1 per cent, but the overall effect on poverty is modest because most poor people do not migrate.

The approach of both of the studies just discussed is to estimate the effect of migration on income, and then the contribution of any increase in income to a reduction in poverty among households with migrants. In this chapter we adopt an alternative approach, linking poverty indices to whether a household has a migrant and to the number of migrants in the household. This is a more direct method of determining the extent of the contribution of migration to poverty alleviation.

The chapter is organized as follows. Section 2 discusses the methodology, including poverty measures and the issues involved in estimating poverty equations. The following section describes the data and clarifies some issues related to the choice of poverty lines, the definition of a migrant and the definition of a household member. Section 4 summarizes the empirical results, and section 5 sets out our conclusions.

2 METHODOLOGY

The poverty measures used in this chapter are the widely used indices proposed by Foster, Greer and Thorbecke (1984). The first is the headcount measure of poverty, defined as the proportion of poor people in the total population. A major weakness of this measure is that it does not distinguish between gradations of poverty; that is, it regards all people living in poverty as the same.

The second index is the poverty gap. In mathematical terms, the poverty gap for an individual is defined as $g_i = (1 - y_i/z)$ when $y_i < z$, and $g_i = 0$ if $y_i \geq z$, where y_i represents the income of individual i and z denotes the poverty line. The mean poverty gap for all individuals can then be expressed by the following formula:

$$pg = \frac{1}{n}\sum_{i=1}^{n} g_i = \frac{1}{n}\sum_{i=1}^{n}\left(1 - \frac{y_i}{z}\right). \tag{6.1}$$

The poverty gap for each individual provides an indicator of the resources needed to lift that person out of poverty but does not reflect the severity of poverty in the community as a whole. The following example illustrates this point. Assume that there are two communities of equal size with an identical poverty line of 100. If one community has five equally poor individuals with an income level of 90, and the other has just one poor person, but that person has an income level of 50, then the poverty gap tells us that poverty is equal in the two places, even though the actual situation in each community is very different.

The third poverty index is the squared poverty gap, defined as:

$$pg^2 = \frac{1}{n}\sum_{i=1}^{n} g_i^2 = \frac{1}{n}\sum_{i=1}^{n}\left(1 - \frac{y_i}{z}\right)^2. \qquad (6.2)$$

The squared poverty gap gives more weight to poor people whose income is far below the poverty line, thereby overcoming one of the main weaknesses of the poverty gap measure of poverty. It would say that poverty is more serious in a community that has fewer poor people, but a greater number with incomes far below the poverty line, than in a community that has more poor people, but with incomes very close to the poverty line.

This study investigates the effect of migration on poverty by linking the three poverty measures just described to some potential determinants of poverty, including a set of migration variables. We use a probit model to estimate the determinants of poverty for the headcount measure of poverty, and a tobit model to estimate the determinants for the poverty gap and the squared poverty gap.

In estimating the effect of migration on poverty, we recognize that the results may suffer from an endogeneity problem. Endogeneity may be caused, first, by reverse causality. Poor households may find it difficult to send family members to the cities because they cannot afford the costs of migration. At the same time, they may have a greater need to send family members to the cities because they need the additional income. The other possible source of endogeneity is the existence of unobserved household and village characteristics that affect both migration behaviour and income, and hence poverty status at the household level.

To account for the effect of endogenous factors on migration, we needed to find an instrumental variable for the migration decision. Following Taylor, Rozelle and de Brauw (2003) and Du, Park and Wang (2005), this study uses the migrant social network at the village level as the instrument for the migration decision.[2] Fortunately our data provide rich information on migration at the village level. Details of the construction of the migrant social network are given in section 4 below.

3 DATA AND DEFINITIONS

This study uses data from the Rural Household Survey, one of three surveys conducted in China under the Rural–Urban Migration in China and Indonesia (RUMiCI) project.[3] The survey was conducted at the beginning of 2008, with a reference year of 2007. It covered some 8,000 rural households, with and without migrant members, in nine provinces (Hebei, Jiangsu, Zhejiang, Anhui, Henan, Hubei, Guangdong, Chongqing and Sichuan). The sample was taken from the standard household income and expenditure surveys conducted annually by China's National Bureau of Statistics. The information on individual and household characteristics was collected at the time of the survey; the household income and expenditure data were copied directly from the bureau's diary records.

To determine the poverty status of a household, one needs an indicator of welfare and a pre-determined poverty line. Both consumption and income are widely used as welfare measures in the poverty literature. However, for this study we decided to use consumption, on the basis that it more accurately captures the resources that households can command for their welfare. Income is a poor indicator of how much households spend on their welfare, because it fails to capture the unobserved effect of savings and borrowings on the capacity of households to spend.

A problem associated with the use of consumption as a welfare measure is the lumpiness of expenditure on durable goods that are purchased within the survey period but used well beyond that period. Unless expenditure on durable goods is spread over the period in which the goods are actually used, the data on expenditure from a household survey will overestimate consumption for the period in which the purchase is made and underestimate it for the period afterwards.

To address this concern, we made two adjustments to the total consumption figures. The first was to replace expenditure on housing by households that reported building or buying a new house with the figure for average expenditure on housing of the other households in the same village. The second was to remove expenditure on equipment from total consumption on the grounds that equipment is a durable good. It should be noted that the two adjustments are incomplete; purchases of vehicles (recorded under expenditure on transport) and purchases of pianos (recorded under cultural expenditure), for instance, were not excluded from total consumption. Nevertheless, adjusted consumption provides a good alternative to total consumption, and in this study we use both, to see if there are differential effects on the analytical results.

Many poverty lines are available to measure poverty in rural China. We selected three of them for use in this study.

The first is the Chinese government's official poverty line. In response to widespread criticism by the World Bank (2001) and others that the line was set at unrealistically low levels, the government increased its official poverty line from 693 yuan per annum in 2006 to 1,067 yuan per annum in 2007. In this study we use the 2007 poverty line.

The second poverty line is the World Bank measure proposed by Ravallion, Chen and Sangraula (2008). According to this poverty line, anyone living on less than $1.25 a day in 2005 can be regarded as living in poverty. Based on purchasing power parity (PPP) consumption of 3.46 yuan per US dollar—the figure estimated by the World Bank's International Comparison Program—this poverty line is equivalent to 1,551 yuan per annum (=1.25*365*3.4) in 2005, or 1,679 yuan per annum in 2007 prices.

The third poverty line is the official rural minimum living standard (*dibao* in Chinese), established by the government to identify and assist regions with a high proportion of poor and chronically unemployed people. The scheme was introduced in 1997 and is gradually being rolled out across the country, although it has still not reached some parts of rural China. The level at which the minimum living standard is set differs between regions, because it takes account of the fiscal capacity and purchasing power of individuals in each region. Among the nine provinces in our sample, Sichuan has the region with the lowest minimum living standard (693 yuan per annum) and Zhejiang the region with the highest (3,120 yuan per annum). The average for all nine provinces is 1,346 yuan, which is higher than the official poverty line of 1,067 yuan per annum in 2007 (see above).

As a poverty standard, the *dibao* has at least two advantages over the other two poverty lines. First, it reflects regional differences in the cost of living, whereas the other two poverty lines are uniform across all regions. Second, it can be used to identify sections of the rural population that are in need of financial support from the government. It therefore has strong policy implications, in contrast to the more academic focus of the other two lines. In consideration of these two advantages, in this chapter we report the results for the *dibao* in preference to those for the two uniform poverty lines, unless the results are sensitive to the choice of poverty line.

Definition of a Migrant

A migrant is defined as anyone aged 16–64 who has moved away from the rural village for at least one month in order to work. Based on this criterion, people who have migrated for non-work reasons, such as marriage, schooling or to join the army, are not migrants. Some studies make a distinction between long-term and short-term migrants based on the number of months a person has worked outside the village of origin (see, for example, Du, Park and Wang

2005). Such a distinction is useful, but the number of months used to differentiate the two types of migrants is necessarily arbitrary. In this study we do not distinguish between long-term and short-term migrants, but we do examine the effect of the duration of migration (the number of months working as a migrant) on poverty among migrant households.

Definition of a Household Member

As noted earlier, the definition of a household member affects the number of persons regarded as being members of a rural household and, consequently, the estimates of per capita expenditure and income for that household. Not only is it a crucial factor in calculations of the per capita income and expenditure of rural households with migrants, but it has a significant effect on comparisons of the per capita income and expenditure of households with and without migrants. Income received and expenditure incurred by migrants in the cities is not normally counted as part of a rural household's income and expenditure. On the other hand, under China's household registration (*hukou*) system, migrants are officially counted as members of their rural households of origin. This gives rise to an inconsistency between the numerator and the denominator when calculating per capita income and expenditure (see also Taylor, Rozelle and de Brauw 2003). To resolve this problem, we needed to find a realistic way of calculating the number of household members.

In most household surveys, the standard practice is to set a cut-off point of six months for identifying a household member; that is, a person who has lived in the household for six months or more in the reference year is defined as a member of that household. An alternative way of defining a household member is to use information on the number of months a person has lived in the household in the year in question to calculate an indicator of the effective number of members in the household. If m is the number of months a person has lived in the household, the ratio of m to 12 months, $m/12$, represents the proportion of the year that the person has been in the household and participated in its consumption activities. Summing the ratio for all members of the same household gives us the effective number of members in that household. We believe that the effective number of household members provides a more accurate representation of household size than the standard way of measuring the number of household members, so we use this measure in our study.[4]

Table 6.1 presents summary statistics for the total sample and for households with and without migrant members. Based on the effective number of household members, households with migrant members are smaller than households without migrant members: on average, they have 2.96 members, compared with 3.46 for households without migrant members. However, based on the unadjusted household size—the total number of household members regard-

Table 6.1　China: Descriptive Statistics for Households with and without Migrants

	Non-migrant Households	Migrant Households	Total Sample
Household size (effective no. of household members)	3.46	2.96	3.26
Household size (as defined by standard practice)	3.43	2.83	3.19
No. of migrants	0.00	1.66	0.68
Age of household head	50.17	50.55	50.33
Years of schooling of household head	7.55	7.37	7.47
No. of years of schooling of family member with the most schooling	8.76	9.45	9.04
Proportion of household members working	62.92	73.07	67.06
Net income per capita (yuan)[a]	5,731	6,360	5,965
Total consumption expenditure per capita (yuan)[a]	4,335	4,760	4,492
Adjusted consumption expenditure per capita (yuan)[a]	3,973	4,253	4,077
Cultivated land per capita (*mu*)[a]	1.33	1.85	1.53

a   The figures for per capita income, expenditure and cultivated land are based on the effective (rather than unadjusted) number of household members. The values based on the unadjusted number of household members are not reported in this table, but the relative sizes of those values are similar to the ones reported here.

Source: Rural Household Survey, 2008.

less of whether or not a member has migrated to a city in the reference year, or for how long—non-migrant households would be smaller: they would have 3.63 members, compared with 4.48 for migrant households. The importance of definition is immediately apparent from this difference in the estimates of household size.

The average age and years of schooling of the household head are similar for households with and without migrant members. However, the number of years of schooling of the family member with the most schooling is much higher for migrant households, as is the proportion of family members defined as being in the labour force.

Households with migrant members have higher per capita incomes than non-migrant households, and higher per capita expenditures. The mean per capita income of migrant households is 6,360 yuan, compared with 5,731 yuan for non-migrant households. Their average per capita expenditure is 9.8 per

Table 6.2   China: Poverty Indices by Poverty Line

	Total Consumption per Capita			Adjusted Consumption per Capita		
	Head-count	Poverty Gap	Squared Poverty Gap	Head-count	Poverty Gap	Squared Poverty Gap
***Dibao* poverty line**						
Non-migrant households	0.062	0.013	0.004	0.072	0.015	0.005
Migrant households	0.026	0.005	0.002	0.030	0.006	0.002
All households	0.048	0.010	0.003	0.056	0.012	0.004
Official poverty line						
Non-migrant households	0.030	0.005	0.002	0.037	0.006	0.002
Migrant households	0.019	0.004	0.001	0.021	0.004	0.001
All households	0.026	0.005	0.001	0.031	0.006	0.002
World Bank poverty line						
Non-migrant households	0.161	0.035	0.012	0.185	0.042	0.014
Migrant households	0.109	0.023	0.008	0.127	0.027	0.009
All households	0.142	0.030	0.010	0.163	0.036	0.012

Source: Rural Household Survey, 2008.

cent higher than that of non-migrant households, and their adjusted consumption is 7.0 per cent higher. Migrant households are also better endowed with land: the area of cultivated land per capita is 1.85 *mu* for migrant households but 1.33 *mu* for non-migrant households.[5]

It is the exclusion of migrant members from the calculation of household size that mainly accounts for migrant households' higher levels of per capita expenditure. If migrants were not excluded, the per capita consumption of non-migrant households would be higher than that of migrant households, that is, 4,335 yuan for non-migrant households but only 3,155 yuan for migrant households. This again confirms the importance of the definition of a household member when comparing the per capita income and consumption patterns of the two types of households.

Table 6.2 assesses the level of poverty among rural households according to the three poverty lines discussed earlier. The most important result to emerge from the table is that poverty is much lower among migrant households than among non-migrant households, regardless of which poverty line is used. Using the *dibao* poverty line, for instance, the poverty rate is 2.6 per cent for migrant households but 6.2 per cent for non-migrant households.

When the poverty line is raised, the number of people falling below the line, and therefore assessed as poor, naturally becomes higher. This is why the World Bank poverty line produces the highest poverty measures and the Chinese government's official poverty line the lowest. Based on the official poverty line, the poverty rate is 3.0 per cent for the nine provinces in our sample, compared with 4.6 per cent for the country as a whole (NBS 2008).

4   THE IMPACT OF MIGRATION ON POVERTY

In this section we investigate the role of migration in poverty alleviation. If y_i is a poverty index for household i, the determinants of poverty may be expressed as follows:

$$y_i = \hat{a}\mathbf{X}_i + \hat{e}M_i + \varepsilon_i \qquad (6.3)$$

where $\mathbf{X_i}$ is a vector of variables for household characteristics (age, years of schooling of household head, household size, the proportion of household members who are working, area of cultivated land per capita); geographical characteristics (whether the household is located in a flat, hilly or mountainous area, whether it is located in a suburb); and county characteristics (whether the county has been identified as a nationally poor county, whether it is located in a revolutionary base area).[6] Provincial dummies are also included to control for provincial characteristics. The variable M_i is a migration indicator. We consider two migration variables. The first is a dummy variable that takes a value of 1 if the household has any migrant members and 0 otherwise. The other is the number of migrants in the household in the reference year, 2007. The latter may be a better indicator of migration than the former, as it captures the 'intensity' of migration at the household level.[7]

One potential problem with equation (6.3) is the possible endogeneity of migration. As discussed earlier, there may be reverse causality between poverty and migration, and there may also be omitted variable(s) that affect both poverty and migration. Two-stage regressions are employed to handle this problem. We use two types of instrumental variables to capture migrant social networks at the village level. The first is the proportion of migrants in the total population of the village. The second is a group of dummy variables whose construction is based on whether the migration destination is within or outside the home province.

Table 6.3 presents the results from the first-stage estimation. The table shows that the estimated coefficients for most of the instruments have the expected signs and are statistically significant at the 1 per cent level, with the exception of two variables that are significant at the 5 per cent level, one that is significant at the 10 per cent level and one that has the right sign but is insignificant.

Table 6.3   China: Regression of Migration Variables on Instrumental Variables[a]

Instrumental Variable	Dependent Variable			
	Migrant Household Dummy		No. of Migrants in 2007	
	OLS	Probit	OLS	Poisson
Proportion of migrants in village population	0.0052	0.0160	0.0108	0.0132
	(12.93)***	(12.52)***	(13.47)***	(14.81)***
Dummies for migration within the province[b]				
21–44% (1/0)	0.0222	0.0773	0.0242	0.0685
	(1.78)*	(2.04)**	(0.98)	(2.01)**
41–60% (1/0)	0.0941	0.2864	0.1479	0.2791
	(4.68)***	(4.72)***	(3.73)***	(5.34)***
61–80% (1/0)	0.1492	0.4470	0.2354	0.3177
	(6.35)***	(6.27)***	(5.08)***	(5.40)***
More than 80% (1/0)	0.0886	0.2695	0.1614	0.2300
	(3.32)***	(3.33)***	(3.06)***	(3.57)***
Dummies for migration outside the province[b]				
21–44% (1/0)	0.0680	0.2154	0.1058	0.2385
	(4.08)***	(4.28)***	(3.22)***	(4.96)***
41–60% (1/0)	0.1489	0.4301	0.2454	0.3984
	(8.51)***	(8.15)***	(7.11)***	(8.30)***
61–80% (1/0)	0.1508	0.4276	0.2195	0.3546
	(8.25)***	(7.78)***	(6.09)***	(7.16)***
More than 80% (1/0)	0.1616	0.4672	0.2227	0.3956
	(6.58)***	(6.37)***	(4.59)***	(6.33)***
Constant	−0.7563	−4.0729	−2.0246	−5.6846
	(6.79)***	(11.13)***	(9.21)***	(14.43)***
No. of observations	7,655	7,655	7,655	7,655
Adjusted R^2 or pseudo R^2	0.1968	0.1651	0.1953	0.1236

* = significant at 10 per cent; ** = significant at 5 per cent; *** = significant at 1 per cent. The absolute values of the z statistics are in parentheses.
a   Variables in the second-stage regression are included in the first-stage regression but are not reported in this table.
b   The dummies are constructed to take a value of 1 if the proportion of migrants migrating within/outside the home province falls within the range shown, and 0 otherwise.
Source: Rural Household Survey, 2008.

   The next step was to obtain the predicted values for both the migrant household dummy and the number of migrants and include them in the poverty index
equations, to determine whether migration plays a role in poverty alleviation.
There were multiple specifications of the equations, given the different definitions of the number of household members as well as the number of poverty
lines and poverty measures. After trying all the specifications, we found that in
most cases the estimates for the explanatory variables, especially the migration
variables, did not change much. We have therefore selected the specifications
using the *dibao* as the poverty line for presentation here. Below, we present
the results of estimating a probit model for the headcount measure of poverty
based on total consumption and adjusted consumption; the results for the other
specifications are available from the authors upon request.

   Table 6.4 presents the results of estimating a probit model for the headcount
poverty measure based on total consumption. The estimated coefficients for
the migration variables are negative, as expected, and statistically significant.
This is true regardless of which migration variable is used, and regardless of
which model is used to regress the migration variables on the instrumental
variables. The negative signs of the coefficients provide evidence that migration helps to reduce the likelihood of a household falling into poverty.

   The coefficient for years of schooling of the household head is negative and
highly significant, meaning that a household with a highly educated head is less
likely to be poor. This again confirms the importance of education in alleviating
poverty. The age of the household head also matters. The estimated coefficient
is positive for the age of the household head and negative for the squared age
of the household head. This indicates that the likelihood of a household falling
into poverty initially increases with the age of the household head, but then
decreases after a certain age. Based on the coefficients in the second column,
the age of the household head is above 85, suggesting that, over the whole life
of a household head, poverty worsens as the household head gets older.

   The number of individuals in the household has a big impact on its poverty status. The positive and statistically significant coefficient for this variable
means that the larger the size of the household, the more likely it is to fall into
poverty. The coefficient for the proportion of family members who are working is far from significant in each of the equations estimated, indicating that
this variable has nothing to do with household poverty. Cultivated land per
capita helps to reduce poverty.

   Geographic location matters: households located in hilly areas are less likely
to be poor, and those located in mountainous areas are more likely to be poor.
Households in the counties officially recognized as poor are less likely to fall
into poverty, perhaps because they are already receiving assistance under the
government's poverty reduction programs. Location in a revolutionary base
county does not seem to affect the poverty status of households. However,

Table 6.4 China: Probit Regression of Headcount on Its Determinants Based on Total Consumption[a]

	Predicted Value of Migrant Household Dummy Based on:		Predicted Value of No. of Migrants Based on:	
	OLS	Probit	OLS	Poisson
Migrant household dummy[b]	−0.6863	−0.7610		
	(4.47)***	(4.82)***		
No. of migrants in 2007[b]			−0.2935	−0.3916
			(3.52)***	(4.03)***
Years of schooling of household head	−0.0463	−0.0464	−0.0457	−0.0460
	(6.57)***	(6.59)***	(6.50)***	(6.53)***
Age of household head	0.0439	0.0390	0.0418	0.0392
	(3.30)***	(3.06)***	(3.05)***	(3.01)***
Age of household head^2	−0.0003	−0.0002	−0.0002	−0.0002
	(2.08)**	(1.77)*	(1.79)*	(1.68)*
Effective no. of household members	0.2149	0.2182	0.2294	0.2311
	(14.10)***	(15.10)***	(16.00)***	(16.97)***
Proportion of family members who are working[c]	0.0008	0.0008	0.0008	0.0007
	(1.07)	(1.09)	(1.07)	(0.97)
Cultivated land per capita (*mu*)	−0.1359	−0.1308	−0.1371	−0.1408
	(6.45)***	(6.17)***	(6.44)***	(6.70)***
Dummy for hilly area	−0.2270	−0.2283	−0.2265	−0.2243
	(2.47)**	(2.49)**	(2.47)**	(2.45)**
Dummy for mountainous area	0.2393	0.2461	0.2472	0.2435
	(1.74)*	(1.78)*	(1.78)*	(1.75)*
Dummy for nationally poor county	−0.2664	−0.2612	−0.2686	−0.2614
	(3.88)***	(3.80)***	(3.92)***	(3.80)***
Dummy for revolutionary base area	0.0770	0.0740	0.0710	0.0662
	(1.70)*	(1.65)*	(1.53)	(1.47)
Dummy for suburb	−0.2870	−0.2786	−0.2679	−0.2642
	(4.95)***	(4.90)***	(4.64)***	(4.66)***
Constant	−3.7612	−3.6252	−3.8355	−3.7055
	(10.73)***	(10.67)***	(10.34)***	(10.61)***
No. of observations	24,785	24,785	24,785	24,785
Pseudo R^2	0.1958	0.1962	0.1950	0.1956

* = significant at 10 per cent; ** = significant at 5 per cent; *** = significant at 1 per cent. The absolute values of the *z* statistics are in parentheses.
a   The provincial dummies were included in the regression but the results are not presented in the table for reasons of space.
b   Predicted values from the first-stage regression.
c   Family members are defined to include those who migrate.
Source: Rural Household Survey, 2008.

households located in city suburbs are much less likely to be poor, reflecting their better access to city services.

Table 6.5 presents the results of estimating a probit model for the head-count measure of poverty based on adjusted consumption. For the most part, the results are similar to those for Table 6.4. The negative and statistically significant signs for the migration variables remain unchanged for three of the four equations estimated. The exception is the coefficient for the number of migrants, which remains negative but becomes statistically insignificant when ordinary least squares (OLS) are used. The other differences are that the coefficients for the two age variables and the coefficient for the dummy variable for a mountainous area become insignificant.

Before proceeding further, it should be noted that the estimated contribution of migration to poverty alleviation remains unchanged even when the number of household members is adjusted using an equivalence scale. The purpose of such a scale is to take account of the fact that the needs of households do not grow directly in proportion to an increase in household size, because resources (such as electricity and space) are shared within the household. We employed two commonly used equivalence scales, the 'old' OECD scale and the modified OECD scale,[8] to re-estimate per capita consumption based on the adjusted numbers of household members. A probit estimation for all three poverty indices using the adjusted per capita consumption figures showed that the estimated coefficients of the migration variables remained negative and statistically significant, but increased in absolute value.[9]

So far, we have examined the effect of migration on poverty at the household level by dividing the sample into migrant households and non-migrant households and examining the differences in poverty status between them. Another way of looking at the role of migration is to limit the sample to migrant households, and see whether these households have some features that apply only to migrants, and that matter to poverty.

Among the households that send migrants, some fall into poverty and some do not. What features do migrant households have in common, but to differing degrees across households, that might account for the poverty status of a household? This is the question we want to explore next.

One such feature is the length of time migrants spend away from their rural villages for work purposes. We wanted to know whether some migrant households were poor simply because their migrant members did not stay in the city long enough to make significant amounts of money. To explore this point, we linked the poverty indices to their determinants, including the maximum number of months a migrant had worked in the destination city. Table 6.6 presents the results of estimating a probit model for the headcount measure of poverty and a tobit model for the squared poverty gap. The number of independent variables included in the table is less than the number included in

Table 6.5   China: Probit Regression of Headcount on Its Determinants Based on Adjusted Consumption[a]

	Predicted Value of Migrant Household Dummy Based on:		Predicted Value of No. of Migrants Based on:	
	OLS	Probit	OLS	Poisson
Migrant household dummy[b]	−0.3111	−0.4598		
	(2.17)**	(3.09)***		
No. of migrants in 2007[b]			−0.1026	−0.2934
			(1.32)	(3.22)***
Years of schooling of household head	−0.0392	−0.0396	−0.0388	−0.0396
	(5.81)***	(5.87)***	(5.76)***	(5.88)***
Age of household head	0.0102	0.0111	0.0069	0.0141
	(0.82)	(0.93)	(0.54)	(1.15)
Age of household head^2	0.0001	0.0000	0.0001	0.0000
	(0.46)	(0.41)	(0.75)	(0.22)
Effective no. of household members	0.2480	0.2437	0.2574	0.2481
	(16.96)***	(17.48)***	(18.65)***	(18.92)***
Proportion of family members who are working[c]	−0.0006	−0.0004	−0.0007	−0.0003
	(0.79)	(0.54)	(0.92)	(0.38)
Cultivated land per capita (*mu*)	−0.1426	−0.1367	−0.1451	−0.1405
	(7.18)***	(6.85)***	(7.23)***	(7.12)***
Dummy for hilly area	−0.2460	−0.2516	−0.2431	−0.2527
	(2.80)***	(2.86)***	(2.76)***	(2.88)***
Dummy for mountainous area	0.1382	0.1520	0.1339	0.1607
	(1.00)	(1.10)	(0.96)	(1.16)
Dummy for nationally poor county	−0.2263	−0.2205	−0.2290	−0.2190
	(3.66)***	(3.56)***	(3.71)***	(3.53)***
Dummy for revolutionary base area	−0.0185	−0.0091	−0.0282	−0.0052
	(0.42)	(0.21)	(0.63)	(0.12)
Dummy for suburb	−0.0392	−0.0396	−0.0388	−0.0396
	(5.81)***	(5.87)***	(5.76)***	(5.88)***
Constant	−2.9226	−2.9222	−2.8972	−3.0365
	(8.97)***	(9.23)***	(8.41)***	(9.32)***
No. of observations	24,785	24,785	24,785	24,785
Pseudo R^2	0.2008	0.2013	0.2005	0.2014

* = significant at 10 per cent; ** = significant at 5 per cent; *** = significant at 1 per cent. The absolute values of the *z* statistics are in parentheses.
a   The provincial dummies were included in the regression but the results are not presented in the table for reasons of space.
b   Predicted values from the first-stage regression.
c   Family members are defined to include those who migrate.
Source: Rural Household Survey, 2008.

*Table 6.6   China: Regression of Headcount and Squared Poverty Gap
Indices for Migrant Households*[a]

	Probit Model for Headcount Based on:		Tobit Model for Squared Poverty Gap Based on:	
	Total Consumption	Adjusted Consumption	Total Consumption	Adjusted Consumption
Maximum no. of months as a migrant worker	−0.0904	−0.1013	−0.0110	−0.0125
	(6.79)***	(8.01)***	(6.28)***	(7.30)***
Years of schooling of household head	−0.0725	−0.0647	−0.0122	−0.0125
	(4.22)***	(3.97)***	(5.50)***	(5.78)***
Age of household head	−0.0076	−0.0254	0.0009	−0.0006
	(0.26)	(0.94)	(0.25)	(0.18)
Age of household head^2	0.0002	0.0004	0.0000	0.0000
	(0.64)	(1.36)	(0.11)	(0.52)
Effective no. of household members	0.3294	0.3117	0.0385	0.0403
	(11.64)***	(11.38)***	(9.71)***	(10.44)***
Cultivated land per capita (*mu*)	−0.2191	−0.2342	−0.0296	−0.0320
	(4.46)***	(5.11)***	(4.60)***	(5.15)***
Constant	−1.9533	−1.3920	−0.2579	−0.2135
	(2.45)**	(1.89)*	(2.53)**	(2.20)**
No. of observations	7,744	7,744	9,226	9,226
Pseudo R^2	0.2938	0.2915	0.5242	0.5328

* = significant at 10 per cent; ** = significant at 5 per cent; *** = significant at 1 per cent. The absolute values of the *z* statistics are in parentheses.
a   The provincial dummies were included in the regression but the results are not presented in the table for reasons of space.

Source: Rural Household Survey, 2008.

Tables 6.4 and 6.5, because some variables were not statistically significant or were very sensitive to the specification, and were therefore dropped from the regressions. Note, however, that the estimated coefficients for all the explanatory variables kept in Table 6.6 change little even if the dropped variables are included.

As Table 6.6 shows, the estimated coefficient for the maximum number of months a migrant spends away from home is negative and highly significant in all the specifications. In fact, the negative and significant coefficient remains unchanged regardless of the poverty line, the definition of the number of households and the welfare measures used to estimate the poverty indices. The results confirm our expectation that the length of time a migrant works in the destination city has a significant impact on the level of poverty experienced by relatives left behind in the village of origin.

5   CONCLUSION

This study has used newly released data from the 2008 Rural Household Survey to investigate the role of migration in alleviating rural poverty in China. We have evaluated the effect of migration on poverty by estimating poverty indices as a function of many factors, including migration. The results show that migration plays an important role in alleviating poverty among rural households in China. The estimated effects of migration on poverty are robust, regardless of the poverty indices used, the definition of household members and so on. In addition, we find that the longer a migrant works in the destination city, the lower the level of poverty among family members left behind in the rural village.

ACKNOWLEDGMENTS

The authors are grateful for the useful comments made by those who participated in the RUMiCI conference at the Australian National University on 10–12 December 2008. We especially thank Bob Gregory, who was the discussant for our paper, and Xin Meng, who made detailed comments and corrections to the paper after the conference. We would also like to thank Beth Thomson, who made many useful corrections and suggestions when editing the chapter.

NOTES

1   See Sen (1966) for a detailed discussion of this subject.
2   See Du, Park and Wang (2005: 699) for a justification of the use of the migrant social network as the instrument for the migration decision.
3   For more details, see Chapter 7 and the project's website, http://rumici.anu.edu.au.
4   We tested the sensitivity of the results to the two measures and found that there was little difference between them.
5   A *mu* is a traditional measure of land area still used in China; 1 *mu* equals 0.33 hectares.
6   Counties that have been designated poor by the central government are eligible to receive assistance under the government's formal poverty alleviation program. Revolutionary base

areas are the areas where the Communist Party of China and its armed forces had established bases prior to 1949.

7   The remittances that migrants send back to their rural households are another potential indicator of the role of migration in poverty reduction. Unfortunately, however, the survey on which this study is based does not contain any information on remittances.

8   For details of the two equivalence scales, see http://www.oecd.org/dataoecd/61/52/35411111. pdf. Meng, Gregory and Wan (2007) use the two equivalence scales for their analyses of urban poverty in China.

9   The results are available from the authors on request.

7 Rural–Urban Migration in China: Survey Design and Implementation

Sherry Tao Kong

1 BACKGROUND AND OVERVIEW OF THE SURVEY DESIGN

The Rural–Urban Migration in China and Indonesia (RUMiCI) project was established in 2006 to study the patterns and effects of migration in China and Indonesia. The goal is to increase understanding of the urbanization process in both countries, and inform policy makers so that they can manage this process more effectively. Given that many existing studies on migration in China are plagued by data limitations, a substantial contribution of the RUMiCI project is to provide a rich, up-to-date dataset for migration studies in both countries.

The China component of the study, Rural–Urban Migration in China (RUMiC), is based on a sample of 5,000 urban households, 8,000 rural households and 5,000 migrant households. We intend to track these households over five years. Three independent surveys are being conducted to collect the data necessary for the research: the Rural Household Survey, the Urban Household Survey and the Urban Migrant Survey. The former two surveys are being conducted by China's National Bureau of Statistics using a random sample from the standard annual household income and expenditure surveys the bureau carries out in cities and rural areas. The Urban Migrant Survey is being conducted by the RUMiC project team in collaboration with Datasea Marketing Research, a Shanghai-based professional survey company.

Background of Migration Surveys in China

While many have articulated the desirability of longitudinal surveys for migration studies (see, for example, Stark 1976 and Bilsborrow 1998), collecting data on migrant populations in developing countries is known to be very difficult. The problems include complications in registering migrants, poor administrative procedures and the mobile nature of the migrant population. Bilsborrow,

Oberai and Standing (1984: 80) have described some of the difficulties typically associated with migrant surveys, especially in less industrialized countries such as Indonesia and China. In Indonesia, for example, the existence of
seasonal and temporary workers makes it difficult to keep track of migrants. In
addition, there are inconsistencies in government decision making, meaning,
for example, that someone recorded as a temporary visitor in one area may be
recorded as a new resident in another area.

In addition to the general challenges facing migration surveys, there are a
number of specific issues complicating the investigation of migration patterns
in China (Day and Ma 1994; Davin 1999). First, defining a migrant can be
problematic, with duration, motivation and distance from home all needing to
be specified. Differences in the definitions used by agencies have inevitably
led to differences in the estimated size and composition of the migrant population. Second, the sheer size of the migrant population, already in the order
of 120 million in 2004 (Sheng and Peng 2005), makes a nationwide survey
of migrants a very challenging and expensive proposition. Third, migrants in
general are a relatively vulnerable group, often treated as second-class citizens. This makes them particularly difficult to interview; out of a sense of
self-preservation, they are naturally reluctant to provide detailed information
on their livelihoods and social networks. Fourth, many migrants are missed by
the usual dwelling-based surveys because they live at or near their workplaces
in makeshift housing and factory dormitories, or in inaccessible locations such
as shanty towns, squatter settlements or slums. To overcome difficulties such
as these, the RUMiC project team developed a set of strategies embedded in
the listing, sampling, interviewing and tracking process. These are discussed
in sections 2–5 of this chapter.

Overview of the Survey Design

The RUMiC survey is one of the largest of its kind and the first large-scale longitudinal survey to focus on patterns of migration in China. It aims to collect
data on three populations: rural households both with and without migrants
(through the Rural Household Survey); urban residents (through the Urban
Household Survey); and rural-to-urban migrants (through the Urban Migrant
Survey). The underlying consideration is to use rural households without
migrants as a control group to study the effects of rural–urban migration on the
living standards, socio-economic conditions and productivity of rural households; and to use urban residents as a control group to study patterns of social
and economic assimilation among rural residents who have migrated to the
city.

This chapter focuses on the design of the Urban Migrant Survey, which
began collecting data in 2008. The target population is all rural–urban migrants,

that is, migrants who were registered in a rural area but living in an urban area in 2008.[1] The Urban Migrant Survey covers 15 cities in nine provinces or metropolitan areas, namely Shanghai, Guangdong, Jiangsu, Zhejiang, Anhui, Hubei, Sichuan, Chongqing and Henan. The first four provinces are China's largest migrant destinations; the remaining five are among the largest sources of migrants.[2] The distribution of the sample across the 15 cities is loosely associated with the overall population size of the city, with larger cities like Shanghai and Guangzhou being allocated larger sample sizes. The sample allocated to each city is shown in Table 7.1 (column 7). The location of the 15 cities is shown in Figure 1.1 on page 4 of this book.

In designing the Urban Migrant Survey, the RUMiC researchers considered the need to (1) obtain an accurate listing of migrant workplaces; (2) institute reliable sampling procedures; (3) develop a comprehensive and meaningful questionnaire; and (4) track migrant households over the life of the study.

Because of the mobile and temporary nature of China's migrant population, there was no existing sampling frame that the RUMiC team could use for the Urban Migrant Survey. This meant that we could not follow the commonly used stratification sampling method. As a result, our first task was to establish a sampling frame that would provide a reasonable representation of the target population. Developing an unbiased, representative sampling frame required us to conduct a pre-survey 'census'—or listing—to gain an overall picture of that population. Using the listing results as a sampling frame, a total of 5,000 migrant households were selected randomly for face-to-face interviews. The information collected through these interviews provided the basis for subsequent research and analysis. The final step in the survey design was to develop a method to track respondents. We intend to interview as many of the respondent households as possible throughout the life of the survey, in order to capture changes over time. This will allow us to compile a genuine longitudinal dataset of Chinese migrant workers over a five-year span.

Throughout the design process, the RUMiC project team worked closely with Datasea to ensure that the survey was tested thoroughly in the field before being implemented. Together with Datasea, the RUMiC team tested the survey design, oversaw the training and supervision of enumerators and conducted quality control. Datasea and its subcontractors were responsible for the recruitment and training of the enumerators, actual data collection and data entry. The enumerators were mainly professional survey staff and university students.

The first questionnaire was drafted in 2006. Between 2006 and 2007, the draft questionnaire was tested twice in Beijing and once in the rural province of Hebei, each time involving 10–20 interviews. The complete listing and sampling procedures were tested between May and July 2007 in two major pilot studies covering 1,000 migrant households. Each involved one large and one medium-sized city: Shanghai and Wuxi in the first instance, and Guangzhou and Shenzhen in the second. The formal listing procedure for the first wave of the survey was conducted between December 2007 and January 2008 in all 15 cities. The sampling and interview process took place between February and April 2008.

The rest of this chapter provides an overview of the Urban Migrant Survey's listing procedures, sampling strategy, questionnaire design and tracking methods. The listing and sampling methods employed in the survey have several innovative features that require some elaboration, so we focus mainly on them. The following description of sampling procedures and survey methodology should provide a useful framework for interpreting the data and research findings described elsewhere in this book.

2   LISTING OF MIGRANT WORKERS AND WORKPLACES

In China, there is a distinct gap in knowledge about the migrant population in any city at a particular point in time, because of problems with the sampling frame used for most household surveys. The existing surveys are generally based on an individual's current residential address and the place of domicile shown in a person's household register (*hukou*).[3] The *hukou* shows the place of registration of the household as a whole, as well as a range of personal details for each individual member of the household. In the case of permanent residents, whether urban or rural, the actual place of residence would usually be consistent with the *hukou*, meaning that there is an official record of the residential addresses of those people. For migrants, students and other temporary visitors, the residential address would be inconsistent with the address shown on the *hukou*. Such persons are required to register with the local authorities as temporary residents, so the authorities' official registers of temporary residents could be expected to provide information on these populations.

In the case of rural-to-urban migrants, however, the official register of temporary residents is largely incomplete. Many migrants do not register at all, and a large number live at their workplaces, without residential addresses as such. These migrants would not be captured by the existing surveys using administrative records of residential address as the basis for migrant survey sampling. The extent of undercoverage of this group of migrants, and how it would affect the results, is difficult to gauge, but it is safe to assume that many of the sampling frameworks used in China are not representative. This bias would in turn compromise the analysis and lead to an incorrect understanding of the migrant situation. The fundamental challenge was therefore to establish a random, representative sampling frame that could provide an accurate picture of the migrant population in all survey cities.

To overcome the problems associated with residential address-based sampling, we decided to conduct a listing covering a large number of workplaces in each city. We included all businesses in randomly selected enumeration areas within defined city boundaries. During the listing, we recorded the total number of staff and the total number of migrant workers in each workplace. This allowed us to estimate the total size of the migrant worker population in each city. The listing-based information on the size of the migrant population was designed to be representative of that city and to provide a sampling frame for subsequent random sampling and the interview process.

The listing procedure was conducted in three steps: we defined each city's boundaries; we divided each city into blocks and randomly selected enumeration areas; and we conducted a listing in each of the selected areas using in-built quality controls.

Defining a City's Boundaries

The Urban Migrant Survey listing did not necessarily cover all areas within a city's administrative territory. Rather, the definition of a city's boundaries took into account both the feasibility of conducting a listing and the necessity to obtain a representative sampling frame. Accordingly, two general principles guided the identification of a city's boundaries: (1) the within-boundary area had to cover as many workplaces as possible where migrants might be employed; and (2) large empty spaces where little economic activity took place would not be included in the within-boundary area. To make sure the boundaries did not exclude any cluster of migrants, we imposed an additional rule: that there should not be any concentrated residential area or production site within 1 kilometre of the defined survey boundaries. If there was such an area, the boundaries would be expanded until this condition was met.

In practice, the areas where most economic activity takes place are far more concentrated than residential areas. As a result, most cities as defined by their survey boundaries proved to be smaller than their actual administrative territories. Although it was admittedly not possible to completely cover the urban city fringe or every business in a survey city, such omissions were minimized by defining the city boundaries to cover as large an area as possible. In Shanghai, for instance, nine of the city's 18 administrative districts were fully within the survey boundaries, and another four were partially within the boundaries.[4]

Dividing Cities into Blocks and Randomly Selecting Enumeration Areas

The area within the survey boundaries of each city was divided into equal-sized blocks averaging 0.25 square kilometres in size, using up-to-date, equal-scale maps. These blocks were numbered in a consistent order.[5] The numbers assigned to the blocks were subsequently used for the random selection of enumeration areas.

The number of blocks randomly selected to be included in the listing process was proportional to the sample size for each city. The actual ratio was 12 per cent of the sample size, of which 10 per cent would be used for the initial listing and 2 per cent would be kept in reserve in case there was a problem with the main sample. In Shanghai, for example, we started with more than 2,000 equal-sized blocks of 500 by 500 metres in size within the identified city boundary. As the sample size for Shanghai was to be 500 households, 60 blocks were selected randomly: 50 for the main sample and 10 for the reserve sample.

The way in which the blocks were selected was as follows. Three groups of random numbers were generated and the blocks with those numbers were marked on the map to indicate the distribution of the enumeration areas. Strictly speaking, each group of blocks had been chosen randomly, so the selection process was statistically sound. However, the businesses where migrants work are not distributed evenly across blocks. Considering this unevenness and the relatively small number of blocks selected for listing, we decided to discard the groups that excluded major clusters of migrant workplaces. For each city, we chose the single group of blocks that covered the most migrant workplaces. In doing so, we admit that we introduced a degree of arbitrariness into the selection of enumeration areas, and acknowledge the potential bias that may result.

Once the choice of enumeration areas was finalized, detailed maps were prepared for the next step in the listing process. These detailed maps allowed the supervisors to delineate the actual boundaries of each enumeration area and identify the main buildings within each block. This was an important step, because although the blocks were of equal size and shape on the map, the actual boundaries needed to take account of the presence of road and transport networks. As one would expect, the end result was irregularly shaped blocks whose boundaries were defined by roads in and around the area. Supervisors then decided the routes that enumerators would follow in conducting the listing.

Conducting the Listing and Ensuring Quality Control

The listing procedure required enumerators to visit every workplace within a defined enumeration area, whether formal or informal, permanent or temporary—or even mobile. The enumerators first recorded the name and address of the business, then went on to enquire about staff. The information collected during this process included total staff numbers, the number of migrant workers employed, the contact details of the person providing the information and a range of basic descriptive indicators on the business, such as floor area and type of industry.

While the normal listing procedure required enumerators to obtain information on every business, we made an exception for large wholesale and retail markets (those with more than 50 stalls) on the basis that the stalls in such markets were likely to be relatively homogenous in size and industry type. In such cases, the enumerators were required to list the total number of businesses in the market and visit 10 per cent of them.

We recognized that taxi drivers, domestic servants, residential cleaners and migrants working in some other occupations would probably not be encountered by enumerators following the normal procedure of visiting workplaces. To ensure that they were not left out of the listing procedure, we developed a number of special procedures to contact such migrants. Where this was not possible, we developed statistical procedures to compensate for the missing information.[6]

An important extra step included in the Urban Migrant Survey listing was to ask enumerators, after they had recorded all the information they could obtain through an enquiry, to record their own subjective assessment of the reliability of the information provided. The enumerators were also instructed to provide their own estimates of the number of migrant workers at each workplace based on observation of such factors as floor area, industry type and the number of migrant workers in neighbouring shops of similar scale. Where business owners refused to provide information, these subjective measures proved particularly useful, although the subjectivity of this information required special treatment.

At the end of the listing process, supervisors compiled all of the information from every enumeration area to obtain a complete set of information that was representative at the city level. The Urban Migrant Survey listing covered more than 100,000 businesses and about 550,000 migrant workers in total. Table 7.1 replicates the summary information from Gong et al. (2008) and provides some basic statistics on the migrant population derived from the listing conducted in December 2007. The first column shows the number of enumeration areas in which a listing was conducted. The second shows the total number of blocks selected for enumeration, including reserve blocks. Column 3 indicates the total number of migrants listed in these enumeration areas. Column 4 presents the migrant population density per enumeration area. Based on the average number of migrants per enumeration area (column 4) and the total number of blocks within the defined city boundary (column 5), we estimated the aggregate number of migrants in each city (column 6).

Among the 15 cities, Dongguan in Guangdong province has the highest density of migrants (2,614 migrants per 0.25 square kilometre), followed by Shenzhen (2,295), Wuxi (1,691) and Guangzhou (1,171) (see column 4). Coinciding with anecdotal evidence, it is apparent that Dongguan, Shanghai, Guangzhou and Shenzhen are some of the most popular destinations for migrants (see column 6). Based on the listing results, the total number of migrants in the 15

Table 7.1 China: Basic Information on the Listing of Migrant Workers by City

Province	City	No. of Enumeration Areas in which Listing Was Conducted (1)	Total No. of Enumeration Areas Selected (main + reserve) (2)	Total No. of Migrants in Enumeration Area (3)	Mean No. of Migrants per Enumeration Area (4) = (3)/(1)	Total No. of Blocks within City Boundaries (5)	Implied Total No. of Migrants (6) = (5)*(4)	Total No. of Migrants to Be Sampled (7)
Guangdong	Guangzhou	40	48	46,822	1,171	1,048	1,226,736	400
	Shenzhen	30	36	68,851	2,295	474	1,087,846	300
	Dongguan	30	36	78,432	2,614	886	2,316,358	300
Shanghai	Shanghai	50	60	40,293	806	2,050	1,652,013	500
Jiangsu	Nanjing	40	48	30,352	759	893	677,608	400
	Wuxi	20	24	33,823	1,691	677	1,144,909	200
Zhejiang	Hangzhou	40	48	45,540	1,139	512	582,912	400
	Ningbo	20	24	18,637	932	249	232,031	200
Hubei	Wuhan	40	48	39,060	977	1,004	980,406	400
Chongqing	Chongqing	40	48	39,792	995	640	636,672	400
Sichuan	Chengdu	40	48	36,145	904	590	533,139	400
Anhui	Hefei	35	42	21,152	604	618	373,484	350
	Bengbu	20	24	5,689	284	121	34,418	200
Henan	Zhengzhou	35	42	28,604	817	655	535,303	350
	Luoyang	20	24	8,600	430	296	127,280	200

Source: Gong et al. (2008).

survey cities is estimated to be 12 million, or slightly less than 10 per cent of the official figure of 126 million for the entire country in 2005 (NBS 2006a).

During the listing period, the enumerators visited around 100,000 businesses. About 30 per cent of them were small groceries, restaurants or cafés and another 10 per cent were clothing wholesalers or retailers. These figures are reflected in the high proportion of migrants in Table 7.2 working in services (34 per cent) and wholesale and retail trade (33 per cent). To illustrate the significance of the sampling frame, Table 7.2 compares the Urban Migrant Survey listing results with those of three other urban-based datasets on migrant workers. The results for the Urban Migrant Survey find more migrant workers engaged in construction and manufacturing, and fewer in wholesale and retail trade.[7] It is possible that the choice of survey cities and the timing of the listing may have contributed to the differences in occupational distribution between the Urban Migrant Survey and the other surveys. However, a more important reason is the underlying sampling method. The three earlier surveys were all based on random sampling of residents in cities. As noted earlier, this approach effectively excludes from the sampling frame all migrants who live at their workplaces.

At the end of the listing process, a group of quality control officers carried out verification procedures to check the completeness of the records of businesses and confirm the accuracy of the information obtained. The officers covered 10 per cent of the enumeration areas in each city during this process, visiting one main street and one smaller street in each area.[8] A 10 per cent margin was allowed for the information completeness check, and a 30 per cent margin was allowed for the accuracy of the information obtained at a specific business. Where there were discrepancies greater than the allowed margins, the listing procedure was repeated for the rest of the enumeration area. If the information for an enumeration area was found to be grossly incomplete or inaccurate, the listing procedure was repeated for all enumeration areas conducted by the enumerator in question. The quality control procedure revealed that the quality of the listing was generally satisfactory. On average, less than 5 per cent of businesses had been omitted and discrepancies in the number of migrant workers ran at around 15 per cent.

3 SAMPLING

The next step was to select a simple random sample of migrants in each city for interview. This section first describes how the sample of migrants was drawn from the listing data. It then discusses how the sampling procedures were implemented in the field.

Table 7.2   China: Listing and Sample Information on the Distribution of Migrant Workers by Industry

City	Construc-tion (%)	Manu-facturing (%)	Educational & Govt Agencies (%)	Other Agencies (%)	Serv-ices (%)	Wholesale & Retail Trade (%)	Total No. of Migrants
Chengdu	10.7	3.1	0.6	6.4	45.8	33.5	36,145
Hangzhou	7.1	17.6	2.5	2.7	37.0	33.2	45,540
Nanjing	16.9	15.9	1.2	10.2	38.2	17.7	30,352
Ningbo	26.1	9.0	5.1	10.1	28.2	21.6	18,637
Shanghai	8.4	10.9	1.5	11.9	41.3	26.1	40,293
Wuhan	5.2	28.9	3.1	2.9	36.5	23.5	39,060
Wuxi	9.4	40.8	2.0	6.0	22.0	19.8	33,823
Bengbu	7.9	13.8	0.3	1.4	30.3	46.2	5,689
Chongqing	9.2	4.7	1.2	0.8	48.8	35.3	39,792
Dongguan	1.2	26.3	3.2	1.7	12.6	55.0	78,432
Guangzhou	1.3	23.2	2.9	6.1	40.1	26.4	46,822
Hefei	10.1	5.4	1.3	8.9	36.3	38.0	21,152
Luoyang	8.3	12.9	2.2	0.5	38.9	37.2	8,600
Shenzhen	7.2	21.8	1.0	2.8	36.3	30.9	68,851
Zhengzhou	21.5	8.2	1.3	1.6	34.5	33.0	28,604
Total	**8.4**	**18.2**	**2.0**	**4.7**	**34.0**	**32.7**	**541,792**
IOE, 1999[a]	4.3	12.7	3.8	0.5	36.6	42.2	1,254
IOE, 2002[a]	5.5	9.8	2.9	0.7	34.1	47.0	3,407
ULS, 2001[b]	10.3	7.3	3.0	0.9	38.7	39.9	2,205
Sample of respondents aged 15+							
(no.)	1,089	1,391	558	285	2,052	2,065	7,440
(%)	10.9	18.8	6.4	4.3	31.9	27.7	100

a   The Institute of Economics (IOE) at the Chinese Academy of Social Sciences conducted two urban-based migrant household surveys, the first covering 13 cities with 780 households (1,785 individuals) in 1999; and the second covering 12 provinces (27 cities) with a total of 2,000 households (5,327 individuals) in 2002. On average, the IOE surveyed less than 100 households in each city.
b   The China Urban Labour Survey (ULS) was conducted by the Institute of Population and Labour Economics at the Chinese Academy of Social Sciences in 2001. Undertaken in five large cities (Shanghai, Wuhan, Shenyang, Fuzhou and Xian), it covered 340 migrant households and 2,365 individuals.

Source: Gong et al. (2008).

Random Selection of the Sample

Theoretically, for each survey city, the total number of migrants working in all enumeration areas could be aggregated from the listing information for each business in each enumeration area. This aggregate number of migrants would then serve as the sampling frame for that city. In practice, however, the execution of this process needed to take account of two things. First, recall that the information collected in large markets did not cover every single business, so the businesses omitted from the listing process would have to be taken into account. Second, in reality it was not always possible to collect information on the number of migrants working in a particular business, because the owners of the business refused to provide the relevant information or the enumerators were refused entry to the premises. In such cases, the enumerators could still record descriptive information such as the industry category, location and estimated size of the business, but crucial information on the number of migrant workers employed in the business would be missing.

We addressed these two issues with the aid of a regression model. First, based on the assumption of homogeneity among businesses in large markets, we used the information collected on 10 per cent of the businesses in each market to estimate the total number of migrants working in all markets in each city. The second step in completing the sampling frame was to account for migrant workers who were not included in the listing. To do this, we constructed a regression model for the number of migrant workers employed in a given workplace, based on determinants such as total number of staff, floor area of the business, type of ownership, industry category and so on. We then used the information we had collected on these factors to predict the probable number of migrant workers in the businesses missed by the enumerators. This exercise was performed for each city to complete the listing information and provide a representative sampling frame for the subsequent sample selection.

To calculate the sampling factor for each city, we divided the sample size by the total number of migrant workers (including predications) in the sampling frame. This factor was assigned to each migrant worker in the sampling frame, giving all migrant workers in the frame an equal probability of being selected.[9] The next step was to randomly select the requisite number of migrant workers for each city, and for each workplace. Recall that the listing database contained business-level information on the number of migrant workers employed at each workplace. Therefore, at the end of this stage, each business was associated with a figure indicating the number of migrant workers to be selected.

Implementation of Random Sample Selection

We now knew the number of migrants to be selected for interview at each workplace. However, to ensure an unbiased sample, we also needed to define a procedure that would enable us to randomly select the designated number of migrants at each workplace. To describe how such a sample was selected in practice, three representative situations are described here.[10]

1   To choose one respondent from a workplace that employed only one migrant worker, sampling officers were instructed to identify the migrant worker and ask him or her to participate in the Urban Migrant Survey.
2   To choose one worker from a workplace that had more than one but less than 10 migrant workers, officers were asked to use the 'random birth-month' method—that is, to select the worker whose birth month was closest to a randomly chosen birth month selected previously.
3   To choose more than one respondent from a workplace with 10 or more migrant workers, sampling officers were instructed to apply a combined 'random interception and random birth-month' method, that is, to randomly intercept migrant workers and choose the ones whose birth months matched a randomly chosen birth month selected before the sampling process took place.[11]

The application of these three methods was supplemented by a set of rules to guide situations where the sampling process was unsuccessful, because of a lack of cooperation, for instance, or because of difficulties in gaining access to a selected workplace. These rules regulated when and how substitution of a selected migrant could take place. In practice, around 60 per cent of the total sample was chosen from businesses randomly selected by the original computer program; selection of the remaining 40 per cent involved substitution during the sampling process.[12] It is important to emphasize that sample substitution took place only between businesses of similar size in the same industry. Sampling officers were not permitted to substitute respondents from small-scale businesses with those from large-scale enterprises, or vice versa. Had such substitutions been allowed, the distribution of migrant workers by occupation and employment would have been biased.

Based on the sample selection, the Urban Migrant Survey collected a wide range of information on migrants and migrant households. The sample covered 5,003 households and 7,440 adult household members (defined as those aged 16 and above). The last two rows of Table 7.2 indicate that the occupational distribution of the sample is broadly consistent with the listing information.

4   QUESTIONNAIRE-BASED INTERVIEWS

The research focus of the RUMiCI project goes beyond the conventional topics of migration determinants and labour market discrimination to cover the welfare status of migrants: their jobs, incomes and physical and mental health, their children's education and health, and the extent to which they assimilate into their city communities. This will allow researchers to explore a number of important aspects of migration that have so far been underresearched. This section briefly describes the structure of the questionnaire and the main survey instruments.[13]

A household-based questionnaire was employed for the Urban Migrant Survey. A household was defined as anyone who was living with the respondent at the time of the survey, sharing income and expenditure. The questionnaire had two main components: one to obtain individual-level information and the other to obtain household-level information. The individual-level component covered four areas: (1) household composition; (2) adult education; (3) adult employment; and (4) children.

Respondents were first asked to provide information to complete a household roster describing the household composition and basic characteristics of each household member: age, marital status, whether or not the individual was a member of an ethnic minority, work capability and so on. This section also included a set of general questions focusing on the mental health of adults.[14]

The sections on both education and employment were targeted at household members aged 16 and above who had completed their schooling. The questions on education focused on schooling and training. The questions on employment were designed to obtain detailed information on the labour market performance of migrant workers and other adults in the same household. This section of the survey first asked a set of general questions to identify the employment status of each individual. It then asked specific questions that differed depending on the respondent's employment status: wage worker, self-employed or not working at the time of the survey. This part of the questionnaire concluded with a set of questions on the migrant's first job in the city. The responses should allow researchers to extract historical information and observe how some labour market indicators, such as migrant workers' wages, change over time.

The final section of the individual component contained about 50 questions on migrant workers' children, defined as the sons or daughters of the household head (or other household members), and either aged under 16 or aged 16 and above and still at school at the time of the survey. Both children who were living in the city with their parents and those who had been left behind in the countryside were covered, to allow researchers to investigate the impact of migration on migrated children's health and education.

The household head (or that person's spouse) was asked to answer the household-level questions in the Urban Migrant Survey. This component covered (1) social networks; (2) lifecycle events; (3) household income and expenditure; (4) household assets; (5) housing conditions; and (6) information on the rural home village. The social networks section contained several subsections covering spouses living separately, adult children living separately, the parents of both the household head and that person's spouse, and general information on the household's social networks, including information on up to five close associates.

All except the social networks section were relatively standard and self-explanatory. The questions on social networks were designed to capture the extent and depth of migrants' social connections, given the substantial literature on the sociological and economic role of social networks. It is well established that social networks have important implications for the intra-family transfer of income and wealth and the internal arrangement of household and social responsibilities (Montgomery 1992; Benabou 1993; Granovetter 2005). This part of the questionnaire therefore sought to gather data that would improve our understanding of the assimilation process.

In summary, the Urban Migrant Survey questionnaire is one of the most comprehensive ever developed for migration studies. It connects closely with the research questions of the RUMiCI project and has the potential to be used to investigate a wide range of questions of interest.

5 TRACKING

The RUMiCI project is designed to provide a longitudinal dataset covering a five-year time span. However, migration is an extremely dynamic process where migrants may move frequently or relocate across vast distances. We therefore designed a set of tracking strategies to enable us to maintain contact with respondents from year to year. The effectiveness of these strategies, and the attrition rate, will become clearer over time. We intend to modify and improve our tracking strategies to deal with problems as they arise, so this section will provide just a brief account of the current plan.

We intend to track respondents so long as they remain in the surveyed provinces and cities. While it would be valuable to follow migrants who return to their rural areas of origin, such an undertaking would not be feasible given the well-known problems and high cost of tracking returning migrants. To reduce the attrition rate, we developed a number of strategies to keep in touch with respondents between waves of the survey. On both the front and last pages of the questionnaire, household heads were asked to supply detailed contact information, including current address, address in the home village, telephone number, and names and contact details of three associates. We intend to contact respondents by telephone every three months and mail small presents to the home village at major festival times. This should help us to maintain an up-to-date list of respondents' contact details, in both the city and the home village, over the coming years. To provide an additional incentive for respondents to stay in touch with the project team, we also set up a lottery scheme in which all respondents were entered at no cost to them.[15]

Of course, despite our efforts, we were aware that we would lose a number of respondents. When we conducted the first round of tracking and lottery activity about five months after the first wave of the survey, we found that we could not contact around 35 per cent of the respondent households. By February 2009, this proportion had reached almost 50 per cent. This high rate of attrition was associated with the severe economic downturn accompanying the global financial crisis. The crisis has had a particularly severe effect on the industries where migrant workers are concentrated, such as manufacturing, construction and services. To address the high rate of attrition, we plan to replace lost respondents with new respondents through a sampling process based on the 2007 listing information.

6 CONCLUSION

The Urban Migrant Survey is an important component of a large-scale study of rural–urban migrants in China and Indonesia. It addresses some of the problems with existing migrant surveys in China, which tend to be dwelling-based, one-off case studies. The project team devised a set of procedures and methodologies to generate a longitudinal dataset covering 5,000 migrant households across 15 Chinese cities. It is one of very few scientifically based, random-sample migration surveys in China. This chapter has highlighted the complex strategies adopted to address the current lack of information on the migrant population.

The first step in the survey design was to conduct a city-level listing to obtain workplace-based information on migrant workers in each city. This allowed us to capture most migrant workers within defined city boundaries. This new approach reduced the sample bias inherent in existing urban-based surveys that have used residential addresses as the basis for sampling. The project team then developed a set of protocols to ensure the randomness and representativeness of the selected sample. The third step was to conduct questionnaire-based, face-to-face interviews with respondent households, where a wide range of information was gathered. Subsequently, respondents have been contacted at regular intervals to ensure that as many as possible participate in future waves of the survey. With the availability of an extensive array of data covering a five-year span, the Urban Migrant Survey should contribute substantially to a better understanding of the patterns and effects of migration in China.

NOTES

1 Unless stated otherwise, in the remainder of this chapter the terms 'migrant' and 'rural–urban migrant' are used interchangeably.
2 According to the 2000 census, Shanghai, Guangdong, Jiangsu and Zhejiang receive 66 per cent of all migrants, while Sichuan, Chongqing, Anhui, Hubei and Henan send 47 per cent of all migrants.
3 On the *hukou* system, see Cheng and Selden (1994), Chan, Liu and Yang (1999), Chan and Zhang (1999) and Liu (2005).
4 The four districts that were partially covered were Baoshang, Minhang, Jiading and New Pudong. The five districts that were excluded from the survey were Songjiang, Jinshan, Qingpu, Nanhui and Fengxian. The official website of the RUMiCI project provides detailed maps and information on the survey boundaries of all 15 cities; see http://rumici.anu.edu.au.
5 During the numbering process, blocks that contained mostly river or parks were excluded, as they would contain few businesses.
6 For a complete account of these procedures, see 'Urban Migrant Survey document: census manual' at http://rumici.anu.edu.au.
7 See Gong et al. (2008: 118–19) for a more detailed discussion of the aggregation of occupational categories as well as background information on previous urban-based surveys.
8 The tasks performed by quality control officers are described in more detail in the Urban Migrant Survey listing procedure; see 'Urban Migrant Survey document: census manual' at http://rumici.anu.edu.au.
9 Most statistical software packages make it easy to generate a random sample once a sampling factor has been specified. We used the STATA statistical package to randomly select the designated number of migrant workers for each city, plus an extra 30 per cent in case a reserve sample was needed.
10 For a detailed account of the procedures used for taxi drivers, street vendors, cleaners and other 'special situations', see 'Urban Migrant Survey document: sampling manual' at http://rumici.anu.edu.au.
11 In the second and third situations, sampling officers were also allowed to use an alternative method based on rosters of workers. In practice, however, this method was hardly used because complete rosters of migrant workers were rarely available.
12 Information on the extent of sampling substitution is based on estimates provided by the local supervisors who conducted the sampling process.
13 For a copy of the questionnaire, see 'Urban Migrant Survey document: interview' at http://rumici.anu.edu.au.
14 These questions were based on the 12-item General Health Questionnaire (GHQ12), which is widely used as a general measure of mental health status. All adult members who were present at the time of the survey were asked to answer this set of questions.
15 The lottery is set up in such a way that about 20 per cent of respondents receive prizes. We are hopeful that the relatively high chance of winning a prize will encourage respondents to stay in touch with the survey team, even though the prizes themselves are modest.

PART II

INDONESIA

8   Assessing the Welfare of Migrant and Non-migrant Households in Four Indonesian Cities: Some Demographic, Social and Employment Characteristics

**Tadjuddin Noer Effendi, Mujiyani,
Fina Itriyati, Danang Arif Darmawan
and Derajad S. Widhyharto**

1   INTRODUCTION

This chapter examines the demographic, social and employment characteristics of migrant and non-migrant households in Indonesia, and assesses their welfare. It is based on a survey of 2,371 households conducted in four Indonesian cities as part of the Rural–Urban Migration in China and Indonesia (RUMiCI) project. In line with the project's longitudinal approach, in both countries the surveys will be conducted annually among the same sample of households for five years. This chapter describes the results of the first round of the Rural–Urban Migration in Indonesia (RUMiI) survey, based on cross-sectional data collected in March–May 2008.

To flag the main findings, we find several important differences between migrant and non-migrant households, but also between recent migrants on the one hand and lifetime migrants and non-migrants on the other. It appears that, over time, migrants take on the characteristics of the resident urban population, suggesting the existence of relatively high levels of social and economic mobility.

The chapter is organized as follows. In the next section, we provide an overview of the history and general patterns of migration in Indonesia. In section 3, we look briefly at methodology. The fourth section describes the main demographic, social and workforce characteristics of individual household heads and family members, as well as household characteristics such as housing conditions and the incidence of poverty. In the fifth section, we focus on differences between migrant and non-migrant households in the four cities studied.

2   AN OVERVIEW OF THE HISTORY AND PATTERNS OF MIGRATION

Historically, research on voluntary migration in Indonesia has focused on the movement of certain ethnic groups across provincial boundaries, for instance, the Bugis from South Sulawesi (Tirtosudarmo 2008: 101–12), the Minangkabau from West Sumatra (Murad 1980) and the Batak and Banjar from North Sumatra and Kalimantan respectively (Naim 1974). These groups migrated from one island to another or from infertile dry-land areas to wet-land paddy areas, mostly looking for agricultural land or opportunities in traditional trading or fishery activities. The pattern of migration was to move permanently from one rural area to another. These kinds of voluntary migrations (*merantau*) were part of the culture of several of these ethnic groups.

The 1960s and 1970s

During the New Order period, lasting from 1965 through to the economic crisis of 1997–98, the focus of voluntary migration shifted from rural-to-rural migration to rural-to-urban migration. This was associated with the spread of development in urban areas—where economic growth rates, investment and job opportunities expanded—and with increasing levels of poverty and landlessness in rural areas. During the 1960s and 1970s, Indonesia's rapidly growing population began to place pressure on human-to-land ratios, leading to fragmentation of land ownership, inequalities in the distribution of land and increasing landlessness, all of which contributed to high levels of poverty. Manning (1998: 46) has estimated landlessness in rural Java at about 30–40 per cent during the 1960s and early 1970s. These high levels of landlessness were associated with a large traditional and non-agricultural sector in which households were engaged in small-scale activities. Earnings were often lower than daily wages in agriculture. This was a symptom of poverty in rural Java where around half of Indonesia's total population lived.

Although there were differences in the distribution of land and rural employment conditions across Indonesia, many regions experienced conditions of surplus labour, low incomes and spreading poverty. It has been estimated that the incidence of poverty during this period exceeded 50 per cent (World Bank 1990 and Hill 1996: 12, cited in Manning 1998: 63). Coupled with a lack of reasonable returns to non-agricultural employment, both off-farm and non-farm, this high incidence of poverty pushed many people to move to urban areas in search of alternative activities offering higher wages (Temple 1974; Suharso et al. 1976; Hugo 1978).

Although many of these rural–urban migrants were successful in building new lives in the city, many others had difficulty accessing the urban labour market, especially the modern sectors, because of a lack of skills and capital. Many ended up in the informal sector, where they worked as construction workers, street vendors, peddlers and food stall vendors in cities like Jakarta (Hugo 1978), Surabaya (Steele 1981) and Makassar (Forbes 1978). While their incomes may have been higher than they would have been in the countryside, they were still low. Some migrants survived by leaving their families behind in the home village and renting huts (*pondok*) in the city. Others squatted in temporary dwellings or lived with friends from the same village in slum areas (Jellinek 1978). The remittances that migrants sent home to support their families had a positive effect on rural household incomes, contributing to a reduction in poverty in rural areas (Hugo 1978: 267–73). The incidence of rural poverty is estimated to have fallen from 20 per cent in 1987 to 14 per cent in 1993 (Manning 1998: 63).

The 1980s and 1990s

In the 1980s and 1990s, rapid development in both rural and urban areas was associated with a marked increase in the tempo of voluntary rural–urban migration (Manning 1987). The central government used the expanded government revenues associated with the oil boom to invest in irrigation, rural and regional infrastructure and social sectors such as health and education. The expansion of cultivated land area and agricultural investment, together with institutional changes, led to a sharp rise in the productivity of rice and other crops, and to a decline in rural employment opportunities.[1] At the same time, there was a rise in urban employment opportunities associated with rapid economic growth and the concentration of manufacturing employment in Java, especially in the vicinity of Jakarta.[2]

Improvements to infrastructure, particularly transport, electricity and communications, led to greater integration of the rural and urban labour markets. The expansion of rural infrastructure made it easier for rural residents to access urban jobs, through better information on job opportunities and improved and cheaper transport (Leinbach 1981; McCawley 1982). Friends and family members who had already migrated to urban areas gave villagers the information they needed to find jobs in the cities and adjust to urban life. For members of poor rural households, moving to an urban area was a rational strategy to improve their income and overcome poverty.

The effect of rural–urban migration goes well beyond consideration of the pressure it placed on urban population sizes and infrastructure. Migrants who moved to urban areas faced numerous difficulties as they adjusted to city life (Pelly 1994). Migration also had implications for household welfare, especially the health and education of children left behind in the countryside. Although the remittances that migrants sent home could be used to pay for the education and other needs of children, these children faced a lack of parental care. This subject needs to be investigated further given that so little is known about the effect of parental absence on children's psychological development.

Although the central government stance on migration was relatively liberal, in practice some of the larger cities introduced regulations and policies that discriminated against migrants.[3] For city governments, migrants were a cause of problems such as unsanitary living conditions, the growth of slum areas and the spread of illegally erected dwellings along river banks or next to the railway tracks. Street vendors, hawkers and peddlers were blamed for all kinds of social ills, such as crime, traffic jams and disturbances to public order. To reduce the flow of rural–urban migrants, some city governments introduced regulations requiring migrants to carry identity cards consistent with the current place of residence; those without the correct city address on their identity cards could be relocated or evicted. Authorities sometimes destroyed the food stalls (*warung*) and temporary dwellings built by migrants. These policies affected not only migrants' incomes but their level of adjustment to, and degree of assimilation and integration into, urban life.

2000 to the Present

In the new century, the main forces driving development are globalization and liberalization. As a result, many more Indonesians are seeking employment overseas. During the economic crisis of the late 1990s, modern sectors such as finance and manufacturing were particularly badly affected. Many manufacturing firms went out of business or had to reduce production, and many employees were retrenched. Workers affected by the downturn either returned to their rural villages or sought employment overseas. In the period 1999–2004, the number of Indonesians officially working overseas rose above 2 million, a figure that excludes a large number of undocumented overseas workers. While the attention of scholars has shifted to international migration (Hugo 1993; Athukorala and Manning 1999), its effect on contemporary patterns of rural–urban migration and the welfare of migrants in both the sending and receiving communities is unknown.

The economic crisis also exacerbated tensions between ethnic groups, leading to riots and conflict in places like Jakarta, West Kalimantan (de Jonge and Nooteboom 2006), Central Kalimantan, Ambon (in Maluku) and Poso (in Sulawesi), and to demands for independence in some regions. One of the causes of the conflict was perceived inequalities in the distribution of revenues between the central government and the regions (Effendi 2000: 175–86). To address this situation, the new, democratically elected government formally implemented a strategy of decentralization in January 2001, giving local (district) governments far greater control over their own revenues and expenditures.

The question naturally arises as to what effect these social and economic changes had on the regions. One would expect that the decentralization policy in particular would have created employment opportunities in some regional centres, attracting migrants from other areas.

3 METHODOLOGY: DEFINING MIGRANTS AND SELECTING THE CITIES

In this study, we define rural–urban migrants as people who lived continuously in a rural area for at least five years before the age of 12, and currently reside in an urban area. Recent migrants are those who moved to a city in the five years preceding the survey, and lifetime migrants are those who moved to a city more than five years before the survey was conducted. Non-migrants are people who were born and raised in a city; thus, this category includes urban-to-urban migrants.

This study focuses on four major cities that have experienced significant inflows of rural–urban migrants over the past few decades: Tangerang in the province of Banten, Samarinda in East Kalimantan, Medan in North Sumatra and Makassar in South Sulawesi. All four are 'melting pots' for people from other parts of the same province as well as from other provinces and islands. The four cities were selected both to capture regional differences and for their differing social and economic characteristics.[4] Two, Tangerang and Samarinda, became major urban settlements only quite recently. The other two cities, Medan and Makassar, have a longer history as major urban areas.

Tangerang is an industrial city on the outskirts of Jakarta with a population of around 1.5 million. After Batam in the Riau Islands, it is the city with the second-largest number of migrant workers in the manufacturing sector. Tangerang has grown very rapidly since the 1980s in response to the twin effects of industrial growth to cater for demand for exports and the movement of Jakartans to the fringes of the city as urban congestion and rising land prices squeezed them out of the city centre. Samarinda is a medium-sized city with a much smaller population of around 600,000. This thriving provincial capital in the resource-abundant region of East Kalimantan is the largest destination for rural–urban migrants from other parts of Kalimantan. Both Tangerang and Samarinda expanded rapidly throughout the 1980s and the first half of the 1990s, at rates above the national average of 4–5 per cent per annum.

The more established cities of Medan and Makassar have grown at a more sedate pace over the past few decades. With a population of over 2 million, Medan is the largest city in the agriculturally rich province of North Sumatra. The region has been a centre of trade between northern Sumatra, Singapore and Malaysia since colonial times. Medan was the main centre of manufacturing outside Java from the late 1960s through to the mid-1980s. The smaller city of Makassar has a population of around 1 million. Although it lacks the strategic location of Medan, it is situated in one of the most densely populated Outer Island provinces, South Sulawesi, and is the largest city in eastern Indonesia. It is the main destination area for migrants from other parts of eastern Indonesia, and has a relatively diversified employment structure.

This study focuses on the demographic, social and employment characteristics of rural–urban migrants in the four cities, and the welfare of rural–urban migrant households relative to non-migrant households. Just under one-quarter of the 2,371 households covered by the 2008 survey are recent migrant households, with the balance distributed fairly evenly between lifetime migrant and non-migrant households.

4   OVERALL FINDINGS

Demographic and Social Characteristics

As one might expect, recent migrants are younger and more likely to be single than lifetime migrants and non-migrants. The average age of the heads of recent migrant households is 26 years, compared with around 45 for the heads of lifetime migrant and non-migrant households (Table 8.1). As we will see, the younger age of the recent migrants is influenced by a significant group of students who have moved from rural to urban areas to continue their studies.

Over two-thirds of household heads are male. However, the share is lower among recent migrants, many of whom are women working in factories or female students studying at the tertiary level. In all cities, a high proportion of recent migrants are single (65 per cent),[5] compared with about 5 per cent for both lifetime migrants and non-migrants. The heads of lifetime migrant and non-migrant households are more likely to be married in all four cities. Among both recent migrants and lifetime migrants, a high proportion of married household heads are living with their spouses in the city (86 per cent). In China, in contrast, rural–urban migrants are far more likely to be single or to be living apart from their spouses.[6]

Table 8.1   Indonesia: Key Characteristics of Sample Households by Migration Status

	Recent Migrants	Lifetime Migrants	Non-migrants	All Households
No. of households	637	884	850	2,371
(%)	(27)	(37)	(36)	(100)
Mean household size (no. of members)	1.8	4.1	4.3	3.6
Characteristics of household head				
Mean age (years)	26	45	44	40
Gender (% female)	31	24	25	26
Marital status (% single)	65	5	6	20

Source: Rural–Urban Migration in Indonesia survey, 2008.

Moreover, in Indonesia, unlike in China, the migrant population tends to be better educated than the non-migrant population. In all four cities, the heads of recent migrant households are slightly better educated than the heads of the other two groups; on average, they have just over 10 years of schooling (Table 8.2). Although not shown in the table, among recent migrant households and, to a lesser extent, non-migrant households, females are better educated than males. This is not the case, however, among lifetime migrants. This is an issue of some importance given our focus on social mobility and migration status in Indonesia. In future rounds of the survey, it will be interesting to see whether these well-educated female migrants exhibit different patterns of social mobility to male migrants.

A comparison of the educational attainment of household heads and their children indicates that, in general, the children have more years of schooling than their parents (see Table 8.2). The exception is recent migrants, because of the large number of single individuals in this group who have migrated to continue their schooling, and of young couples whose children are not yet in school or still in primary school. The discrepancy between household heads and their children is most pronounced for lifetime migrants, suggesting the possibility of high rates of social mobility among longer-term migrants.

Labour Force and Employment Characteristics

In many countries, labour force participation rates tend to be highest among recent migrants. Rates are generally lower among longer-term migrants and

*Table 8.2   Indonesia: Mean Years of Schooling of Household Heads and
Children Who Have Finished School by Migration Status and City*

	Recent Migrants		Lifetime Migrants		Non-migrants	
	Household Heads	Children	Household Heads	Children	Household Heads	Children
Younger cities						
Tangerang	10.0	9.6	9.8	12.5	8.7	10.2
Samarinda	10.8	11.1	9.6	11.1	10.7	10.6
Established cities						
Medan	12.1	9.3	9.9	11.4	9.5	11.3
Makassar	13.5	0.0[a]	10.8	12.0	10.7	10.6
All cities	**10.2**	**9.9**	**10.0**	**11.6**	**9.8**	**10.8**

a   In Makassar, no children of recent migrants had finished school.
Source: Rural–Urban Migration in Indonesia survey, 2008.

non-migrants, who are more likely to be studying or outside the paid work-force (Standing 1978). In line with their lower average levels of schooling, migrants tend to be concentrated in blue-collar jobs and the informal sector, although they make up a significant share of the manufacturing workforce in countries that exhibit rapid rates of industrial growth, such as China.

There are some interesting departures from these patterns among our Indo-nesian sample. We find that there is very little difference in the labour force participation rates of males and females in each of the three migration-status groups. As one would expect, less educated recent migrants (those with less than nine years of schooling) have the highest participation rate (see Figure 8.1). However, in contrast to the usual pattern in other countries, a much *lower* proportion of *more educated* recent migrants are in the labour force. As noted above, one of the features of this more educated group of migrants is the large number of individuals attending school, especially at the tertiary level. Less educated migrants display the same pattern as in other countries: most have come to the city to work and most are engaged in less skilled activities.

Among lifetime migrants and non-migrants, housekeeping is the main activity of less educated women outside the labour force. This may reflect the difficulties that women—especially less educated women—face in finding jobs in the city.[7]

The data on occupation presented in Table 8.3 indicate that a high propor-tion of the labour force is engaged in blue-collar work. The rates are espe-cially high among recent migrants, where 87 per cent of males and 84 per

Figure 8.1   Indonesia: Labour Force Participation Rates by Migration Status, Gender and Years of Schooling

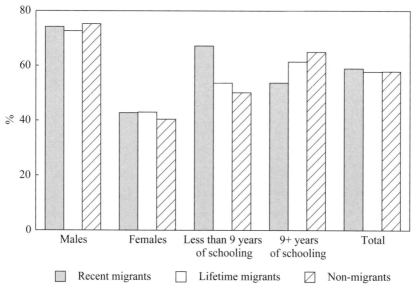

Source: Rural–Urban Migration in Indonesia survey, 2008.

Table 8.3   Indonesia: Share of Blue-collar Workers in Total Employment by Migration Status, Gender and City (%)[a]

	Recent Migrants		Lifetime Migrants		Non-migrants	
	Males	Females	Males	Females	Males	Females
Younger cities						
Tangerang	89	89	82	82	80	79
Samarinda	88	79	74	58	64	59
Established cities						
Medan	80	79	75	73	74	75
Makassar	84	69	64	60	73	66
All cities	87	84	74	76	75	72

a   Blue-collar jobs are unskilled jobs and semi-skilled jobs in trade, services, production, transport and similar activities.

Source: Rural–Urban Migration in Indonesia survey, 2008.

*Figure 8.2   Indonesia: Sector of Employment by Migration Status and
              Gender*

Source: Rural–Urban Migration in Indonesia survey, 2008.

cent of females are blue-collar workers. This is related to the relatively low
educational attainment of the employed population in general, and of recent
migrant workers in particular; the average number of years of schooling of the
employed population in all four cities is less than 12 years. The lower rates of
blue-collar employment among lifetime migrants suggest that most migrants
enter the urban labour market through blue-collar jobs, but that, over time, they
experience some occupational mobility into white-collar occupations.

The services and trade and restaurants sectors absorb the largest numbers
of lifetime migrant workers and non-migrant workers in all cities, while the
manufacturing sector absorbs the largest numbers of recent migrant workers
(Figure 8.2). Employment in government and community services (such as
education and health) is especially important for lifetime migrants and non-
migrants, but of much less significance for recent migrants.

The employment data raise two points of comparison with the data presented for China in earlier chapters of this book. First, in Indonesia, the construction sector plays only a minor role in absorbing workers, accounting for
around 10 per cent of male workers in all three migration-status groups. This

is a fairly recent phenomenon dating from the 1997–98 economic crisis, which led to a large drop in government spending on roads, housing and other public infrastructure, and a corresponding decline in the ability of the construction sector to soak up workers. Second, over half of all female workers in the recent migrant category are employed in manufacturing. As in China, the employment of young female migrants has become an important feature of industrial development in Indonesia.

Although not shown in Figure 8.2, in all cities the data indicate that close to two-thirds of respondents are wage earners, about one-third are self-employed and a small proportion are working as unpaid family workers. Wage earners are most prominent among recent migrants who have come to the city in search of manufacturing and construction jobs. Among recent migrants, a higher share of females than males are in wage employment, probably because of the high proportion of females in this group employed in the manufacturing sector.[8]

Looking to the data on workers in the formal versus informal sectors, we find that a high proportion of self-employed workers in all three migration-status groups are engaged in running small enterprises in the informal sector. In contrast, wage earners in the informal sector (wage employees in enterprises with less than five workers) constitute only a small proportion of all workers in this sector—less than 23 per cent in the case of recent and lifetime migrants. In all cities, a higher proportion of wage earners in all three migration-status groups work in enterprises with over 100 workers; they also tend to be better educated, although they do not necessarily earn higher wages (see also Chapter 10 of this book).

One might expect a high level of labour utilization among wage workers in the recent migrant category. Overall, however, there do not seem to be any big differences in the number of hours worked by migrants and non-migrants in any of the cities. With the exception of lifetime migrants in Medan, self-employed workers work slightly more than 48 hours (our definition of a normal working week, including eight hours of overtime). Unpaid family workers work close to a normal working week, with the exception of recent migrants in Medan.

To sum up, the differences in the demographic, social and occupational characteristics of migrants and non-migrants in the Indonesian sample appear to be less marked than those in the Chinese sample, especially those discussed in Chapters 3 and 4 of this book. Recent migrants do display individual features that set them apart from lifetime migrants and non-migrants—they are younger, more likely to be single and more likely to work in wage jobs in manufacturing. But these differences tend to fade once rural–urban migrants have lived for long periods in the cities. This is especially noticeable among the children of migrants who have been brought up in the city and are in the workforce. Although more careful econometric work is required to confirm the determinants of occupation, Indonesia's relatively open regulatory regime

Figure 8.3   Indonesia: Housing, Cooking and Communication Facilities by Migration Status[a]

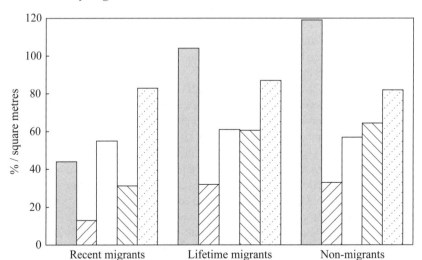

a   Living area is in square metres; others are percentages.
Source: Rural–Urban Migration in Indonesia survey, 2008.

with regard to rural–urban migration appears to have resulted in a more even distribution of the population in terms of key individual characteristics than has occurred under China's more regulated regime.

Household Characteristics

The information we collected on housing and communications illustrates the difficulty of drawing conclusions about household welfare with reference to just one or two variables. Figures 8.3 and 8.4 both present information on household welfare but show quite different patterns across the three migration-status groups. Figure 8.3 provides information on living area, drinking water, sanitation (whether the house has a bathroom and toilet), the availability of kerosene for cooking and access to a fixed-line or mobile phone. On most of these indicators, recent migrant households are at a disadvantage to the other two groups. The major differences concern access to piped water and the living area available to recent migrants in the city. These differences are partly explained by home ownership patterns. Single recent migrants are more likely

Figure 8.4   Indonesia: Poverty Incidence by Migration Status

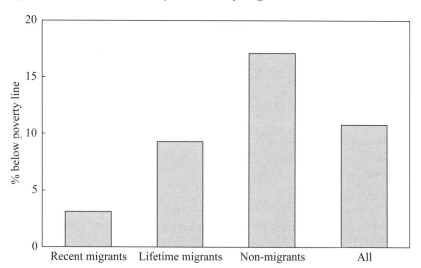

Source: Rural–Urban Migration in Indonesia survey, 2008.

to rent a single room, often in makeshift housing in urban slum areas, and to depend on communal cooking, water, bathing and toilet facilities. Most non-migrants, on the other hand, occupy standalone housing with a regular supply of water and electricity (although there are some important regional variations, described in section 5 below).[9]

Does this mean that recent migrants are worse off than the other two migration-status groups? Not necessarily. While non-migrants enjoy better housing conditions, ironically, poverty incidence appears to be lowest among recent migrants and highest among non-migrants. Indonesia's central statistics agency, Statistics Indonesia, defines poverty in terms of per capita expenditure per month on a basket of essential food and non-food items, the latter including housing, clothing, health care and education (Statistics Indonesia 2007: 117–20). In calculating the national and provincial poverty lines, Statistics Indonesia distinguishes between urban and rural areas.[10] When we apply the urban poverty lines for the four provinces in this study (see Statistics Indonesia 2007: 62),[11] we find that migrants (both recent and lifetime) are better off than non-migrants as measured by the proportion of households living below the poverty line (Figure 8.4).[12] The overall incidence of poverty for the entire sample is 10.8 per cent, or slightly lower than the rate for all urban Indonesia recorded in 2007 (12.5 per cent). Of course, as indicated in Chapter 11 of this book, the sample on which the survey is based is not necessarily representative of all urban Indonesia.

Table 8.4   Indonesia: Poverty Incidence by Migration Status and City (%)

	Recent Migrants	Lifetime Migrants	Non-migrants	All Households	Incidence of Urban Poverty[a]
Younger cities					
Tangerang	4.3	2.4	11.3	6.0	7.2
Samarinda	3.2	20.5	15.6	14.3	6.6
Established cities					
Medan	0.0	13.3	18.9	15.3	7.2
Makassar	1.8	11.7	23.6	12.6	5.7
All cities	3.1	9.3	17.1	10.8	12.5

a   Incidence of urban poverty in the province in which the city is situated according to the 2007 National Socio-Economic Survey.

Source: Rural–Urban Migration in Indonesia survey, 2008; Statistics Indonesia (2007).

In all cities except Samarinda, a smaller proportion of migrants than non-migrants live in poverty, and in all cities except Tangerang, a smaller proportion of recent migrants than lifetime migrants live under the poverty line (see Table 8.4). The low incidence of poverty among recent migrant households is partly explained by the high proportion of young, single workers and students from middle-class backgrounds in this group. The single workers are better off than other recent migrants because they mostly do not have dependants, and because some of them are employed in large manufacturing companies offering higher wages. Students, too, are slightly less likely to be living in poverty, because they receive financial support from their parents and generally do not have dependants.[13] Thus, while recent migrants appear to be worse off than the other two groups as measured by their living conditions, they are by no means worse off as measured by their current levels of consumption.

5   INTERCITY VARIATIONS

As noted above, our sample of four cities comprises two relatively recently established cities (Samarinda and Tangerang) and two well-established cities (Medan and Makassar). The former two cities were small urban settlements at the beginning of the New Order period, whereas Medan and Makassar were the hubs of their respective regional economies. As might be expected, some (but certainly not all) of the regional variations in the characteristics of individuals and households according to migration status can be attributed to these differences in the growth profiles of the two sets of cities.

From the outset it should be noted that Medan stands out from the other three cities for the small number of recent migrants in the survey sample (Table 8.5). Medan experienced large inflows of migrants in the 1970s and 1980s but since then its population growth has slowed. Makassar, too, has not experienced any significant growth in its population for at least a decade. But it stands out for the large number of students who have moved to the city from rural areas to continue their studies, a great number of whom were captured by our survey. The proportion of recent migrants, lifetime migrants and non-migrants is therefore relatively even in Makassar and the two rapidly growing cities.

Of the total sample of 2,371 households, 32 per cent reside in Tangerang, 19 per cent in Samarinda, 27 per cent in Medan and 22 per cent in Makassar (Table 8.5). The average household size is 3–4 in each of the cities, although it is smaller among recent migrants in Tangerang and Makassar (because of the high proportion of single migrants).

Demographic and Social Patterns

As discussed above, the heads of recent migrant households have a much lower average age than the heads of the other two groups, partly because of the large number of students in this group. This is especially apparent in the established city of Makassar, where students from rural areas dominate the sample and the average age of recent migrants is just 24 years, compared with 26–30 in the other three cities (Table 8.5). Thus, recent migrants who have moved to an urban area to study (as in Makassar) tend to be younger than those who have moved to an urban area to work in the manufacturing sector (as in Tangerang). The large number of students pursuing educational opportunities in Makassar and other Indonesian cities reflects a general improvement in educational facilities at the tertiary level, attributable in part to initiatives taken since regional autonomy was introduced in 2001.

A high proportion of household heads are female, especially among recent migrants in the established cities of Makassar (45 per cent) and Medan (43 per cent) (see Table 8.5). In the case of Makassar, many of the household heads enumerated in the census blocks surrounding the university campus are young, single, better-educated female students. This points to an improvement in female access to education, even in staunchly Islamic regions such as South Sulawesi where Makassar is located.[14] In the more rapidly growing cities of Tangerang and Samarinda, recent migrant households have a higher proportion of female household heads than the other two groups, probably for similar reasons: children from rural households are migrating to urban areas either to work or to study.

Table 8.5   *Indonesia: Characteristics of Households and Household Heads*
               by City and Migration Status

	Younger Cities		Established Cities		All Cities
	Tangerang	Samarinda	Medan	Makassar	
No. of households					
Recent migrants	251	152	31	203	637
Lifetime migrants	251	161	310	162	884
Non-migrants	248	137	299	166	850
All	750	450	640	531	2,371
%	32	19	27	22	100
% of households					
Recent migrants	33	34	5	38	27
Lifetime migrants	33	36	48	31	37
Non-migrants	33	30	47	31	36
All	100	100	100	100	100
Mean household size (no. of members)					
Recent migrants	1.6	2.1	2.3	1.6	1.8
Lifetime migrants	3.5	4.0	4.6	4.1	4.1
Non-migrants	4.3	3.6	4.4	5.1	4.3
All	3.1	3.4	4.4	3.6	3.6
Mean age of household head (years)					
Recent migrants	26	29	30	24	26
Lifetime migrants	41	44	49	44	45
Non-migrants	44	41	46	46	44
All	37	39	47	38	40
Gender of household head (% female)					
Recent migrants	27	17	43	45	31
Lifetime migrants	7	9	50	17	24
Non-migrants	12	12	49	15	25
All	15	12	49	26	26
Marital status of household head (% single)					
Recent migrants	65	47	52	80	65
Lifetime migrants	5	3	2	12	5
Non-migrants	3	11	4	6	6
All	25	17	5	33	20

Source: Rural–Urban Migration in Indonesia survey, 2008.

One important social dimension of migration in many countries is its effect on household members, particularly children left behind in the countryside. However, this does not appear to be a major problem in Indonesia, where only a small minority of household members are left behind in the home village. The share is understandably higher among recent migrants, who are less well established in the city than lifetime migrants. The share is also higher in Tangerang, where circular migration is more common than in the other cities. Circular migrants are those who move between a permanent place of residence outside the city and a workplace in the city, usually on a weekly, monthly or three-monthly basis. In Tangerang, 19 per cent and 12 per cent of recent migrant and lifetime migrant household members respectively are living in households in which the head is a circular migrant.

The average age of children left behind in the home village ranges from around seven to ten years. Most of these children live with their grandparents. The high cost of living in the city is the main reason given by parents for leaving their children in the countryside.[15] However, it should be stressed once again that the numbers of left-behind children are small compared with those in some Chinese cities (see Chapter 2).

As might be expected, the average number of years of schooling of recent migrant household heads is higher in the more established cities of Makassar and Medan (13.7 and 12.1 years respectively) than in the more rapidly growing cities of Samarinda and Tangerang (10.8 and 10 years respectively). In Makassar and Medan, a higher proportion of recent migrant household heads (some of them still studying) are educated at the tertiary level: 75 per cent of recent migrants in Makassar and 45 per cent in Medan, compared with just 26 per cent in Samarinda and 4 per cent in Tangerang (where the majority of recent migrants have a senior high school education). As discussed elsewhere, Makassar is a centre of tertiary education in eastern Indonesia and many families from other parts of Sulawesi and from Maluku and Papua send their children there to study. Makassar is also regarded as a relatively secure environment for students, an important consideration for parents concerned about the security situation (mainly ethnic conflict) in the province of origin. In Tangerang, many recent migrants are employed as factory workers. Such workers are generally recruited at the junior or senior high school level.

The differences between cities in the educational attainment of recent migrants may be related to the reasons that migrants give for moving to the city. In the more established cities, fewer recent migrants say that they have come to the city to work, and more to study. In Makassar, over 60 per cent of male recent migrants and 67 per cent of female recent migrants stated that they had moved to the city to study; only 12 per cent said they had moved there to work. In Medan, 36 per cent of recent migrants had moved to the city to study and 20 per cent to work. This is in marked contrast to both of the rapidly grow-

The Great Migration

Table 8.6   Indonesia: Female Labour Force Participation Rates by
          Migration Status and City (%)

	Recent Migrants	Lifetime Migrants	Non-migrants
Younger cities			
Tangerang	69	48	42
Samarinda	34	39	33
Established cities			
Medan	42	46	45
Makassar	13	35	37
All cities	43	43	41

Source: Rural–Urban Migration in Indonesia survey, 2008.

ing cities; in Tangerang, for example, only 2 per cent of recent migrants stated that they had moved to the city to study, and 71 per cent to work.

It is interesting to note that the children of migrants living in Samarinda have a higher level of educational attainment than their parents (Table 8.2). This may reflect the improvements in access to education that have drawn migrants to Samarinda in recent years, based on the government revenues generated by rapid economic development. In addition, the large coalmining firms and oil companies operating in the resource-rich province of East Kalimantan have begun to provide scholarships to students as one manifestation of their corporate social responsibility programs (Bandiyono, Mujiyani and Purwaningsih 2003).

Labour Force and Employment Patterns

The differences between cities in labour force participation rates are closely related to the demographic and educational trends discussed above. In the case of females, however, cultural factors also play a part. Thus, female participation rates are much lower among all migration-status groups in the more strongly Islamic cities—that is, lower in Samarinda than in Tangerang among the rapidly growing cities, and lower in Makassar than in Medan among the more established cities (Table 8.6). Although both Tangerang and Samarinda have grown rapidly in recent years, the tradition of female employment outside the home is less well established in Samarinda, where nearly half of all female recent migrants report housekeeping as their main activity.

Looking at employment patterns by industry, it is clear that the more rapidly growing cities offer a higher share of manufacturing employment than the

Table 8.7   *Indonesia: Share of Employment by Migration Status, Gender and City (%)*

	Recent Migrants		Lifetime Migrants		Non-migrants	
	Males	Females	Males	Females	Males	Females
Younger cities						
Tangerang						
Manufacturing	45	63	43	39	29	29
Trade & services	45	35	49	59	58	69
Other	11	2	9	1	13	2
Total	**100**	**100**	**100**	**100**	**100**	**100**
Samarinda						
Manufacturing	26	62	15	22	17	29
Trade & services	48	28	54	69	59	69
Other	26	10	31	9	25	3
Total	**100**	**100**	**100**	**100**	**100**	**100**
Established cities						
Medan						
Manufacturing	11	33	18	9	22	15
Trade & services	69	67	66	88	64	83
Other	21	0	16	3	14	3
Total	**100**	**100**	**100**	**100**	**100**	**100**
Makassar						
Manufacturing	23	31	8	12	15	20
Trade & services	75	63	78	87	66	80
Other	2	6	13	1	20	0
Total	**100**	**100**	**100**	**100**	**100**	**100**
All cities						
Manufacturing	36	58	22	19	22	22
Trade & services	51	39	61	78	62	76
Other	13	4	17	3	17	2
Total	**100**	**100**	**100**	**100**	**100**	**100**

Source: Rural–Urban Migration in Indonesia survey, 2008.

more established cities (Table 8.7). This is especially evident in the case of female recent migrants, who are engaged mainly in export-oriented activities such as textiles and footwear in Tangerang, and in the wood-based and mining enterprises that predominate in East Kalimantan where Samarinda is located.

The proportion of migrants (both male and female) engaged in manufacturing is higher in Tangerang than in Samarinda, reflecting its importance as a major industrial centre. Tangerang has developed rapidly since the late 1960s, chiefly as a result of its strategic location near the capital, Jakarta. Its many factories making textiles, garments, shoes, electronic goods, ceramics and other products have attracted sizeable inflows of migrants from countless remote rural regions over the past few decades (Warouw 2006). Although some of these factories closed down during the economic crisis of the late 1990s, Tangerang is still an attractive destination for migrants in search of jobs. This is reflected in its high population growth rates: during the period 1990–2000, Tangerang's population grew at an average rate of 4.1 per cent per annum, well above the national rate of 1.4 per cent (Statistics Indonesia 2000: 161, 171).

Samarinda's growth as a major commercial centre was initially based on timber, with migrants from Java and other islands quick to take advantage of the opportunity to find jobs in the wood-processing sector. More recently, Samarinda has become a centre for businesses servicing East Kalimantan's coalmining and oil industries, where male migrants in particular are likely to find jobs. As in Tangerang, several factories have closed down in Samarinda in the past few years, including at least five large sawmills.[16] The closure of these factories can be traced to the difficult economic conditions of the past few years, as well as the declining availability of timber (Forest Watch Indonesia 2001).

In the more established cities of Medan and Makassar, employment in trade and services dominates both male and female employment in all three migration-status groups. In Medan, for example, 88 per cent of female lifetime migrants and 83 per cent of female non-migrants are engaged in trade and services (see Table 8.7).

The contrast between the two sets of cities is particularly marked in the case of female employment. This is demonstrated very clearly in Table 8.8, which shows the ratio of female employment in manufacturing (and in trade and services) in *each* city relative to total female employment in manufacturing (and in trade and services) in *all* cities. The ratio for manufacturing is higher in the two rapidly growing cities than in the two slower-growing cities. In the slower-growing cities of Medan and Makassar, on the other hand, females are overrepresented in trade and services.

The smaller proportions of migrants and non-migrants employed in manufacturing in Medan and Makassar reflect these cities' more diversified economies. Both received significant manufacturing investments in the past but now have a variety of trade and service industries catering to the needs of their rich agricultural hinterlands (Rutz 1987: 176). In addition, both have strong educational sectors to service their large populations. As already noted, Makassar in particular is a centre of higher education in eastern Indonesia.

As suggested by the small number of recent migrants captured by the survey in Medan, this city is no longer a popular destination for rural–urban migrants

Table 8.8   Indonesia: Ratio of Female Employment in Each City to Total Female Employment in All Cities by Migration Status, Sector and City

	Recent Migrants	Lifetime Migrants	Non-migrants
Manufacturing			
Younger cities			
Tangerang	1.1	2.0	1.3
Samarinda	1.1	1.2	1.3
Established cities			
Medan	0.6	0.4	0.7
Makassar	0.5	0.6	0.9
All cities (%)	**58**	**19**	**22**
Trade & services			
Younger cities			
Tangerang	0.9	0.8	0.9
Samarinda	0.7	0.9	0.9
Established cities			
Medan	1.7	1.1	1.1
Makassar	1.6	1.1	1.0
All cities (%)	**39**	**78**	**76**

Source: Rural–Urban Migration in Indonesia survey, 2008.

in search of jobs. With the significant increases in the price of palm oil in the international market in recent years, the rubber and palm oil plantations outside Medan, and the associated processing factories, have become more attractive destinations for these migrants. These trends are reflected in Medan's population growth rates over time. Between 1971 and 1980, the population of Medan grew by 8.9 per cent a year, well above the national rate of 2.3 per cent (Statistics Indonesia 2000: 161). But between 1990 and 2000, the growth rate fell to 0.97 per cent, compared with 1.2 per cent for the province in which it is situated, North Sumatra (Statistics Indonesia 2000: 263).

Patterns of Household Welfare

Across cities, patterns of access to living space, drinking water and sanitation tend to favour lifetime migrants and non-migrants. However, the differences that exist between cities are related to historical patterns of urban growth and a

Table 8.9   Indonesia: Housing, Cooking and Communication Facilities by Migration Status and City

	Mean Living Area (m²)	Piped Water (%)	Bathroom & Toilet (%)	Kerosene for Cooking (%)	Fixed-line or Mobile Phone (%)
Younger cities					
Tangerang					
Recent migrants	21.0	1.6	52.2	31.2	75.9
Lifetime migrants	64.1	8.8	71.9	32.1	87.5
Non-migrants	156.3	5.6	81.0	28.6	71.4
Samarinda					
Recent migrants	106.4	26.6	60.4	75.0	84.6
Lifetime migrants	135.5	45.6	86.1	71.0	84.4
Non-migrants	95.1	60.1	88.5	59.4	90.6
Established cities					
Medan					
Recent migrants	48.5	48.4	93.5	74.2	87.0
Lifetime migrants	119.3	41.4	96.4	77.2	86.6
Non-migrants	116.8	33.8	96.0	73.8	84.1
Makassar					
Recent migrants	33.6	13.0	53.2	73.9	80.5
Lifetime migrants	102.1	35.1	45.7	60.6	88.2
Non-migrants	95.8	37.9	78.6	64.4	96.6

Source: Rural–Urban Migration in Indonesia survey, 2008.

range of other variables, not just migration status. Access to drinking water, for example, is better in the less densely populated cities of Medan and Samarinda than in Makassar and Tangerang (Table 8.9).[17] The main sources of cooking fuel are chiefly related to the availability and cost of gas versus kerosene in each city.[18] Similarly, a high proportion of households in all cities have access to a fixed telephone line or mobile phone—the share ranges from 76 per cent in Tangerang to 91 per cent in Medan in the case of mobile phones. This simply reflects the improvement in communications that has taken place across Indonesia in recent years, accompanying the greater availability and spread of technology.

What about the incidence of poverty? The lower rates of poverty among recent migrants, discussed above, are common across all four cities. Whether this holds once we control for a range of other household variables would need careful econometric examination. It is, however, consistent with the better health outcomes found for recent migrants in Chapter 9 of this book.

We have already suggested several reasons for the low rates of poverty among recent migrant households: the high proportion of middle-class students in this group, and of single workers without dependants. Many of the single recent migrants are employed in large manufacturing firms in Tangerang and Samarinda, where they earn respectable wages. In Samarinda, for instance, the average monthly net income of skilled wage earners is about Rp 2 million, compared with Rp 1.4 million in Tangerang, Rp 1.5 million in Medan and Rp 1.9 million in Makassar. Students are prominent among recent migrants in Makassar and Medan. In Samarinda, the living allowances received by students from their parents—ranging from Rp 0.5 to Rp 1 million a month—put them above the urban poverty line for East Kalimantan.

With the exception of lifetime migrants in Samarinda, a higher proportion of non-migrants than migrants live below the poverty line in all four cities (see Table 8.4). However, there is no clear pattern of difference in poverty incidence between the younger and more established cities. As related in Chapter 9, the characteristics of individuals and households play a major role in determining poverty incidence, regardless of place of residence.

6   CONCLUSION

While there have been a number of intensive studies of rural-to-urban migration in Indonesia, most were conducted in the 1970s and 1980s when migration was a response to rural poverty and urban growth. Since that time relatively little research has been conducted on this important topic. We know little about how those earlier migrants fared in the urban labour market, how migration affected their welfare or how it influenced non-migrant and urban communities. In the 2000s, we would expect globalization, decentralization and the advent of a more democratic government to have affected the distribution of benefits from rural–urban migration in ways that are quite different from those in earlier periods.

This chapter has provided a broad array of information on the demographic and social characteristics, labour force behaviour and household welfare of migrants, drawn from the first round of an annual survey of migrant and non-migrant households. Some general conclusions emerge from this survey. First, insofar as there are different patterns between recent migrants, lifetime migrants and non-migrants, they tend to be between recent migrants on the one hand and lifetime migrants and non-migrants on the other. In other words, over time lifetime migrants appear to take on the characteristics of the resident urban population, suggesting the possibility of relatively high levels of social and economic mobility.

Second, empirical evidence suggests that more females than males migrated from rural to urban areas in the 2000s, either to find work or to continue their studies. Moreover, the females who had migrated to an urban area within the preceding five years were better educated than those who had arrived more than five years ago. The educational and work opportunities available to these better-educated females are not much different from those available to male migrants.

Finally, differences in the local economic and social environments of the four cities do seem to be important for understanding the effect of rural–urban migration in Indonesia. Industrial cities and younger cities (such as Tangerang and Samarinda) exhibit different patterns of employment and poverty to the more established cities (such as Makassar and Medan).

One important challenge is to identify the factors that account for these differences and the extent to which they influence outcomes for migrant households. Chapter 9 takes up this topic, asking whether migrants 'make it' in the cities. It looks at migrants' income, health and education, and the extent to which differences in the earnings of migrants versus non-migrants explain the contrasts in household economic status and poverty identified in this chapter. Another issue of interest is the extent to which the inclusion of students among migrant households changes the outcome compared with rural–urban migration studies that focus mainly on employment relationships. This and a number of other subjects will need to be addressed when we examine the results of the second and subsequent rounds of the RUMiI survey.

NOTES

1 See especially Martin-Schiller (1980), Budiono et al. (1982: 9), Collier et al. (1982) and Manning (1998: 89).
2 See, for example, Donges, Stecher and Wolter (1980: 368), Mather (1983) and Forbes (1984: 4).
3 For example, in the early 1970s the Jakarta city government had a 'closed city' policy preventing migrants from moving to the capital (Hugo 1978: 211), and in the past few years it has carried out operations to ensure that only migrants who hold the correct identity card and have a permanent job are allowed to stay in Jakarta.
4 The criteria for the selection of the four cities are discussed in detail in Chapter 11.
5 These single individuals are classified as household heads because they reside alone in the cities, even though many of them are actually the dependants of families living in rural areas.
6 The Chinese sample is based on enumeration of individuals at the workplace, whereas the Indonesian sample is based on enumeration at the place of residence (see Chapters 7 and 11). This difference in the sampling procedure may partly explain the higher proportion of Indonesian migrants living with their spouses in the cities.
7 In Tangerang, which has a high proportion of young recent migrants, a lack of childcare facilities may also be hindering young mothers from entering the labour market.

8   A high proportion of better-educated workers are in wage employment regardless of migra-
     tion status. Less educated migrants and non-migrants, on the other hand, are more likely to be
     self-employed in all four cities.

9   When living area is adjusted for household size, we find that the difference between recent
     migrants and the other two groups narrows, although the area available to recent migrants
     (around 12 square metres per capita) is still around half that available to lifetime migrants and
     non-migrants (25 and 22 square metres respectively).

10   The poverty line for urban Indonesia is Rp 188,000 per capita per month, and the poverty line
     for rural Indonesia is Rp 147,000 per capita per month (Statistics Indonesia 2007: 62).

11   The urban poverty lines for the provinces in which the four survey cities are located are as
     follows: South Sulawesi (Makassar): Rp 149,000; Banten (Tangerang): Rp 188,000; North
     Sumatra (Medan): Rp 205,000; and East Kalimantan (Samarinda): Rp 240,000.

12   To take account of changes in the cost of living between 2007 (when Statistics Indonesia pub-
     lished its poverty lines) and March–May 2008 (when we conducted our survey), we adjusted
     the Statistics Indonesia poverty lines by 10 per cent. (Note that the year-on-year inflation rate
     climbed from 7.4 per cent in February 2008 to 10.4 per cent in May 2008.) Because of these
     cost-of-living adjustments, the statistics in this chapter on poverty incidence differ slightly
     from those reported in Chapter 9.

13   We checked to see whether excluding students or single-person households made any differ-
     ence to the incidence of poverty among recent migrant households. We found that it made
     only a small difference, with the percentage of recent migrant households in poverty rising
     from 3.1 per cent to just 4 per cent in the case of both students and single-member house-
     holds.

14   The access of females to education increased significantly over the three decades from the
     1960s, leading to a decline in the female illiteracy rate from 60 per cent in 1960 to 17 per cent
     in 1990 (Statistics Indonesia, Bappenas and UNDP 2001).

15   Unfortunately the study did not ask about the location of the home village or its distance from
     the city in which the migrant was residing. The only relevant information we had on this topic
     was the migrant's place of birth, from which it was possible to establish whether or not the
     person was born in the same province or district or had moved there from another location.

16   This information was obtained through interviews and field observation in January 2009.

17   In Medan, the local water authority has made great strides in improving the availability and
     quality of piped water; see Statistics Indonesia Medan (2006: 202) and www.kabarindonesia.
     com, accessed 2 February 2009.

18   In Tangerang, for instance, the government policy of providing liquid petroleum gas (LPG) at
     subsidized prices since oil prices increased in 2005 has made it cheaper for households to use
     gas rather than kerosene for cooking.

9 The Socio-economic and Health Status of Rural–Urban Migrants in Indonesia

**Budy P. Resosudarmo, Asep Suryahadi,
Raden M. Purnagunawan, Athia Yumna
and Asri Yusrina**

1 INTRODUCTION

The movement of people from rural to urban areas, popularly known as urbanization, is a common phenomenon observed all over the world during a country's process of development. The Harris–Todaro model has long been used to explain this phenomenon. In general, the prevalence of higher average incomes in urban areas has attracted large numbers of rural people to move to urban areas (Harris and Todaro 1970). Some rural residents move to urban areas to work in the formal sector and some to study, but many are self-employed or work illegally in some of the lowest-paid jobs in the informal sector. These rural–urban migrants have to adapt to a city lifestyle and compete to earn an income that meets their expectations. Some succeed but others certainly fail.

It is also a well-established observation that migrants have to work harder to achieve the urban income they expect. They need to be willing to endure harsher conditions than non-migrants living in the same city. In pursuit of a better life, they often end up sacrificing their own health and that of their children (Garnier et al. 2003). In many cases, the hard work and anti-social hours worked by adult migrants divert their attention away from their children, particularly their children's educational performance (Batbaatar et al. 2005; Liang and Chen 2007).

In Indonesia, rates of rural-to-urban migration increased during the 1970s and 1980s. During this period, Indonesia implemented a number of economic reforms that were successful in attracting foreign investment and improving the socio-economic conditions of the populace. Levels of education increased, the status of women rose, and the quality of roads and transportation improved (Hill 2000b; Thee 2001; Resosudarmo and Kuncoro 2006). Most foreign investment initially went into resource extraction industries, and later into export-oriented, labour-intensive industries such as garments and footwear. Together with complementary domestic investment in industry and services, the high levels of foreign investment contributed to the growth of urban and industrial agglomerations in several major cities. The movements of population that took place during these decades, particularly from rural to urban areas, saw people moving short and long distances, temporarily and permanently.[1]

The literature on the performance of rural–urban migrants in the urban labour market is relatively well established in the Indonesian case, especially for the period of rapid economic growth leading up to the economic crisis of 1997–98.[2] Less is known about the relationship between migration and health, especially for migrants who have moved to the city in the post-Soeharto period. Fewer studies yet have evaluated whether or not rural–urban migrants succeed in achieving a socio-economic and health status that is at least comparable to that of their non-migrant counterparts in the same cities.

The main goal of this chapter is to determine whether or not the families of rural–urban migrants in Indonesia 'make it', by studying both their own perceptions of improvement as well as more objective measures of their income and educational and health status. Following the practice of the central statistics agency, Statistics Indonesia, this study distinguishes between rural–urban migrants who have moved to a city within the preceding five years (recent migrants) and those who have lived in a city for more than five years (lifetime migrants). Like the other chapters in this section of the book, this study focuses on rural–urban migrants in four cities: Medan, Tangerang, Samarinda and Makassar. The data on which the study is based are derived from the Rural–Urban Migration in Indonesia (RUMiI) survey, conducted in Indonesia in 2008 as part of the Rural–Urban Migration in China and Indonesia (RUMiCI) project.[3]

To find out whether or not rural–urban migrants make it, we look at a number of socio-economic and health indicators for households, adults and children. First, we examine household expenditure per capita and the probability of a household being poor as defined by Statistics Indonesia's regional poverty lines. Second, we examine the probability of an adult being significantly underweight or overweight, or of normal weight, based on body mass index (BMI). We then establish the probability of a dependent child being significantly underweight or overweight, using both BMI-for-age and weight-for-age. Finally, we examine educational attainment among children and the probability of a child entering elementary school late. To measure the net effect of migration, we compare the results for recent and lifetime migrants with those of a control group, namely local urban residents (non-migrants) living in the same city.

The remainder of the chapter is organized as follows. The next section reviews the literature on rural-to-urban migrants in Indonesia. Section 3 describes the method used in the chapter to determine whether or not migrants make it in the cities. Section 4 presents and discusses the econometric results, and section 5 summarizes our conclusions.

2 LITERATURE REVIEW

Most of the literature on rural–urban migration analyses patterns and causes of migration,[4] migrant earnings in the urban labour market[5] and the effects of migration on the areas that migrants leave, or those they move to.[6] As noted earlier, little attention has been given to the question of whether or not rural–urban migrants make it in the city. Of the studies that have considered the success or otherwise of rural–urban migrants, most have focused on only one or a few of the indicators observed in this chapter.

The findings of studies on whether or not migrants make it are mixed. An example of a study that finds that migrants *do* make it is Garnier et al. (2003). From 1995 to 1999, the authors conducted a longitudinal study of 331 Senegalese adolescent girls, 36 per cent of whom were non-migrants and the remainder rural-to-urban migrants working as maids in the city. They observed the nutritional and growth status of the girls as measured by height-for-age, weight-for-age, BMI and fat mass index, and researched their determinants. Garnier et al. concluded that, in general, the nutritional and growth status of the migrants was better than that of the non-migrants.

A study by Batbaatar et al. (2005), however, illustrates that many migrants do not make it in the cities. The authors explored the effect of rural-to-urban migration on the well-being of children in Mongolia, focusing in particular on access to education. Their sample consisted of 964 households, of which 326 were migrant households. They observed that, in some of the rural areas left by migrants, more children were out of school than in urban areas of high in-migration. However, in the latter areas, fewer migrated than non-migrant children were attending school.

Consistent with the findings of several chapters in this book, Sato (2006) finds that migrants in China are doing it tough in terms of housing. Sato observed the cost and condition of housing among rural–urban migrant households in mega-urban areas in China at the end of the 1990s. He based his findings on data from the 1999 Chinese Academy of Social Sciences (CASS) survey, which covered more than 3,900 households of urban origin and 790 migrant households of rural origin as defined by the household registration (*hukou*) system. For the purposes of the study, Sato confined his attention to 'settled' migrants of rural origin; that is, he included only migrant households with stable home addresses in urban areas, and excluded those living in communal housing such as factory dormitories.

He found that, as a proportion of total expenditure, migrants spent far more on rent, utilities and other housing-related expenditure than non-migrant households. Although the quality of housing had generally improved, there was still a wide gap in the housing conditions of migrant and non-migrant households; the proportion of households living in houses with their own toilet and bathroom, for example, was 33 per cent among non-migrant households but only 6 per cent among migrant households. Conditions were worse in the provincial capitals than in the subprovincial or county-level cities. Despite this, rents were much higher in the provincial capitals. Sato found that socio-political factors such as party membership together with individual factors such as years of employment, years of education and household income were important in explaining the cost of housing in Chinese cities.

Weber et al. (2007) examined a subsample of the US Panel Study of Income Dynamics dataset for 1993, consisting of 701 household heads aged 25–64 residing in non-metropolitan counties. To find out whether there were any differences in the poverty status of households that had migrated versus those that had not, the authors tracked the movements of the households between 1993 and 1999, and assessed their poverty status in the latter year. They employed a two-stage probit model to explain the direct and indirect effects of education on the probability of a household being poor and to control for the fact that better-educated rural adults were more likely to move to urban areas and to access better-quality jobs.

Weber et al. found that the educational attainment of the household head was a strong direct and indirect determinant of poverty: the higher the household head's level of education, the lower the probability of the household being poor. Other important determinants were the gender and age of the household head, and family size. They found that migration status was not important, probably because rural populations in developed countries such as the United States tend to be quite wealthy. This suggests that, for people with an equivalent level of education, the risk of poverty among those who are likely to move is no different to the risk of poverty among those who are likely to stay behind in a rural area.

Although not described in detail here, a number of other studies have analysed rural–urban migration at the household or individual level. They include a study by Liang and Chen (2007) on the educational consequences of migration for children in China and a study by Bogin and MacVean (1981) on the health consequences of migration for children in Guatemala. Bogin and MacVean found that the children of rural-to-urban migrants in Guatemala were smaller than the children of non-migrants.

3 METHODOLOGY

Building on the literature discussed above, we employ a number of models to find out whether or not migrants make it. The general form of these models is as follows:

$$Y_i = f(M_i, IC_i, HC_i, DC_i, VC_i, MS_i) \qquad (9.1)$$

where Y_i is socio-economic and health status; M_i is a vector of migration status (recent and lifetime migrant dummies with non-migrants as the control group); IC_i is a vector of individual characteristics; HC_i is a vector of household characteristics; DC_i is a vector of city dummies (where Tangerang is the control group); VC_i is the distance to the subdistrict (*kecamatan*) office, representing the level of development in the village of origin; and MS_i is the migration strategy, proxied by the age at which a person leaves the village of origin.

The first set of equations consists of an equation for per capita household expenditure, estimated using the ordinary least squares (OLS) method, and an equation for the probability of being poor, estimated using the probit method. A 'poor' household is defined as a household whose per capita expenditure is below the poverty line for the region where the household is located, as assessed by Statistics Indonesia. Since this is a household-level analysis, no characteristics for individuals are included in the models. The household characteristics are the gender, age, educational attainment, work status and labour classification of the household head, as well as the size of the household.

The second set of equations consists of equations for the probability of an adult having a normal BMI, being severely underweight or being severely overweight, estimated using the probit method. BMI is weight (in kilograms) per square of height (in metres). The range of a normal BMI is 18.5–25. People with a BMI below 16.5 are considered severely underweight and those with a BMI above 30 are considered severely overweight. Household characteristics are proxied by per capita household expenditure. The individual characteristics are gender, age, work status, labour classification, disability status, smoking status, religion and having health insurance (as a proxy for concern about health).

The third set of equations consists of equations for the probability of a dependent child being severely underweight or severely overweight, estimated using the probit method. Both conditions are measured using BMI-for-age and weight-for-age. Severely underweight children are those with a BMI or weight that falls within the lowest 5 per cent for their age group, and severely overweight children are those with a BMI or weight that falls within the top 5 per cent. Household characteristics are proxied by per capita household expenditure and whether or not other members of the family are severely underweight or overweight. The latter is important, since it is a measure of whether or not the child's weight is an inherited characteristic or due to lifestyle factors. The

Table 9.1   Indonesia: Socio-economic and Health Indicators by Migration Status

	Recent Migrants	Lifetime Migrants	Non-migrants
Households			
Average household expenditure per capita (Rp million)	9.5	7.0	6.3
% of poor households	4.7	10.7	21.2
Adults			
% of adults with normal BMI	66.2	63.4	62.4
% of severely underweight adults	5.3	3.5	4.4
% of severely overweight adults	1.5	4.1	3.8
Dependent children			
% of severely underweight children based on BMI	12.5	12.8	9.8
% of severely overweight children based on BMI	28.9	26.5	26.1
% of severely underweight children based on weight-for-age	11.7	6.1	6.5
% of severely overweight children based on weight-for-age	14.8	20.0	14.9
Average educational attainment (years of schooling)	4.3	5.1	4.9
% of children who entered school late	39.3	24.9	30.4

Source: Rural–Urban Migration in Indonesia survey, 2008.

individual characteristics are gender, age, religion and whether or not the person has health insurance.

The final set of equations comprises equations for educational attainment and the probability of being late to enter elementary school, among the children of recent and lifetime migrants relative to the children of non-migrants. The former equation is estimated using the OLS method and the latter using the probit method. Household characteristics are proxied by per capita household expenditure. The individual characteristics are gender, age and religion.

4   FINDINGS AND DISCUSSION

In this section we discuss the results of the equations, using data from the 2008 RUMiI survey. Table 9.1 sets out some basic socio-economic and health

*Figure 9.1   Indonesia: Migrant Perceptions of Their Average Household
           Income*

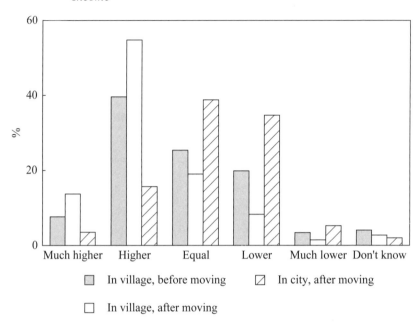

Source: Rural–Urban Migration in Indonesia survey, 2008.

indicators for the samples of households, adults and children analysed in this
chapter.

The Perception Paradox

To find out whether migrants themselves felt they had made it, at least in terms
of household income as measured by per capita household expenditure, we
asked them the following three questions.

1   Before moving to the city, how do you think your family income compared
    to the average income of others in the same village?
2   After moving to the city (right now), how do you think your family income
    compares to the average income of families who stayed in the village?
3   How do you think your family income compares to the average income of
    families in the city in which you live?

The responses are shown in Figure 9.1.

*Figure 9.2   Indonesia: Average Household Expenditure per Capita
            by Migration Status*

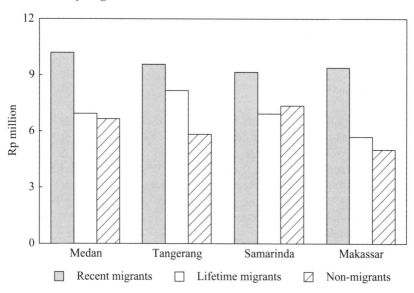

Recent migrants   Lifetime migrants   Non-migrants

Source: Rural–Urban Migration in Indonesia survey, 2008.

The answers to questions (1) and (2), shown in the first and second bars of Figure 9.1, reveal that a high proportion of migrants think they have made some progress since moving to the city. As the figure indicates, the proportion of migrants who think they have a higher or much higher income than the average income in the village of origin is far higher than the proportion who think that their income is lower than the average income in the village.

Figure 9.1 also reveals migrants' perceptions about their income relative to that of non-migrants in the same city. Most migrants think that their income is lower than or equal to the average household income in the city in which they live. That is, while most migrants think that the move from a rural to an urban area has made them better off, they believe that they are not as well-off as their non-migrant counterparts in the same city.

However, when we look at household income as measured by per capita household expenditure, we find that the reality is somewhat different. Figure 9.2 shows that, on average, migrants are actually *better off* than non-migrants in all four cities surveyed. This is the paradox surrounding migrants' perceptions of income.

Our estimates of per capita household expenditure, arrived at after controlling for various household, village-of-origin and city characteristics, as well as migration strategy, confirm that both recent and lifetime migrants are significantly better off than non-migrants (Table 9.2, column 1). Similarly, the estimation results for the probability of being poor show that migrant households are significantly less likely to be poor than non-migrants living in the same city, taking into account their various characteristics (column 2). Hence, one can only conclude that migrants do make it as measured by improvements in their socio-economic status.

Health Status

To survive in the city, migrants must work hard and endure harsh living and working conditions. Evidence from a number of countries suggests that this affects their own health and that of their children.

In the Indonesian context, it is particularly important to find out whether rural–urban migrants sacrifice their health and that of their dependents, because we have just shown that they are generally successful in improving their socio-economic status. Does this success come at the cost of their health? That is the issue we examine here.

We analysed the health status of adult migrants and dependent children separately, mainly to take account of the different ways in which the health status of adults and children is measured. For adults (those aged 16 years or above), BMI is the dominant measure of health, and there is universal consensus on the weight ranges for normal-weight, severely underweight and severely overweight adults. For children, however, weight-for-age is the preferred measure of health; where BMI is used, the analysis should be based on BMI-for-age. Moreover, there is no universal consensus on the weight ranges for a normal-weight, severely underweight or severely overweight child. The most common practice is to define a child as being severely underweight if his or her BMI (or weight) falls within the range of the lowest 5 per cent for children of the same age in the same region, and as severely overweight if the child's BMI (or weight) falls within the range of the highest 5 per cent. Hence, the ranges for BMI-for-age and weight-for-age may differ from one region to another.

To set the appropriate BMI-for-age and weight-for-age ranges for children, we used data from the 2000 round of the Indonesian Family Life Survey rather than the data we had collected ourselves through the RUMiI survey. This was because the Indonesian Family Life Survey used the same method to measure weight and height, but had a much larger dataset. We then applied the results to our own data to determine whether or not the health status of the dependent children of migrants was worse than that of the dependent children of non-migrants in the same city.

Table 9.3 shows the results for the econometric analysis of adults' health status. It can be seen that, after controlling for individual, household and city characteristics, the probability of a migrant (either recent or lifetime) having a

Table 9.2   Indonesia: Estimation Results for Household Expenditure per Capita and the Probability of Being Poor

	Household Expenditure per Capita (OLS) (1)	Probability of Being Poor (Probit) (2)
Migration status		
Lifetime migrant	0.217***	−0.749***
Recent migrant	0.358***	−0.960***
Household characteristics		
Gender of household head (female = 1)	0.056	0.050
Age of household head	0.019***	−0.060***
Age of household head^2	−0.000*	0.001***
Educational attainment of household head	0.051***	−0.082***
Household head is a professional worker[a]	0.324***	−0.450***
Household head is a clerical worker[a]	0.169***	−0.336**
Household head is a manual worker[a]	0.114**	−0.169
Household head is an agricultural worker[a]	−0.115	0.216
Household head is a student (yes = 1)	0.397***	−0.909***
No. of household members	−0.132***	0.233***
City characteristics		
Medan	−0.077**	−0.385***
Samarinda	−0.092***	−0.058
Makassar	−0.371***	0.200*
Village characteristics		
Distance to subdistrict office	−0.003**	0.005
Migration strategy		
Age of household head on leaving village	−0.006***	0.015**
Constant	14.845***	0.687
No. of observations	2,371	2,371
R^2 (or equivalent)	0.368	0.215

*** = significant at the 99 per cent confidence level; ** = significant at the 95 per cent confidence level; * = significant at the 90 per cent confidence level.
a   Professional, clerical, manual and agricultural workers are dummies for work status. The control group is household heads who are unemployed or not in the workforce.
Source: Rural–Urban Migration in Indonesia survey, 2008.

Table 9.3   Indonesia: Estimation Results for the Health Status of Adults

	Normal BMI (Probit)	Severely Underweight (Probit)	Severely Overweight (Probit)
Migration status			
Lifetime migrant	0.022	−0.099	0.017
Recent migrant	0.009	0.022	−0.072
Individual characteristics			
Gender (female = 1)	−0.121**	0.191**	0.129
Age	−0.018***	−0.078***	0.107***
Age^2	0.000**	0.001***	−0.001***
Professional worker[a]	0.076	0.053	−0.117
Clerical worker[a]	0.021	0.044	−0.014
Manual worker[a]	0.135**	0.081	−0.223**
Agricultural worker[a]	−0.103	−0.091	0.010
Student (yes = 1)	−0.134*	0.321***	−0.218
Disabled (yes = 1)	0.207	0.520	
Smoking among those aged 18+	0.009	0.016	−0.101
Catholic (yes = 1)	0.039	0.021	0.240
Non-Muslim, non-Catholic	0.102*	−0.091	0.083
Has health insurance	−0.016	0.065	−0.057
Household characteristics			
Log(expenditure per capita)	−0.044	−0.153***	0.035
City characteristics			
Medan	−0.137***	0.080	0.261***
Samarinda	0.092*	0.205**	−0.245**
Makassar	−0.039	0.399***	−0.068
Constant	1.489***	1.781**	−4.532***
No. of observations	5,474	5,474	5,438
R^2 (or equivalent)	0.011	0.082	0.083

*** = significant at the 99 per cent confidence level; ** = significant at the 95 per cent confidence level; * = significant at the 90 per cent confidence level.

a   Professional, clerical, manual and agricultural workers are dummies for work status. The control group is people who are unemployed or not in the workforce.

Source: Rural–Urban Migration in Indonesia survey, 2008.

normal BMI is not significantly different from that of a non-migrant. Similarly, the probability of a migrant being severely underweight or severely overweight is not significantly different from that of a non-migrant.

Gender and age seem to be the important factors determining the health performance of adults. Females are less likely to have a normal BMI; they are more likely to be severely underweight than males with the same characterstics. The older a person is, the less likely he or she is to be severely underweight, but the more likely to be severely overweight. Other important determinants of the probability of being severely underweight are being a student (perhaps unsurprisingly) and per capita household expenditure. Being a manual worker is an important determinant of having a normal BMI or being less likely to be severely overweight. It is interesting to note that there are significant differences between the four cities in the probability of being severely underweight or overweight.

Table 9.4 presents the results for the econometric analysis of dependent children's health status. When BMI-for-age is used, the dependent children of lifetime migrants have a higher probability of being severely underweight. However, when weight-for-age is used, it is the dependent children of recent migrants that have a higher probability of being severely underweight. Based on weight-for-age, the dependent children of lifetime migrants have an increased probability of being severely overweight, at the 90 per cent confidence level. Given these inconclusive findings, it seems safe to conclude that, in general, the dependent children of migrants are no more likely than the children of non-migrants to have an increased probability of health problems.

It is interesting to observe in Table 9.4 that the existence of other family members with similar health problems is a significant determinant of the probability of health problems among dependent children. It makes no difference whether they are the dependent children of migrants or non-migrants. This indicates that obesity or being severely underweight may be inherited conditions, although further research would be needed to verify this.

Finally, we can conclude that there is no evidence in the case of Indonesia that migrants have to sacrifice their health in order to be able to survive in the city. Moreover, there is only limited evidence that the health of their dependent children suffers. In general, the health status of migrants and their dependent children is the same as that of non-migrants.

Dependent Children's Educational Status

Our grounds for wishing to observe the educational status of children are two-fold. First, migrants are suspected of working long hours and unsociable shifts. This raises the question of whether they are able to pay sufficient attention to their children's development, in particular their educational performance.

Table 9.4   Indonesia: Estimation Results for the Health Status of Dependent Children

	BMI-for-Age (Probit)		Weight-for-Age (Probit)	
	Severely Underweight	Severely Overweight	Severely Underweight	Severely Overweight
Migration status				
Lifetime migrant	0.217***	−0.012	0.026	0.139*
Recent migrant	0.148	−0.132	0.347**	−0.135
Individual characteristics				
Gender (female = 1)	−0.083	−0.107*	−0.062	−0.140**
Age	−0.034***	−0.046***	−0.021*	−0.023***
Disabled (yes = 1)	0.203			
Catholic (yes = 1)		0.332*	−0.637	0.151
Non-Muslim, non-Catholic	−0.392**	0.241**	−0.501**	0.356***
Has health insurance	−0.205**	0.129*	−0.169	0.063
Household characteristics				
Other members with similar health problem	0.249*	0.277***	0.245*	0.256**
Log(expenditure per capita)	−0.125**	0.087	−0.097	0.282***
City characteristics				
Medan	0.063	−0.418***	0.303**	−0.246***
Samarinda	0.086	0.064	0.153	0.116
Makassar	0.151	−0.089	0.499***	0.041
Constant	0.909	−1.482*	−0.042	−5.114***
No. of observations	1,885	1,923	1,929	1,929
R^2 (or equivalent)	0.032	0.039	0.046	0.041

*** = significant at the 99 per cent confidence level; ** = significant at the 95 per cent confidence level; * = significant at the 90 per cent confidence level.

Source: Rural–Urban Migration in Indonesia survey, 2008.

Second, the children of migrants have limited, or sometimes even no, access to schools in the city. As Liang and Chen (2007) have shown for China, and Batbaatar et al. (2005) for Mongolia, the act of migration can have serious consequences for the educational performance of migrants' children.

Because our survey was conducted in urban areas, this study is only able to observe the educational status of dependent children living in the city, not those remaining behind in the village. We use two indicators to represent edu-

Table 9.5   Indonesia: Estimation Results for the Educational Status of Dependent Children

	Educational Attainment (OLS)	Late School Entry (Probit)[a]
Migration status		
Lifetime migrant	0.117**	−0.133*
Recent migrant	−0.004	0.195
Individual characteristics		
Gender (female = 1)	0.081	−0.026
Age	0.895***	0.044***
Disabled (yes = 1)	−1.766*	0.483
Catholic (yes = 1)	0.090	−0.008
Non-Muslim, non-Catholic	0.109	−0.095
Household characteristics		
Log(expenditure per capita)	0.274***	−0.242***
City characteristics		
Medan	0.211***	−0.783***
Samarinda	0.161*	−0.483***
Makassar	0.226**	−0.651***
Constant	−9.142***	3.183***
No. of observations	1,474	1,470
R^2 (or equivalent)	0.835	0.066

*** = significant at the 99 per cent confidence level; ** = significant at the 95 per cent confidence level; * = significant at the 90 per cent confidence level.
a   Probability of entering elementary school one or more years late, that is, at age seven or above.

Source: Rural–Urban Migration in Indonesia survey, 2008.

cational status: educational attainment as measured by years of schooling (the main indicator) and the probability of a child entering elementary school late (the supplementary indicator). The results of the econometric estimation are shown in Table 9.5.

We found no evidence that the educational performance of the dependent children of migrants is worse than that of the dependent children of non-migrants—on the contrary, the children of lifetime migrants actually perform better than those of non-migrants. Lifetime migrants also seem to send their children to elementary school at the correct age (six years old). The educational performance of the children of recent migrants, meanwhile, is similar to that of the children of non-migrants.

The age of the household head and per capita household expenditure are important determinants of children's educational performance, regardless of migration status. Higher-income households are more likely to send their children to elementary school at the right age. The city in which a child lives has a significant effect on the educational performance of the child.

5   CONCLUSIONS

In this chapter, we have sought to ascertain whether or not rural–urban migrants make it in the city, that is, whether they are able to achieve at least the same socio-economic and health status as their non-migrant counterparts. We have also investigated whether migrants sacrifice their health, and the health and education of their dependent children, in the attempt to improve their socio-economic status.

This study constitutes the first attempt to use data from the RUMiI survey to tackle the issue of whether or not migrants make it in the Indonesian context. A number of caveats should be attached to the results. First, the study uses the socio-economic and health status of non-migrants as the benchmark to determine whether or not rural–urban migrants succeed, whereas some might argue that the status of residents in the rural village of origin would be the correct counterfactual. Second, if it is the case that only the most motivated persons in a village actually migrate, then the data on rural–urban migrants may suffer from a selection bias problem. Third, it is conceivable that we have not conducted the post-estimation tests properly, so that the results suffer from endogeneity or a missing variable bias.

Taking these caveats into account, this study provides strong evidence that rural–urban migrants in Indonesia do indeed make it. After controlling for various characteristics, the income of migrant households is found to be significantly higher than that of non-migrant households, and they have a significantly lower probability of being poor. The health of migrants and their children is no different to that of non-migrants and their children. There is only weak, and not robust, evidence that the children of migrants have a higher probability of being severely underweight. The educational performance of migrants' children does not lag behind. In fact, there is evidence that the educational attainment of the children of lifetime migrants is significantly better than that of non-migrants' children.

Hence, it can be inferred that, in Indonesia, the process of rural-to-urban migration is not harmful, and may in fact lead to improvements in the socio-economic status of migrants. In Indonesia as in other countries, poor rural people will continue to migrate to the cities in search of a better life. To allow this process to happen naturally, governments need to remove the barriers currently preventing rural people from moving to urban areas. These include the high cost of travel, the need to hold an identification card permitting a person to live and work in an urban area, and unequal access to urban public facilities. Further research is needed to determine the full extent and nature of those barriers, and the most appropriate policy responses.

NOTES

1   Chapter 8 of this book describes these trends in more detail. See also Hugo (1995), Jones (1997), Manning (1998) and Firman (2004).
2   See Chapter 10 of this book, and also Krausse (1979), Azis (1997) and Manning (1998).
3   See Chapter 11 for a description of the design and methodology underpinning the RUMiI survey. More details on the dataset and other background material can be found at http://rumici. anu.edu.au.
4   See, for example, Fields (1975), Mazumdar (1976), Zhao (1999b), Lucas (2004) and Dubey, Palmer-Jones and Sen (2006).
5   See, for example, Meng and Zhang (2001), Hazans (2004) and Davila and Mora (2008).
6   Studies on the effect of migration on the areas migrants leave include Hetler (1989), Skeldon (1997), Rozelle, Taylor and de Brauw (1999) and Goldsmith, Gunjal and Ndarishikanye (2004). Studies on the effect of migration on the areas migrants move to include Zhang and Song (2003), Au and Henderson (2006) and Lu and Song (2006).

10 Making It in the City: Recent and Long-term Migrants in the Urban Labour Market in Indonesia

Armida Alisjahbana and Chris Manning

1 INTRODUCTION

The crucial role of the urban labour market in providing jobs for rural people is well documented in the case of Indonesia, from the time economic growth began to accelerate almost half a century ago.[1] Research on rural-to-urban migration over the past several decades has focused in particular on the engagement of circular migrants in the informal sector in petty trade, transport and construction, as well as the movement of unskilled rural workers into the country's expanding export-oriented industries. However, there have been few studies examining how these cohorts of migrants have fared over time in the urban labour market, or comparing their jobs and wages with those of non-migrants. The present study seeks to fill this gap.

This chapter examines the earnings and other employment characteristics of migrants and non-migrants working in the formal, small business and informal sectors in four Indonesian cities. One research question relates to the extent to which rural–urban migrants have been disadvantaged in the job market compared with more established urban residents. Another concerns the experience of recent and longer-term migrants in the cities, drawing attention to the potential for greater occupational mobility among the longer-term migrants. We examine the performance of migrants and non-migrants during two very different periods of economic performance: before the economic crisis in 1998 when the Indonesian economy was growing quite rapidly, and during the decade since 1998 when formal-sector job expansion faltered.

In the context of the comparison between China and Indonesia, three points should be noted. First, there have been few formal constraints on migration from the villages to the cities in Indonesia, despite periodic but short-lived attempts by city authorities to limit the movement of people from rural to urban areas. Although migrants are required to hold identity cards based on their place of residence, this has not been a major obstacle to permanent rural–urban migration, unlike in China, where the household registration (*hukou*) system has been used to discourage migrants from moving permanently to the cities. Second, migration to the cities has occurred over a much longer time period in Indonesia. It accelerated from the late 1960s, when the economy began to grow strongly on a sustained basis for the first time since Indonesia achieved independence in 1945. And third, Indonesia's rural–urban migrants are heavily engaged in the informal sector, especially petty trade and the sale of processed food, in contrast to the much greater involvement of migrants in wage employment in China (Meng and Zhang 2001).

To foreshadow some of the main results, we observe differences in labour market outcomes between both recent and long-term migrants relative to non-migrants. But the patterns are quite different for the two migrant groups. Whereas longer-term migrants actually receive higher wages than non-migrants, the opposite is true for recent migrants. Recent migrants fare worse than non-migrants in terms of earnings, even though they are more likely to be concentrated in wage jobs rather than self-employment. In this chapter, we examine variables associated with these different wage outcomes for each of the three migration-status groups and speculate on the reasons for the contrasting results for recent and long-term migrants.

The next section of the chapter examines some of the literature on the role migrants have played in the urban labour market in Indonesia and other developing countries. In the third we discuss methodology, the sample and the definition of key variables. The fourth compares the occupations held by migrants and non-migrants through the application of a multinomial logit model. We then examine earnings differentials and their determinants for the three groups, paying some attention to gender differentials.

2   MIGRATION AND THE URBAN LABOUR MARKET

The shift of labour out of agriculture is frequently associated with a spatial shift to a more urbanized economic environment, where economies of scale and scope offer a much greater range of job opportunities (World Bank 2009). Where such a shift occurs, one important question relates to how migrants fare in the urban labour market relative to non-migrants, and the extent to which these patterns change over time as migrants are assimilated into the urban labour force (Lucas 1997).

In the case of Indonesia, both the shift of labour out of agriculture and rural–urban migration have been features of the labour market since the late 1960s when economic growth began to accelerate.[2] The share of total agricultural employment fell from close to 60 per cent in the early 1970s to 40 per cent on the eve of the economic crisis 25 years later, and has remained relatively constant since then (Manning 1998).[3] Urban employment grew at rates of around 5–6 per cent per annum over the same period. This was roughly two to three times the rates of growth in rural employment, which were negative towards the end of the period in some of the better-integrated labour markets in parts of Java and Bali.[4]

Studies of migration in Indonesia have noted that migrants were most likely to enter the informal sector, except for a brief period in the late 1980s and early 1990s when export-oriented manufacturing played a dominant role in job creation (Hugo 2000). Over the past three decades, the informal sector share of total employment has remained relatively constant, except during the decade that preceded the economic crisis.[5] Estimates suggest that it continued to expand after 1998, to account for 36 per cent of all urban jobs in 2007 (Manning 2008).

In this chapter, we distinguish between migrants who entered the urban labour market before the height of the economic crisis in 1998 and those who entered it afterwards. It makes good sense to distinguish between these two periods because of their differing rates of economic growth, separated by a severe economic downturn and regime change. During the former, 'Soeharto' period, Indonesia experienced sustained growth of approximately 7–8 per cent over 30 years, with very few periods of significant economic downturn.[6] In the latter period, economic growth rates almost halved to an average of 4–5 per cent per annum (after a sharp decline in living standards in 1998), although they accelerated to close to 6 per cent between 2006 and 2008 (McLeod 2008). Whereas formal sector jobs grew quite quickly under Soeharto, demand for labour in this sector grew less rapidly subsequently, as economic growth rates slowed in the post-Soeharto period (Manning 2008). We might expect these trends to be reflected in the structure of jobs taken up by more recent migrants to the cities.

Outcomes in the urban labour market depend partly on the occupational mobility of migrants after they settle in the cities and partly on the extent to which governments allow migrants to settle permanently. We look briefly at each before turning to an assessment of labour market effects in the four surveyed cities.

Occupational Mobility

Both the segment of the labour market a migrant initially enters and the degree of occupational mobility in the labour market play a major role in determining the income of migrants relative to non-migrants. Initial entry into wage employment in the formal sector, especially export-oriented labour-intensive industries, is common in countries where wage employment is growing rapidly, as in China in recent decades. In many other, less rapidly growing, economies, migrants tend to start out in informal sector jobs rather than in wage employment. This is particularly true if several conditions hold: there is an excess supply of labour at going wage rates in the agricultural sector; formal sector employment is relatively small and its growth is slow; and wages in the formal sector are held above market-clearing levels by institutional factors (Mazumdar 1994). Under such conditions, migrants typically crowd into informal sector jobs in trade and services in the towns and cities.

At the same time, it is a mistake to assume that migrants are occupationally immobile, even within the informal sector, or that they remain in the same low-wage jobs that they first take up in the cities (Katz and Stark 1986). Over time, opportunities for mobility into higher-income jobs arise as migrants accumulate skills and experience. The extent to which migrants avail themselves of these opportunities is therefore important.

The more general literature on occupational mobility suggests that migrants do not always view the informal sector as a stepping stone for movement into the formal sector, as assumed by some of the early models of rural–urban migration.[7] In his seminal work on transition between the formal and informal sectors in Mexico, for example, Maloney (1998) distinguishes several distinct yet overlapping segments of the informal sector (including self-employed workers, informal salaried workers and contract workers) on the basis of differences in earnings, as well as labour mobility in relation to the formal sector. Labour tends to flow both in and out of the informal sector, making for a much greater 'churning' of labour markets than many had imagined, as has been identified in Latin America more generally (IADB 2004).

Government Restrictions

While there is widespread agreement that migrants benefit economically from having access to the urban labour market, the extent of the gain depends partly on government policies with regard to migration. One can imagine two extreme situations, with most policy regimes lying between the two. On the one hand, migration may be tightly controlled in an authoritarian context, through permits that control either the mobility or the place of residence of rural households. On the other hand, the movement of migrants may be quite seamless. In such an environment, migrants compete with one another and urban residents for jobs, largely unencumbered by government regulation.

The institutional environment in Indonesia is closer to the latter scenario, despite some (largely unsuccessful) efforts to slow urban growth by limiting the intake of rural–urban migrants.[8] Rural–urban migrants are required to report to the local authorities, where their current address is registered on a new identity and family card. In addition, from time to time city authorities have attempted to curtail migration from rural areas by banning informal sector activities from some parts of the larger cities. While sometimes costly and time consuming, these restrictions do not appear to have posed significant obstacles for migrants. Bribery has tended to undermine the controls that city authorities have sought to impose through registration systems. Unlike in China, urban slums have proliferated in many Indonesian cities.

The effectiveness of government restrictions has also changed over time. Since the fall of Soeharto's authoritarian regime in 1998, the police and military have proved less able to prevent rural people from crowding into the urban informal sector. Thus, compared with China, one might expect rural–urban migrants to blend in more easily with urban residents, and to share similar jobs and incomes, after taking differences in human capital into account.

3   APPROACH AND METHODOLOGY

The analysis is conducted in two stages. First, we examine the extent to which job allocation across the formal, small business and informal sectors is related to migration status, after controlling for a range of other personal, employment and regional characteristics of the working population. A multinomial logit model of job placement is adopted for this analysis. The second, and main, part of the analysis focuses on the determinants of earnings among the three migration-status groups, overall and by gender.

The sample covers all employed persons earning an income from work, and aged 15 and above, in the four cities studied: Tangerang near Jakarta in Banten (West Java), Medan in Sumatra, Samarinda in Kalimantan and Makassar in South Sulawesi.[9] The focus is on 'earnings' workers, that is, permanent and casual wage employees, employers and self-employed persons. Family workers are not included in the analysis.

The three groups of interest are recent migrants, long-term migrants and non-migrants. To meet the definition of a rural–urban migrant, both recent and long-term migrants must have spent at least five years continuously in a rural area before turning 12 (see Chapter 11 for details). Note, however, that our definition of recent migrants is slightly different to that used in the other chapters on Indonesia in this book. We define recent migrants as all employed persons who moved to their current place of residence in one of the four cities studied in 1998 or later—rather than in the five years preceding the survey, as in Chapters 8 and 9 of this book. We adopt this approach on the grounds that a recent migrant's current sector of employment is likely to have been heavily influenced by the economic crisis of 1998, when labour market conditions changed significantly.

Long-term migrants are all employed persons who moved from a rural area to one of the four cities before 1998. Non-migrants are all employed persons who were not raised in a rural environment and currently reside in one of the four cities covered by the survey. Note that, under this definition, the 'non-migrant' group includes not only workers who were born and raised in one of the four cities but a group of urban–urban migrants who moved to one of the cities from another urban area.

Of particular interest in the analysis is the allocation of jobs between the formal, small business and informal sectors, and the extent to which participation in any one of these sectors affects the earnings differential between migrants and non-migrants. The three sectors of employment are defined in the following way. The formal sector grouping seeks to describe places of employment that provide relatively regular employment and earnings, such as large businesses and the public sector. Individuals included in the small business group deploy relatively small yet not insignificant amounts of capital and/or employ a small number of non-family employees (defined as 5–19 workers).[10] The third group, the informal sector, covers self-employed persons who invest smaller amounts of capital, wage employees in micro enterprises and workers engaged by larger firms on a casual basis; this group in particular is likely to suffer considerable uncertainty in their wages and employment. Appendix A10.1 and Figure A10.1 describe the classification of the three sectors in greater detail.

Total earnings are defined as the net earnings of wage workers, employers and the self-employed from their main job in the month preceding the survey, including fringe benefits (food, transport and housing allowances, and the value of in-kind payments) and other emoluments accruing to wage and non-wage employees. The in-kind payments made to employees vary depending on the nature of their employment contract with the firm: whether they are permanent, contract or casual employees, and whether they are paid on a monthly or daily basis. Even in the formal sector, a high proportion of total earnings are in the form of cash payments; only 20 per cent or so of all wage employees receive some in-kind payments, and for these employees the payments amount to a quite small share of total monthly earnings. Thus, unlike in China, where allowances and other forms of in-kind income account for a significant portion of the difference in earnings between migrant and non-migrant workers (see Chapter 3 of this book), in Indonesia this is not the case.

What are the main hypotheses? We examine three with the help of a multinomial logit model and regression analysis.

First, we expect recent migrants to be more heavily concentrated in less stable, easy-to-enter activities in the informal sector, in contrast to non-migrants, who are more likely to be engaged in the formal and small business sectors. Earlier studies of migration have pointed to such a pattern in Indonesia. The

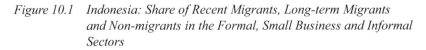

Figure 10.1   Indonesia: Share of Recent Migrants, Long-term Migrants and Non-migrants in the Formal, Small Business and Informal Sectors

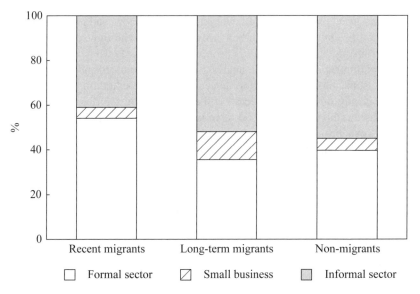

Source: Rural–Urban Migration in Indonesia survey, 2008.

fact that the formal sector grew much less quickly after the 1998 crisis, and hence migrants had fewer opportunities to gain work there, would increase the likelihood of recent migrant engagement in the informal sector. Longer-term migrants might be expected to lie somewhere between non-migrants and recent migrants in terms of participation in the formal sector.

Second, we anticipate that the earnings of recent migrants would be lower than those of the other two groups, with earnings highest among non-migrants. Long-term migrants, with their intermediate levels of city connections and accumulated human capital, could be expected to fall between the other two groups in terms of earnings.

And third, the sector of employment in which a worker is engaged (formal, small business or informal) is predicted to play an important role in explaining earnings differentials, in addition to the standard demographic and human capital characteristics (age, gender, experience and schooling), other demand-side variables (industry of employment and occupation) and location.

Figures 10.1 and 10.2 provide an overview of the distribution of the three migration-status groups across sectors, and of their hourly earnings. Contrary to expectation, we find that recent migrants are concentrated in formal rather than informal sector jobs, whereas long-term migrants and non-migrants tend

*Figure 10.2   Indonesia: Index of Hourly Earnings of Recent Migrants,
            Long-term Migrants and Non-migrants by Sector of
            Employment*

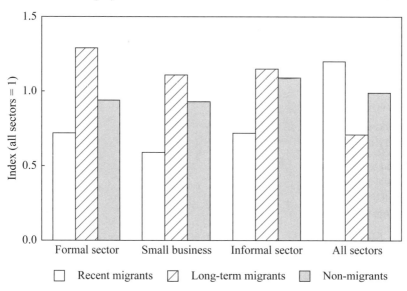

Source: Rural–Urban Migration in Indonesia survey, 2008.

to work in the informal sector (Figure 10.1). Thus, at first glance, there is little
evidence of a process of progression from informal sector to formal sector jobs
as migrants became more familiar with an urban environment. Second, a higher
proportion of longer-term migrants are employed in small business: 13 per
cent, compared with just 5 per cent for non-migrants and recent migrants. Thus,
migrants who moved to the city before 1998 are more likely to be engaged in
small business than the other two groups, although we have not distinguished
between those who started out in such activities (owing to greater opportunity
or to the specific characteristics of this early cohort of migrants) and those who
moved subsequently into business after migrating to the city.

    There is relatively little difference in the mean monthly and hourly earnings
of migrants and non-migrants (Table 10.1). However, there is some indication
that our second hypothesis may be on the right track. From Figure 10.2, it is
very clear that recent migrants in each sector of employment earn considerably
less per hour than long-term migrants and non-migrants. Thus, while the average hourly earnings of recent migrants range from Rp 5,400 to Rp 8,100 (about
US$0.60–0.70), those of long-term migrants range from Rp 8,600 to Rp 15,000
(US$1.10–1.30). While the magnitude of the difference appears large within
each sector, the higher earnings of long-term migrants than recent migrants was

Table 10.1   Indonesia: Index of Mean Monthly Earnings, Hours Worked and Earnings per Hour by Migration Status and Sector of Employment

	All Migrants	Non-migrants	Total Sample
Mean monthly earnings			
Formal sector	1.1	1.0	1.1
Small business	1.3	1.6	1.4
Informal sector	0.8	0.9	0.8
Total (index)	1.0	1.0	1.0
Total (Rp thousand)	1,566	1,526	1,545
Mean hours worked			
Formal sector	0.96	0.99	0.98
Small business	1.16	1.25	1.20
Informal sector	1.00	0.97	0.98
Total (index)	1.00	1.00	1.00
Total (hours)	52.2	49.6	50.8
Mean hourly earnings			
Formal sector	1.1	1.0	1.0
Small business	1.5	1.3	1.4
Informal sector	0.8	1.0	0.9
Total (index)	1.0	1.0	1.0
Total (Rp)	9,020	8,818	8,913

Source: Rural–Urban Migration in Indonesia survey, 2008.

expected. The consistently higher earnings of long-term migrants than non-migrants regardless of sector of employment was not anticipated, however, and deserves special attention when interpreting the multivariate analysis.[11]

The differences in hourly earnings do not appear to be explained by more intensive work on the part of recent migrants. All three groups work relatively uniform hours, at just over 50 hours a week, although recent migrants work slightly more hours than the other two groups (Table 10.2).[12]

To put these figures in perspective, the average monthly earnings of long-term migrants are more than 50 per cent higher than the 2008 minimum wage, which varies from around Rp 800,000 to Rp 1.2 million per month depending on the region. In contrast, the monthly earnings of recent migrants working in the informal and formal sectors are barely above the minimum wage, and only

Table 10.2   Indonesia: Descriptive Statistics for the Main Variables

	Recent Migrants			Long-term Migrants			Non-migrants		
	No. of Observations	Mean	Standard Deviation	No. of Observations	Mean	Standard Deviation	No. of Observations	Mean	Standard Deviation
Monthly earnings (Rp thousand)	587	1,273	1,084	853	1,804	2,368	1,554	1,578	4,259
Working hours (per week)	587	52.89	17.73	853	52.39	22.02	1,554	50.33	20.16
Hourly earnings (Rp)	587	6,353	5,922	853	10,904	21,705	1,554	9,042	24,065
Log of hourly earnings	587	8.51	0.72	853	8.73	1.03	1,554	8.56	0.96
Age	587	27.13	7.56	853	42.99	10.47	1,554	35.50	11.75
Age^2	587	793	532	853	1,957	963	1,554	1,399	934
Work experience (years)	587	2.36	2.84	853	12.22	9.97	1,554	7.55	8.77
Years of schooling	587	10.22	3.00	853	10.14	3.99	1,554	10.63	3.69
Household head[a]	587	0.74	0.44	853	0.75	0.43	1,554	0.44	0.50
Marital status[a]	587	0.47	0.50	853	0.04	0.20	1,554	0.30	0.46
Gender[a]	587	0.66	0.47	853	0.72	0.45	1,554	0.65	0.48
In good health[a]	587	0.97	0.17	853	0.94	0.24	1,554	0.96	0.19

a   Categories: household head: 1 = head, 0 = other; marital status: 1 = single, 0 = married, widowed or divorced; gender: 1 = male, 0 = female; in good health: 1 = in very good/good health, 0 = in poor health (subjective appraisal).

Source: Rural–Urban Migration in Indonesia survey, 2008.

30 per cent higher among small business operators. The average monthly earnings of non-migrants fall between these two extremes.

It should be noted that the disadvantage in the labour market experienced by recent migrants is not necessarily inconsistent with the findings in Chapters 8 and 9 of this book that recent migrants have higher levels of expenditure and lower levels of poverty than non-migrants, and a comparable health status. Both long-term migrants and non-migrants have a higher average age than recent migrants—43 and 36 years respectively, compared with just 27 for recent migrants (see Table 10.2)—and are more likely to be married with children. Given that they are supporting more dependants, it is not surprising to find that their per capita incomes are lower than those of recent migrants, many of whom are young and single.[13]

4 MIGRATION STATUS AND THE ALLOCATION OF JOBS

A major theme in the literature is the contrasting ways in which migrant and non-migrant workers adapt to urban labour market conditions and opportunities. In this section, we examine some of the similarities and differences between the two groups of workers in terms of job allocation.

What factors help determine the allocation of jobs between migrant and non-migrant workers? We constructed a multinomial logit model to examine the factors that influence job placement among recent migrants, long-term migrants and non-migrants. The dependent variable for this equation is the individual's current job. The three job classifications are the formal sector, the small business sector and the informal sector, with the informal sector used as the base category.[14] The explanatory variables tested in relation to job attainment are migration status, individual and human capital characteristics, occupation, industry and location (in one of the four cities included in the study). The reference groups are non-migrants for the migration status variable, technical jobs for the occupation variable, trade for the industry variable and the city of Tangerang for the location variable. The estimated coefficients are interpreted relative to these reference groups.

The results are shown in Table 10.3.[15] They indicate that migration status does not appear to be a major influence on job placement in the formal sector or the small business sector, relative to employment in the informal sector. Neither of the migration dummies (recent or long-term migrant relative to the omitted category, non-migrant) are significant in explaining the apparent greater participation of migrants than non-migrants in the formal sector. Thus, the greater engagement of recent migrants than non-migrants in the formal sector (shown in Figure 10.1), and the greater likelihood that non-migrants will

Table 10.3   Indonesia: Multinomial Logit Results for Employment Attainment among Migrants and Non-migrants[a]

	Formal Sector			Small Business Sector		
	Coef-ficient	$P > z$	Marginal Effects[b]	Coef-ficient	$P > z$	Marginal Effects[b]
Migration dummies						
Long-term migrant	0.163	0.151	0.031	**0.276**	0.073	0.014
Recent migrant	−0.006	0.968	−0.006	0.147	0.543	0.010
Individual characteristics						
Age	−0.002	0.957	−0.003	**0.087**	0.034	0.006
Age^2	−0.000	0.245	−0.000	**−0.001**	0.074	−0.000
Years of schooling	**0.191**	0.000	0.044	**0.077**	0.000	−0.000
Household head	0.126	0.346	0.048	**−0.608**	0.007	−0.046
Marital status	**0.338**	0.016	0.103	**−0.847**	0.003	−0.054
Male	0.059	0.639	0.001	**0.478**	0.030	0.028
In good health	0.093	0.701	0.013	0.376	0.271	0.019
Work experience (years)	**0.012**	0.088	0.003	0.001	0.897	−0.000
Dummies for occupation						
Professional/manager	−0.317	0.162	−0.063	−0.496	0.114	−0.021
Clerk	0.092	0.801	0.043	−1.134	0.149	−0.048
Unskilled	0.026	0.903	0.028	**−0.782**	0.005	−0.051
Other occupation	**−0.554**	0.008	−0.114	**−0.634**	0.013	−0.025
Dummies for industry						
Manufacturing	**1.620**	0.000	0.401	**−0.785**	0.003	−0.077
Services	−0.089	0.524	0.009	**−1.338**	0.000	−0.068
Transport	**0.402**	0.024	0.101	−0.068	0.773	−0.015
Construction	−0.307	0.149	−0.046	**−1.720**	0.000	−0.061
Other industry	**0.443**	0.040	0.122	−0.509	0.096	−0.036
Dummies for location						
Medan	**−0.689**	0.000	−0.158	−0.061	0.737	0.014
Samarinda	**−0.324**	0.013	−0.075	−0.055	0.789	0.005
Makassar	**−0.477**	0.001	−0.098	**−0.519**	0.023	−0.020
Constant	**−1.901**	0.005		**−3.547**	0.001	
No. of observations	2,994.00					
LR chi^2(44)	1,052.49					
Pseudo R^2	0.19					
Log likelihood	−2,271.49					

a   All variables significant at the 5 per cent level or higher are shown in bold. The base category is informal sector employment. Omitted categories: dummy for migration = non-migrant; dummy for marital status = married, widowed or divorced; dummy for gender = female; dummy for in good health = in poor health; dummy for occupation = technical; dummy for industries = trade; dummy for location = Tangerang.
b   Marginal effects are evaluated at the variable mean.

Source: Rural–Urban Migration in Indonesia survey, 2008.

be placed in the informal sector, are not statistically significant, after taking the influence of personal characteristics, labour demand variables and location into account. The dummy for long-term migrants is, however, found to be significant and positive (at the 5 per cent level or higher) in helping to explain this group's greater participation in small business relative to non-migrants, after controlling for other variables. The greater likelihood of long-term migrants being engaged in small business is consistent with the bivariate relationship, which shows that this group is more than twice as likely to be engaged in small business as the other two groups.

These findings are of interest, since they do not support the surprising bivariate finding that recent migrants are more likely to work in the formal than in the informal sector. If anything, after controlling for other variables, recent migrants are *less* likely to work in the formal sector (the coefficient is negative, although very small), which is in line with our hypothesis. Second, the greater engagement of long-term migrants in small business makes sense, given that these people have spent at least 10 years in an urban area and at least 10 years in the workforce. It is understandable that these more experienced individuals would show a greater propensity to work in small business, and to make the transition from formal or informal sector jobs into small business, as they gain experience in the workforce.

What other variables influence job placement in the formal and small business sectors compared with placement in the informal sector? A range of variables related to personal characteristics, experience, occupation and industry are significant for placement in small business relative to the informal sector as the base category. Thus, almost all of the personal characteristics are significant, except good health. Workers engaged in small business are also more likely to work in technical occupations and the trade sector. The small coefficient for work experience is not so surprising in the case of small business. We know that one characteristic of this sector in Indonesia and many other countries is high rates of new start-ups and attrition.

A narrower range of variables helps explain placement in the formal sector relative to the informal sector. Only years of schooling, work experience in the current job and marital status are significant at the 5 per cent level or higher, among the individual and human capital characteristics. The findings on schooling and work experience are to be expected. Compared to informal sector workers, formal sector workers tend to be selected on the basis of completed schooling, especially in the public sector, and to remain for long periods in the same job.

For formal sector workers, engagement in manufacturing and location in the city of Tangerang are found to be significant (the coefficients for all of the location dummies are significantly negative relative to the omitted category, Tangerang). We suspect both results are influenced by characteristics attributable to recent migrants. That is, recent migrants tend to be more heavily engaged in manufacturing—over 40 per cent in the total sample, or almost twice the proportion for the other two migration-status groups. And over half of all recent migrants in the sample reside in Tangerang, compared with 25–30 per cent among long-term migrants and non-migrants.

To conclude this section on job placement, insofar as we expect the earnings of non-migrants to be significantly higher than those of recent and long-term migrants, these differences do not appear to be the result of non-migrants' greater representation in sectors where earnings are anticipated to be high— that is, the formal and small business sectors.

5 EARNINGS AND MIGRATION STATUS

What factors influence the earnings of migrant versus non-migrant workers? To examine this, we compute a Mincerian earnings function in which average hourly earnings are related to a range of human capital, labour demand and contextual variables.

The Mincerian earnings function estimated here includes five main sets of variables, estimated separately for migrants and non-migrants working in the formal, small business and informal sectors:

$$W_{im} = f(EMSTS_{im}, INHHD_{im}, OCC_{im}, IND_{im}, R_{im}) \qquad (10.1)$$

where the dependent variable W_{im} represents hourly wages for each migration-status group. (In the equations it is estimated in logs.) $EMSTS_{im}$ is a vector of employment status, with the informal sector as the omitted category; $INHHD_{im}$ is a vector of individual and household social and demographic characteristics; OCC_{im} and IND_{im} are vectors of occupation and industry characteristics respectively; and R_{im} is a vector of city dummies (where Tangerang is the control group).

Table 10.2 above provides some descriptive statistics for the three migration-status groups. Recent migrants differ from the other two groups on a number of key variables: their earnings are lower; they are younger and have less experience in the current job; and they are more likely to be single. In addition, a higher proportion of recent migrants are found in the formal sector and in manufacturing; more are unskilled or semi-skilled; and fewer (13 per cent) are engaged in services. However, they have a similar number of years of schooling (10 years, equivalent to passing the first year of senior high school).

Long-term migrants and non-migrants, on the other hand, display similar characteristics, although long-term migrants tend to be older and to have more work experience. In addition, a higher proportion of long-term migrants are male, and almost all are married, widowed or divorced rather than single. Even though a higher proportion of long-term migrants work in small business, their employment characteristics are quite similar to those of non-migrants in terms of industry and occupation. Both groups are also fairly evenly distributed across the four cities, in contrast to recent migrants, who are more highly concentrated in Tangerang.

Earnings Differentials by Migration Status

The above discussion suggests that a major challenge in computing the earnings functions is to explain why wages are lower among recent migrants, and higher among long-term migrants, than among non-migrants. The Mincerian earnings equation is estimated separately for each migration-status group, with employment in the formal sector, the small business sector or the informal sector included as an explanatory variable, together with other socio-demographic and job characteristics.

Table 10.4 presents the results for the earnings function estimations. First, we should note that, with the exception of non-migrants in the small business sector, employment status is a consistent predictor of earnings among all migration-status groups. This is especially true for long-term migrants. Thus, hourly earnings tend be higher if migrants, either recent or lifetime, are employed in the formal or small business sectors rather than in the informal sector. The fact that recent migrants tend to be concentrated in the formal sector does not appear to be a factor in their lower average earnings relative to the other two groups. Put differently, even though a high proportion of recent migrants are employed in the formal sector, where they earn lower wages than long-term migrants and non-migrants working in the same sector, it is not simply placement in this sector that contributes to their lower earnings. Rather, it is the jobs that they perform in the formal sector that sets recent migrants apart from long-term migrants and non-migrants.

Thus, the earnings of recent migrants are lower because they work in unskilled occupations or, to a lesser extent, low-wage service industries; for recent migrants, the coefficients for both variables are negative and the unskilled worker dummy is significant. While age and experience are both important predictors of higher earnings among long-term migrants and non-migrants (both significant at the 5 per cent level or higher), this is not the case for recent migrants, most of whom are relatively young and have limited work experience. Nor does the fact that recent migrants are concentrated in manufacturing contribute significantly to their lower earnings.

Among long-term migrants and non-migrants, gender (the male dummy indicating positive effects), years of schooling and the dummies for place-

Table 10.4   Indonesia: Determinants of Hourly Earnings by Migration Status[a]

	Recent Migrants		Long-term Migrants		Non-migrants	
	Coefficient	$P > t$	Coefficient	$P > t$	Coefficient	$P > t$
Dummies for sector of employment						
Formal sector	**0.174**	0.010	**0.228**	0.003	**0.162**	0.001
Small business sector	**0.214**	0.094	**0.265**	0.007	0.112	0.153
Individual characteristics						
Age	0.020	0.245	**0.072**	0.001	**0.026**	0.033
Age^2	−0.000	0.526	**−0.001**	0.000	**−0.000**	0.096
Work experience (years)	0.010	0.314	**0.018**	0.000	**0.016**	0.000
Years of schooling	**0.063**	0.000	**0.062**	0.000	**0.084**	0.000
Household head	**0.307**	0.000	−0.127	0.270	0.071	0.280
Marital status	−0.042	0.541	−0.059	0.719	−0.060	0.375
Gender (male)	0.050	0.452	**0.381**	0.001	**0.223**	0.000
In good health	**0.472**	0.003	−0.023	0.855	0.164	0.155
Dummies for occupation						
Professional/manager	−0.067	0.759	**0.525**	0.000	−0.121	0.235
Clerk	−0.357	0.387	**0.490**	0.048	−0.048	0.778
Unskilled	**−0.367**	0.044	−0.040	0.770	**−0.439**	0.000
Other occupation	**−0.323**	0.084	0.122	0.362	**−0.351**	0.000
Dummies for industry						
Manufacturing	0.102	0.261	**0.281**	0.012	0.076	0.288
Services	−0.082	0.409	**0.210**	0.032	−0.024	0.701
Transportation	**0.266**	0.028	0.097	0.445	−0.113	0.177
Construction	**0.228**	0.078	**0.287**	0.069	**0.168**	0.092
Other industry	−0.226	0.168	0.198	0.156	0.107	0.304
Dummies for location						
Medan	**−0.228**	0.033	**−0.229**	0.005	**−0.095**	0.087
Samarinda	0.027	0.703	0.015	0.871	**0.159**	0.016
Makassar	0.108	0.197	0.001	0.993	−0.053	0.432
Constant	6.871	0.000	6.015	0.000	6.898	0.000
No. of observations	587		853		1,554	
F	8.56		15.73		24.24	
Prob. > F	0		0		0	
R^2	0.2503		0.2943		0.2583	
Adjusted R^2	0.221		0.2756		0.2477	
Root MSE	0.63128		0.87837		0.83099	

a   All variables significant at the 5 per cent level or higher are shown in bold. Omitted categories: dummy for marital status = married, widowed or divorced; dummy for gender = female; dummy for in good health = in poor health (subjective appraisal); dummy for occupation = technical; dummy for industries = trade; dummy for location = Tangerang; dummy for migration = non-migrant. Dummy for household head = spouse/other.

Source: Rural–Urban Migration in Indonesia survey, 2008.

ment in certain industries and occupations are all significant in the earnings equation, in addition to age and experience in the current job. For long-term migrants, the coefficients for professional and clerical workers are also positive and significant, as are those for engagement in manufacturing and services compared with the omitted category, trade. Among non-migrants, involvement in unskilled jobs contributes negatively to hourly earnings, while engagement in the construction sector (surprisingly) has a positive and significant coefficient.

Finally, the regional dummies are not significant in most cases, although location in Medan rather than another city produces a negative and significant coefficient for all three migration-status groups, whereas location in the city of Samarinda produces a positive and significant coefficient among non-migrants. The negative coefficients for the city of Medan are a little puzzling given that it has historically attracted migrants from other parts of Indonesia owing to its thriving agricultural and manufacturing sectors.

Earnings Differentials by Gender

Gender is typically an important variable in helping to explain wage differentials, after controlling for a number of other factors. It is pertinent, therefore, to examine whether there are important differences in the level of engagement of male and female migrant and non-migrant workers in the urban economy. First, it is worth noting that female participation rates are quite high among both migrants and non-migrants (see Chapter 8) and that the distribution of females across employment status groups is quite similar to that of males (see Table 10.5). The one notable difference is that, among recent migrants, more females are engaged as formal sector (wage) workers.

Among long-term migrants and non-migrants, the earnings regressions discussed above indicate a positive and significant coefficient for being male. However, unlike in China (see Chapter 3), in the Indonesian case there is no obvious pattern of difference in the age–earnings profiles of migrant versus non-migrant workers, for either males or females. Indeed, the opposite pattern to that observed in China seems to apply in the case of males: in Indonesia, it is the age–earnings curve for migrants rather than non-migrants that rises more steeply at older ages. For both males and females, earnings rise steadily to reach a peak between the ages of 40 and 50, then decline steadily thereafter (see Figure 10.3). However, the earnings of migrants rise more steeply when they are in their forties and fifties whereas the earnings of non-migrants level off. This pattern is not apparent for females, who experience a dip in average earnings in their thirties. The latter may be related to their choice of jobs during the childbearing and early childrearing years.

The education–earnings profiles of migrants and non-migrants are similar for both genders, rising gradually to year 12 (the final year of secondary

*Table 10.5   Indonesia: Distribution of Migrants and Non-migrants by
            Gender and Sector of Employment*

	Recent Migrants	Long-term Migrants	Non-migrants	Total
Males				
Formal	49	39	41	42
Small business	5	12	8	9
Informal	45	49	51	49
Total	100	100	100	100
Average	20	30	50	100
No.	384	578	964	1,926
Females				
Formal	66	28	37	41
Small business	4	13	9	9
Informal	29	59	54	50
Total	100	100	100	100
Average	21	24	56	100
No.	197	227	535	959

Source: Rural–Urban Migration in Indonesia survey, 2008.

school), and then steeply thereafter. Again, this is in contrast to the situation in China, where migrant workers have a much flatter education–earnings profile than non-migrant workers. In the case of Indonesia, male earnings appear to rise more gradually than female earnings, starting at lower levels of schooling (from lower secondary level) (Figure 10.4). Female earnings per hour are relatively flat and then rise steeply at the upper secondary and tertiary levels.

It is pertinent to ask if the same variables are significant in separate earnings equations for males and females. Table 10.6 shows the results of the earnings regressions for male and female migrant and non-migrant workers. Among migrants, the coefficients for both the formal sector and the small business sector are significant for males only, relative to the omitted value, the informal sector. For women, employment in the formal or small business sectors does not appear to have a significant effect on earnings relative to women working in the informal sector. In other words, females who are engaged in the formal sector or in business do not appear to have an advantage over their counterparts in the informal sector. Either migrant women are relegated to lower-paying jobs in the former two sectors, or they tend to take up better-paying jobs in the informal sector. Table 10.5 suggests that both explanations are probably relevant—although neither explanation entirely suffices, as there is simply

Figure 10.3   Indonesia: Age–Earnings Profiles of Migrant and Non-migrant
Workers by Gender[a]

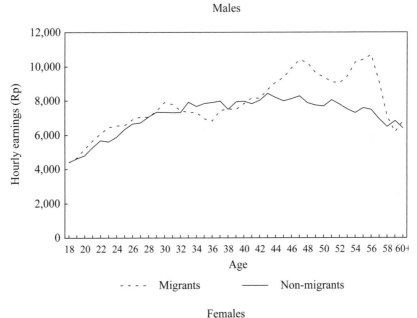

Males

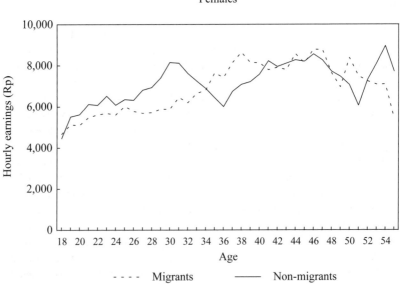

Females

a   Data smoothed, five-year moving averages.

Source: Rural–Urban Migration in Indonesia survey, 2008.

Figure 10.4   Indonesia: Education–Earnings Profiles of Migrant and Non-migrant Workers by Gender

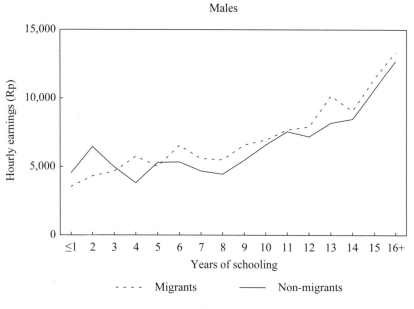

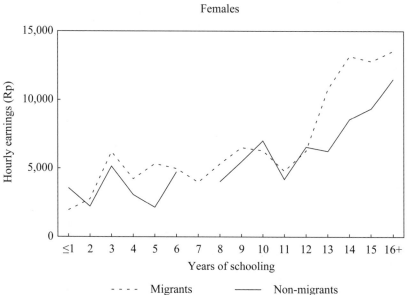

Source: Rural–Urban Migration in Indonesia survey, 2008.

Table 10.6 Indonesia: Determinants of Earnings by Migration Status and Gender[a]

| | Migrants | | | | Non-migrants | | | |
| | Males | | Females | | Males | | Females | |
	Coefficient	$P > t$	Coefficient	$P > t$	Coefficient	$P > t$	Coefficient	$P > t$
Individual characteristics								
Age	0.067 ***	0.000	0.053 **	0.021	0.020	0.146	0.042	0.112
Age^2	-0.001 ***	0.000	-0.001 ***	0.005	-0.000	0.351	-0.000	0.167
Years of schooling	0.056 ***	0.000	0.076 ***	0.000	0.082 ***	0.000	0.090 ***	0.000
Household head	0.260 **	0.010	0.095	0.371	0.097	0.232	0.047	0.772
Married	0.109	0.212	-0.047	0.738	-0.060	0.477	-0.058	0.651
In good health	-0.016	0.891	0.275	0.115	0.146	0.279	0.180	0.399
Work experience (years)	0.012 *	0.001	0.032 ***	0.000	0.011 ***	0.001	0.025 ***	0.000
Dummies for sector of employment								
Formal sector	0.260 **	0.000	0.074	0.516	0.080	0.147	0.350 ***	0.001
Small business sector	0.279 ***	0.001	0.152	0.335	0.034	0.705	0.235	0.116
Dummies for occupation								
Professional/manager	0.258 *	0.053	0.864 ***	0.001	-0.183	0.114	-0.016	0.936
Clerk	0.328	0.140	0.703	0.132	-0.288	0.165	0.243	0.428
Unskilled	-0.192	0.106	0.195	0.405	-0.525 ***	0.000	-0.290	0.130
Other occupation	0.036	0.765	0.094	0.672	-0.495 ***	0.000	-0.060	0.738

Dummies for industry

	Coef.	p	Coef.	p	Coef.	p	Coef.	p
Manufacturing	0.179 **	0.035	0.222	0.153	0.024	0.764	0.187	0.196
Services	0.103	0.236	0.024	0.847	-0.061	0.422	0.025	0.818
Transport	0.123	0.198	0.220	0.650	-0.139	0.106	-0.117	0.634
Construction	0.304 ***	0.005	(dropped)		0.110	0.267	0.650	0.256
Other industry	-0.046	0.688	0.614 **	0.023	0.054	0.616	0.070	0.815
Dummies for location								
Medan	-0.145 **	0.048	-0.376 ***	0.002	-0.122 *	0.054	-0.044	0.687
Samarinda	0.096	0.158	-0.224 *	0.068	0.163 **	0.024	0.150	0.273
Makassar	0.115	0.135	-0.102	0.447	-0.124	0.108	0.115	0.383
Constant	6.306 ***	0.000	6.094 ***	0.000	7.455 ***	0.000	6.146 ***	0.000
No. of observations	1,005		435		1,005		549	
F	13.94		12.08		17.13		7.81	
Prob. > F	0		0		0		0	
R^2	0.2295		0.3684		0.2679		0.2372	
Adjusted R^2	0.213		0.3379		0.2523		0.2069	
Root MSE	0.76612		0.82219		0.75255		0.95767	

* = significant at 10 per cent; ** = significant at 5 per cent; *** = significant at 1 per cent.

a   Omitted categories: dummy for marital status = married, widowed or divorced; dummy for gender = female; dummy for in good health = in poor health (subjective appraisal); dummy for occupation = technical; dummy for industries = trade; dummy for location = Tangerang; dummy for migration = non-migrant; dummy for household head = spouse/other.

Source: Rural–Urban Migration in Indonesia survey, 2008.

not enough variation across the three employment sectors to identify a precise parameter estimate.

Among personal characteristics, the coefficients for age, experience and years of schooling are significant at the 1 per cent or 5 per cent level and help to explain the earnings of both male and female migrants. The positive result for work experience among females is noteworthy, suggesting a greater degree of attachment to jobs than is often found for female workers. However, most of the coefficients for the dummy variables for occupation and industry are not significant in the separate regressions for male and female migrants.

The findings for non-migrants are less conclusive. Among females, the coefficient for formal sector workers is significant, relative to informal sector workers as the omitted category. But engagement in neither the formal sector nor the small business sector is significant for male non-migrants, which is a little puzzling given the strong (positive) result for formal sector engagement reported in Table 10.4. The difference becomes less puzzling, however, when one considers the disaggregated results in Table 10.6. It appears that, for both males and females, the small business dummy is still quite imprecisely estimated, while the formal sector dummy is more precisely estimated and strongly positive for the female subsample of non-migrants. The results for the female sample appear to be driving the results in Table 10.4.

For male and female non-migrants, both years of schooling and experience are positively and significantly related to earnings. But, as in the case of migrants, the industry and occupation dummies are not significant in the case of female non-migrants.

6   CONCLUSIONS

The focus of this chapter has been on job allocation and earnings among recent and long-term migrants versus non-migrants. This topic is important given the potential disadvantage that rural–urban migrants suffer in the urban labour market in terms of both jobs and wages. Two important innovations in the analysis have been: (1) the focus on migrants over two periods (before the economic crisis in 1998 when the economy was growing quite rapidly, and since 1998 when it was not); and (2) the differentiation between the small business and informal sectors when comparing the experience of the three migration-status groups in the urban labour market.

The analysis indicates that migrants who entered the labour market after 1998 are likely to be at a disadvantage to longer-term migrants and non-migrants. On the other hand, longer-term migrants compete quite favourably with non-migrants, providing some evidence that this group does tend to 'make it' in the city after a number of years. But we do not know whether this is because longer-term migrants entered the urban labour market before 1998, when conditions were more conducive, or because they have had longer than recent migrants to adjust to an urban environment. Both factors are probably important.

The earnings of recent migrants are lower either because they are younger and less experienced or because they are engaged in unskilled occupations. Although more research is needed, we suspect that the turnover of unskilled jobs has increased since 1998, and that this may have contributed to the relative disadvantage of recent migrants. Their average years of experience in the current job of just over two years suggests that this may be the case.

The findings with regard to both the job placement and earnings of longer-term migrants are instructive, especially in comparison with the results for China (see Chapter 3 of this book). The raw data suggest that wages are significantly (over 15–30 per cent) higher among longer-term migrants than among non-migrants in all three sectors of employment—the formal sector, the small business sector and the informal sector. Although we have not presented data on occupational mobility, it seems probable that long-term migrants are more likely than non-migrants to change jobs or to adopt strategies to improve their living standards.[15] In this respect, they appear to have fared much better than rural–urban migrants in China, the great majority of whom are unable to settle in the city and become 'long-term migrants'. It is also worth noting that female migrants in Indonesia appear to have done better in the urban labour market than their Chinese counterparts; age, experience and education are the main determinants of earnings for this group.

Standard human capital and labour demand variables help to clarify some of the differences in jobs and earnings between the three migration-status groups. Indeed, the conventional human capital variables that are generally expected to affect job allocation tend to be more significant among long-term migrants than among recent migrants or non-migrants in the case of Indonesia. Our preliminary conclusion from this part of the study is that labour markets have been relatively open over time, especially with regard to the access of migrants to higher-paying formal sector jobs (particularly in manufacturing) and opportunities in small business.

We reiterate that the lower earnings of recent migrants reported in this chapter are not necessarily inconsistent with the findings reported in Chapters 8 and 9 of higher levels of expenditure, lower levels of poverty and comparable health status among recent migrants relative to non-migrants. While earnings from work are the main source of income for most households, the level of individual earnings may not correlate closely with household welfare, especially if the size of the household and the number of dependants differ systematically across migrant groups. We find this to be the case for the migrants and non-migrants studied here. The seeming contradiction appears to be reconciled by the fact that a higher proportion of both lifetime migrants and non-migrants are married with children, whereas recent migrants, on average, are much younger and mostly single.

We conclude that, as measured by wages, most migrants do as well as non-migrants in the labour market in Indonesia, and long-term migrants do significantly better. But we also note that a clear wage disadvantage is experienced by migrants who entered the labour market after the economic crisis in 1998, even though many are able to get formal sector jobs. Further analysis is needed to determine both the factors that have contributed to higher wages among long-term migrants as well as those that have influenced lower wages among recent migrants. In this context, we suggest that factors such as social networks and job search and occupational mobility would be worthy of closer examination.

ACKNOWLEDGMENTS

We would like to acknowledge the excellent research assistance provided by Pipit Pitriyan and the comments on an earlier draft by Sudarno Sumarto from the SMERU Institute in Jakarta.

NOTES

1   See Chapter 8 of this book for a short overview of the history of migration in Indonesia.
2   Nevertheless, as in neighbouring Malaysia and Thailand, a dynamic export-oriented cash crop sector has meant that the agricultural sector continues to play a major role in employment and economic growth—although Indonesia has been a net food importer for several decades (Butzer, Mundlak and Larson 2003).
3   In August 2007, 41 per cent of employed persons still worked in agriculture, according to the National Labour Force Survey.
4   Some of the difference in rates of urban versus rural employment growth can be attributed to the official reclassification of rural regions as urban areas, as the infrastructure and social services associated with urban areas were extended into the countryside.
5   The central statistics agency, Statistics Indonesia, defines the informal sector to cover all casual, self-employed and family workers, excluding self-employed workers who are professionals and managers. See Appendix A10.1 and Figure A10.1 for more details.
6   The economy is estimated to have experienced negative economic growth only once (in 1982) during this 30-year period (Hill 2000a).
7   Most notably, these included extensions of the Harris–Todaro model of rural–urban migration. See Mazumdar (1994) and Lall, Selod and Shalizi (2006) for a critique of some of the assumptions of the early models of rural–urban migration.
8   This subsection draws on Hugo (1978, 2000), Abeyasekere (1987) and Firman, Kombaitan and Pradono (2007).
9   See Chapter 11 for details of the sampling procedures adopted to select the sample in each of the four cities.
10 Statistics Indonesia distinguishes between small firms (those with 5–19 employees) and cottage establishments (those with less than five employees).

11   This finding should be qualified in one important respect. Our definition of migrants excludes people who were raised in an urban environment and subsequently moved to one of the four surveyed cities. It is possible that the inclusion of these urban–urban migrants in the non-migrant group may have contributed to the higher share of informal sector work and lower earnings found among non-migrants compared with long-term migrants.

12   Not surprisingly, people working in small business work the longest hours regardless of migration status—close to 60 hours a week (data not shown in Table 10.2).

13   Another factor that may have contributed to the contrasting results for individual earnings, as against other indicators of household welfare, is the high proportion of recent migrants who are still at school and have a relatively high socio-economic status (see Chapter 8). For the most part these students are outside the labour force (because they are receiving transfers from their middle-class parents in the home village), and hence are not included in the analysis of job placement and earnings in this chapter.

14   The coefficients for the formal sector and business sector groups should be compared with those for the informal sector group. The marginal effects of the regressors on the probabilities are also calculated.

15   In both the first and second rounds of the survey (conducted in 2008 and 2009), we collected data on first job in the city and current job, so in subsequent analyses we will be able to test this tentative conclusion more rigorously.

APPENDIX A10.1   DEFINITION OF FORMAL, SMALL BUSINESS AND INFORMAL SECTOR EMPLOYMENT

Formal Sector

- All private sector employees with permanent (*tetap*) employment status, or working on contracts, who are employed in businesses with five employees or more.
- All civil servants (including teachers and health care workers on the government payroll), military personnel and police.
- All employers or self-employed persons with productive assets of at least Rp 100 million (about US$10,000 at March/April 2008 prices).
- All employers with productive assets of less than Rp 100 million who employ 20 or more non-family workers.

Small Business Sector

- All employers or self-employed persons with productive assets of Rp 5–100 million who employ less than 20 workers.
- All employers with productive assets of less than Rp 5 million who employ 5–19 workers.

Informal Sector

- All employees with casual (*tidak tetap/lepas*) employment status, regardless of the size of the firm.
- All employees in firms with less than five workers, regardless of whether they are casual, permanent or contractual employees.
- All employers or self-employed persons with productive assets of less than Rp 5 million, or who employ less than five workers.
- Others not covered as formal sector or small business sector workers.

Figure A10.1   Indonesia: Definition of Sector of Employment for Employees and Self-employed/Employers

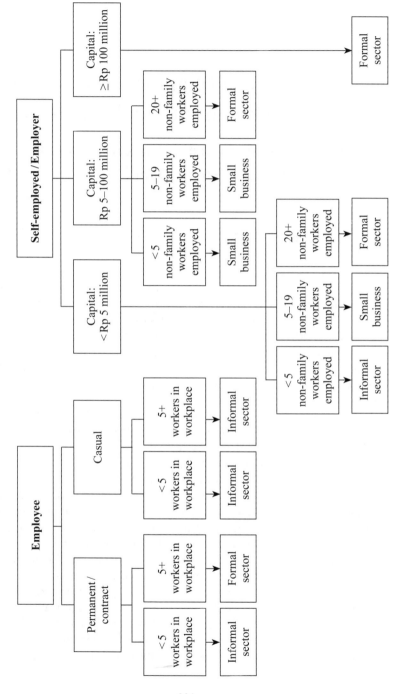

11 Rural–Urban Migration in Indonesia: Survey Design and Implementation

Budy P. Resosudarmo, Chikako Yamauchi and Tadjuddin Noer Effendi

1 INTRODUCTION

This chapter summarizes the study design of the Rural–Urban Migration in Indonesia (RUMiI) project, part of the Rural–Urban Migration in China and Indonesia (RUMiCI) project. We first discuss the overall distribution of migrants in Indonesia and the selection of survey cities. Next, we describe the process of identifying the migration status of each household in the sampling frame, using a pre-survey listing. This is followed by a discussion of the sampling method, focusing on the oversampling of migrant households. The timeline of the survey is then discussed and the questionnaire is summarized. Finally, we provide some concluding remarks.

The study design is based on the research objectives of the RUMiCI project. The first of these objectives is to investigate the labour market activities and welfare of individuals who have moved from rural to urban areas. Thus, one population of interest is households whose heads have moved from a rural to an urban area. We focus on this group of households because they are the most likely to experience profound changes in relation to jobs, incomes and educational attainment; these changes in turn can be expected to provide the impetus for dynamic socio-economic and demographic change in the regions they move to and those they leave behind. The focus on rural-to-urban migrant households facilitates the second main objective of the RUMiCI study, a comparison of migrant households in China and Indonesia.

The other population of interest is a comparison group consisting of households whose heads were raised mainly in an urban area. Information on this group is used to ascertain the degree of assimilation of migrant households. The migration status of the household head is considered to represent the migration status of that household, as the behaviour of the head is likely to significantly affect the well-being and behaviour of other members. This definition also simplifies the study design.

The longitudinal nature of the RUMiCI study together with the frequent collection of data are likely to increase understanding of the diversity of migrants and changes in their well-being. While existing cross-sectional data for Indonesia delivered through national censuses and intercensal population surveys provide information on migrants at a particular point in time, they do not shed light on changes in the welfare and behaviour of migrants. The Indonesian Family Life Survey is a good source of longitudinal data on migrants, but it is conducted at relatively infrequent intervals, making it difficult to examine year-to-year changes (see Strauss et al. 2009). The lack of annual panel datasets specifically on migrants has made it difficult to conduct any detailed investigation of their assimilation and income mobility patterns.

The RUMiI study aims to fill this gap by providing rich information on 1,521 Indonesian households headed by rural–urban migrants, and another 850 headed by non-migrants, in four municipalities. The group of migrant households consists of 637 recent migrant households (those whose head arrived from a rural area within five years of the initial interview, conducted in 2008) and 884 lifetime migrant households (those whose head arrived more than five years before the initial interview). The researchers intend to track as many of those households as possible over the five years from 2008 until 2012.

The Indonesian and Chinese studies differ in several ways. First, during its first two years (2008 and 2009) the Indonesian survey was conducted in urban areas only, whereas the Chinese study was carried out in both urban and rural areas. Second, the definition of a rural–urban migrant differs significantly between the two countries: the Chinese definition is based on the household registration (*hukou*) system, while the Indonesian definition is based on birth area and extended experience in a rural environment during childhood (see section 3 below). Third, the Indonesian survey is based on visits to residential structures, while the Chinese sample is based on visits to workplaces, such as factories and stores. Because the Indonesian study does not capture migrants living in non-residential structures, the Indonesian sample is likely to comprise migrants who have settled more permanently in the destination area.[1]

2   SELECTION OF SURVEY CITIES

Four cities or municipalities (*kota*) with a large number of migrants were selected for the RUMiI study. Although the scope of the study was not large enough to obtain a nationally representative sample, these four cities are likely to capture some of the diversity of the migrant experience in Indonesia. The municipalities were chosen to represent four broad geographic regions: (1) Sumatra;

(2) Java and Bali; (3) Kalimantan; and (4) Sulawesi, Papua, Maluku and Nusa Tenggara (that is, eastern Indonesia). Sumatra, Java, Kalimantan, Sulawesi and Papua are the five largest islands in Indonesia. They have diverse cultures, languages and socio-economic characteristics.[2] All except Papua have at least one large urban enclave of rural–urban migrants. One of the largest enclaves in each region was chosen for the survey, taking into consideration survey costs and the availability of local staff. Information on the concentration of migrants was drawn from the 2005 intercensal population survey (Survei Penduduk Antar Sensus, or Supas). The location of the four cities is shown in Figure 1.2 on page 5 of this book.

Definition of a Rural–Urban Migrant

The Supas is a nationally representative, cross-sectional household survey. It is conducted every 10 years between two censuses. The last three censuses were conducted in 1980, 1990 and 2000; the last three intercensal surveys were conducted in 1985, 1995 and 2005. The Supas provides information on residence at time of birth for all individuals, and residence five years previously for individuals aged six or above.

Information from the Supas allows us to distinguish between two types of migrant households: long-term and short-term. A long-term migrant is someone whose current residential area is different from his or her birth area.[3] If the birth area of that person is rural, then the person is classified as a long-term rural–urban migrant. A short-term migrant is someone whose current residential area is different from his or her residential area five years ago. If the residential area of that person five years previously is classified as rural, then the person is considered a short-term rural–urban migrant.

The distinction between urban and rural areas is based on the classification provided by the central statistics agency, Statistics Indonesia, in 2005. Based on population density, the proportion of households engaged in agriculture, the availability and quality of infrastructure and other socio-economic characteristics (Surbakti 1995), the agency defines an area as being either a rural district (*kabupaten*) or an urban municipality (*kota*) (Statistics Indonesia 2006).

The characteristics of migrants can be refined further by considering the age at which a person leaves the place of origin and the degree of attachment to it. For example, an individual who was born in a rural area and moved to an urban area after just a few months or years might well be indistinguishable in skills and experience from an individual born in an urban area. Based on this consideration, the RUMiI study collected information on whether an individual had lived in a rural area for a total of five years or longer before graduating from primary school. The study also obtained information on past residence, the frequency of visits to the area of origin and the amount of time spent there, to allow comparison of the different ways of defining migrants. In analysis based on the Supas, however, the definition has to be based on past residence, because this is the only source of data available.

Individuals residing in places other than residential buildings are excluded from the Supas, and from our survey. The Supas enumerates households residing in legal residential buildings; thus, it would not cover people living in temporary dwellings or non-residential buildings.[4] Our sampling framework is based on the same list of households as that used for the Supas, so this applies to our survey as well.

The rural/urban classification provided by Statistics Indonesia provides a rough indicator of the rural/urban status of an individual's community (village) of origin when that person left the community. Of course, it is possible that an area's status may have changed over time, or that a rural area contains some urban communities (and vice versa). However, in the absence of community-level information on past place of residence in the Supas, or the capacity to establish the exact rural/urban status of every area in the year of birth of each individual, we rely on the 2005 Statistics Indonesia definition. To the extent that municipalities may have contained rural communities when individuals left their area of origin, the estimated number of rural–urban migrant households is likely to provide a lower bound for the estimated number of rural–urban migrants.

Enclaves of Migrants in Four Regions

Estimates founded on the residence-based definitions of long-term and short-term migrants indicate that long-term rural–urban migrants comprise a significant proportion of the urban population, and short-term rural–urban migrants a relatively small proportion (see Table 11.1). Of the 44 million individuals living in municipalities in 2005, 16 million (36 per cent) were long-term migrants (their area of birth was outside their current area of residence). Of these, 11 million people (67 per cent of all long-term migrants, or 24 per cent of the total urban population) were born in areas that were considered rural in 2005, making them long-term rural–urban migrants. These estimates suggest that around one in four urban residents is from a rural area. Of the 40 million individuals aged six or above in 2005, 3 million (8 per cent) had lived in a different area five years previously, forming a group of short-term migrants. Of these, 2 million (61 per cent of all short-term migrants, or 5 per cent of the total urban population aged six or above) had lived in a rural area five years previously, making them short-term rural–urban migrants.[5]

As Table 11.1 indicates, Java/Bali absorbs large numbers of short-term and long-term migrants, reflecting its high share of the total population. In 2005 the region had a population of 27.5 million (62 per cent of the total urban

Table 11.1 Indonesia: Distribution of Long-term and Short-term Migrants by Region, 2005[a]

Region	Total Population in Urban Areas	Long-term Migrants				Urban Population Aged 6+	Short-term Migrants			
		Migrants[b]		Rural–Urban Migrants[c]			Migrants[d]		Rural–Urban Migrants[e]	
	(no.)	(no.)	(%)	(no.)	(%)	(no.)	(no.)	(%)	(no.)	(%)
Java & Bali	27,409,290	10,040,589	36.6	6,570,415	24.0	25,182,585	2,007,422	8.0	1,196,742	4.8
Sumatra	9,516,854	3,101,800	32.6	2,034,105	21.4	8,599,925	740,977	8.6	421,451	4.9
Kalimantan	2,902,837	1,163,982	40.1	851,035	29.3	2,611,588	207,629	8.0	134,615	5.2
Eastern Indonesia[f]	4,434,862	1,610,492	36.3	1,263,075	28.5	3,977,781	335,331	8.4	239,803	6.0
Indonesia	**44,263,843**	**15,916,863**	**36.0**	**10,718,630**	**24.2**	**40,371,879**	**3,291,359**	**8.2**	**1,992,611**	**4.9**

a The total population is estimated based on the weights provided in the Supas. The distinction between an urban area (*kota*) and a rural area (*kabupaten*) follows the 2005 classification developed by Statistics Indonesia.

b Individuals in urban areas whose birth area is different from their current residential area.

c Individuals in urban areas whose birth area is different from their current residential area *and* the birth area is rural.

d Individuals in urban areas whose residential area five years previously is different from the current residential area.

e Individuals in urban areas whose residential area five years previously is different from the current residential area *and* the residential area five years previously is rural.

f Sulawesi, Papua, Maluku and Nusa Tenggara.

Source: 2005 Supas; Statistics Indonesia (2006).

population), including 6.5 million long-term migrants from rural areas (61 per cent of all long-term rural–urban migrants) and 1.2 million short-term migrants from rural areas (60 per cent of all short-term rural–urban migrants). Sumatra was the second-largest region with a population of 9.5 million (22 per cent of the total urban population) in 2005. This included 2 million long-term rural–urban migrants (19 per cent of all long-term rural–urban migrants) and 421,000 short-term rural–urban migrants (21 per cent of all short-term rural–urban migrants). That is, in both regions the number of rural–urban migrants was roughly proportional to the region's share of the total urban population. Kalimantan and eastern Indonesia had far fewer inhabitants: only 3 million (7 per cent of the total urban population) in the case of Kalimantan and 4 million (10 per cent of the total urban population) in the case of eastern Indonesia. However, with more than 851,000 and 1.2 million long-term rural–urban migrants respectively, both had slightly higher shares of this group of migrants relative to total population than the other two regions—at least 28 per cent, compared with 24 per cent or less for Java/Bali and Sumatra.

The results from the Supas confirmed that each region had a major enclave of migrants from rural areas.[6] In Java, the five municipalities that make up the capital, Jakarta, had 2.4 million long-term and 430,000 short-term migrants from rural areas in 2005. Medan, the largest enclave in Sumatra, had 275,000 long-term and 55,000 short-term rural–urban migrants. The next largest was Batam, with 222,000 long-term and 70,000 short-term migrants. The largest enclave in Kalimantan was Samarinda, which had 189,000 long-term and 29,000 short-term migrants from rural areas. The next largest was Balikpapan, which had 144,000 long-term and 25,000 short-term rural–urban migrants. Among the eastern Indonesian islands, one municipality stood out as a major enclave: Makassar with 331,000 long-term and 82,000 short-term migrants of rural origin.

In most cases, the largest enclave in each region was selected for the survey: Medan in Sumatra, Samarinda in Kalimantan and Makassar in eastern Indonesia. The exception was Tangerang in Java, which had a smaller number of rural–urban migrants than some Jakarta municipalities. But although the capital absorbed the largest number of migrants, the cost of conducting a survey there was expected to be high, and the neighbouring municipality of Tangerang was considered a good substitute. Tangerang is the eighth largest enclave in Java, with 348,000 long-term and 65,000 short-term migrants from rural areas. Many of them are likely to work in Jakarta, and probably share some characteristics with migrants living in the capital. These four municipalities—Medan, Samarinda, Makassar and Tangerang—together with the capital city of Jakarta cover 33 per cent of all long-term and short-term migrants of rural origin in Indonesia.

3   THE PRE-SURVEY LISTING

For each of the selected municipalities, we obtained the list of households in randomly selected census blocks prepared by Statistics Indonesia for enumeration of the 2007 National Socio-Economic Survey (Survei Sosial Ekonomi Nasional, or Susenas).[7] The Susenas is a large-scale, nationally representative, repeated cross-section survey conducted since the 1960s. A census block is a group of residential segments with some clear borders, each containing about 100 dwellings. Every year, Statistics Indonesia selects about 12 per cent of the census blocks and conducts interviews with 16 households in each block.

Statistics Indonesia regularly updates its information on households residing in the selected census blocks, so the 2007 Susenas list gave us access to recent information on residents in the municipalities to be surveyed. Our sampling frame consisted not only of households interviewed for the Susenas, but all households in the selected census blocks. In Tangerang, we added the list of households living in surrounding areas, because the municipality contained fewer households than the other three municipalities. Many of the individuals in the additional households would have worked in Tangerang even though they did not live there. Altogether, the 2007 Susenas list yielded information on 20,682 households for our four survey sites. The top row of Table 11.2 provides a breakdown across the four municipalities.

Because the Susenas list does not contain information on the migration status of household heads, we conducted a pre-survey listing to obtain this information. The objective was to classify households into three groups according to the migration status of the head: (1) non-migrant households;[8] (2) recent rural–urban migrant households (those that had arrived in an urban area within the last five years); and (3) lifetime rural–urban migrant households (those that had lived in an urban area for more than five years). There were two main reasons for separating recently arrived households from other rural–urban migrant households. First, we felt that recent migrants were likely to exhibit more dynamic changes during the five years of the study. And second, we intend to compare this group of migrants with a similar group of Chinese migrants during the course of the study. However, recently arrived migrants are a relatively small group, as the 2005 Supas shows. We hoped to overcome this difficulty by separating recent from lifetime migrants and oversampling the former group to facilitate the statistical analysis.

The rural versus urban status of a household was decided on the basis of three questions in the pre-survey listing. The first question was: 'Did the household head live in a village (rural area) for a total of five years before the completion of primary school?' 'Village' in this case was subjective: if the household head regarded the place of origin as a rural area and answered 'yes', then the household was counted as a rural–urban migrant household; if

Table 11.2 Indonesia: Results of the Pre-survey Listing by City[a]

	Medan (no.)	(%)	Tangerang (no.)	(%)	Samarinda (no.)	(%)	Makassar (no.)	(%)	Total (no.)	(%)
Total no. of households	**5,363**	**100.0**	**6,416**	**100.0**	**4,568**	**100.0**	**4,335**	**100.0**	**20,682**	**100.0**
No. of households not contacted	914	17.0	916	14.3	410	9.0	760	17.5	3,000	14.5
Reason for not being contacted										
Dwelling & name of household head was repeated in the sampling frame	19	0.4	65	1.0	1	0.0	3	0.1	88	0.4
Dwelling or household could not be found	191	3.6	451	7.0	30	0.7	74	1.7	746	3.6
Dwelling was non-residential	28	0.5	0	0.0	0	0.0	5	0.1	33	0.2
Dwelling was not occupied	371	6.9	316	4.9	300	6.6	476	11.0	1,463	7.1
Resident could not be contacted	180	3.4	65	1.0	63	1.4	200	4.6	508	2.5
Resident refused to be interviewed	122	2.3	0	0.0	16	0.4	1	0.0	139	0.7
Unclear	3	0.1	19	0.3	0	0.0	1	0.0	23	0.1
No. of households that had lived in the area for less than one month	4	0.1	6	0.1	2	0.0	20	0.5	32	0.2
No. of households that had lived in the area for more than one month	4,445	82.9	5,494	85.6	4,156	91.0	3,555	82.0	17,650	85.3
Non-migrant	2,692	60.6	2,785	50.7	1,547	37.2	1,715	48.2	8,739	49.5
Lifetime migrant	1,685	37.9	2,166	39.4	2,386	57.4	1,331	37.4	7,568	42.9
Recent migrant	68	1.5	543	9.9	223	5.4	509	14.3	1,343	7.6

a Non-migrant households are those whose household head did not spend a total of five years in a rural area before finishing primary school. Among migrant households, lifetime migrant households are those whose household head had lived in the municipality for more than five years, and recent migrant households are those whose household head had arrived in the municipality within the previous five years. See the text for more detail.

Source: Rural–Urban Migration in Indonesia survey, 2008.

the household head regarded it as an urban area and answered 'no', then the household was not counted as a rural–urban migrant household. Rural–urban migrant households were then asked the following two questions: 'How long (years and months) has the household head lived in this municipality?', and 'How long (years and months) has the household head lived in any municipality, including this municipality?' If the head had lived in either the current municipality or some other municipality for more than five years, then the household was categorized as a lifetime rural–urban migrant household. If the head had lived in a municipality for less than five years, then the household was classified as a recent rural–urban migrant household. In the small number of cases where the head of a rural–urban migrant household had arrived in the urban area within the previous month, and therefore may have been residing there only temporarily, the household was excluded from the sample.

Of the 20,682 households on the 2007 Susenas list, we were able to obtain information on the migration status of 17,682 households, or 86 per cent (Table 11.2). The other 3,000 households could not be contacted for a variety of reasons: 746 (about a quarter) because the information on household name and address was unclear;[9] 1,463 (about half) because the dwelling was unoccupied;[10] 508 (17 per cent) because the resident could not be located;[11] and 139 (5 per cent) because the resident refused to be interviewed. Most of the latter cases were in Medan, where field observation suggested that many Chinese households declined to be interviewed. Overall, however, refusal was not a significant cause of no contact.

After excluding 32 households whose head had lived in the municipality for less than one month, we were left with 17,650 households as the basis of the sample. About half of these households could be classified as rural–urban migrant households. Of these, 15 per cent (8 per cent of the total sample) were recent migrant households.

4   SAMPLING

The study aimed to obtain a sample of about 2,500 migrant and non-migrant households. To maximize the accuracy of the estimates, we hoped to obtain roughly equal sample sizes for non-migrants, lifetime migrants and recent migrants in each of the four cities. However, the listing results suggested that we would fall short of the target for recent migrants in Medan. Also, we had already allocated more local staff to the two larger cities, Medan and Tangerang, in the expectation that they would have more heterogeneous populations.[12] Based on these factors, the sample was allocated as indicated in Table 11.3. The main (target) sample for all four cities was 918 non-migrants, 918 lifetime migrants and 664 recent migrants. The target samples for Samarinda

Table 11.3 *Indonesia: Allocation of the Sample by City*[a]

	Medan	Tangerang	Samarinda	Makassar		Total
Non-migrant households						
Sampling frame	2,692	2,785	1,547	1,715		8,739
Training sample	14	12	8	8		42
Main sample	303	250	183	182		918
Reserve sample[b]	61	50	37	36		184
Lifetime migrant households						
Sampling frame	1,685	2,166	2,386	1,331		7,568
Training sample	14	12	8	8		42
Main sample	303	250	183	182		918
Reserve sample[b]	61	50	37	36		184
Recent migrant households				1 Member[c]	2+ Members[c]	
Sampling frame	68	543	223	269	240	1,343
Training sample	4	12	8	2	6	32
Main sample	54	250	178	34	148	664
Reserve sample[b]	10	150	36	7	29	232

a   See the notes to Table 11.2 for a definition of non-migrant, lifetime migrant and recent migrant households.

b   The reserve sample (20 per cent of the main sample) was used if all households in the main sample had been visited but the number of households interviewed still fell well below the target sample size for each municipality and migration category. The reserve sample was increased to 60 per cent of the main sample for recent migrant households in Tangerang in order to supplement the sample size for this migration category.

c   The sample of recent migrant households in Makassar was divided into single and multiple-member households to take account of the disproportionately high number of students in the city, most of them single and living alone. This group could provide only limited information on labour market activities and the well-being of household members, including children. Households with more than one member, which were unlikely to be student households, were oversampled.

Source: Rural–Urban Migration in Indonesia survey, 2008.

231

and Makassar were around 180 households in each of the three migration categories, while the target sample for Tangerang was 250 in each category. Because of the small number of recent migrant households in Medan, a target sample of 54 households was allocated to this category, with a larger sample of 303 assigned to the other two migration categories.

In addition to the main sample, a reserve sample (in most cases 20 per cent for each group) was drawn up, to be used if the number of interviews fell short of the target due to refusal or some other interview failure. Also, to increase the size of the recent migrant sample, the reserve sample of recent migrant households in Tangerang (the largest source of recent migrants) was increased to 60 per cent of the target sample. Another modification to the basic sampling framework was required in Makassar. Pilot tests and local knowledge told us that a high proportion of recently arrived single migrants were likely to be students, a group of limited interest to us because of the study's focus on labour market analysis.[13] Also, we wanted to avoid the problem of high levels of attrition that would result if a large number of the students moved to Jakarta or some other large city to work during the five years of the survey—a common choice among students living in Makassar. We therefore decided to divide recent migrant households in this municipality into single-member and multiple-member households, and undersample the former group.

Tables 11.4–11.6 show the number of households in the sampling frame, and the number approached for interview (visited), for each of the three migration categories. The number of households visited varied across cities and migration categories. In Makassar, only the main sample was used for non-migrant and lifetime migrant households (Tables 11.4 and 11.5 respectively), because the target sample sizes were more or less reached. However, both the main and reserve samples were used for recent migrant households (Table 11.6), because many households listed as recent migrants turned out to have been listed incorrectly. In Medan, both the main and reserve samples as well as the training sample were used for all migration categories, mainly to increase the sample size for recent migrant households.[14] In the other two municipalities, the main and reserve samples were used for all categories.

The initial sampling factor was computed for each migration category and municipality as the number of households visited divided by the number of households in the sampling frame. The attempt to attain a similar sample size across groups of differing migration status resulted in a higher sampling factor for migrant—particularly recent migrant—households. In Medan, for instance, the sampling factor was 0.14 for non-migrant households, 0.22 for lifetime migrant households and 1.00 for recent migrant households. Recent migrant households had the highest between-municipality gap in the sampling factor, ranging from 0.15 for single-member households in Makassar to 1.00 in Medan, where all households in the base population were included in the sample.

The overall response rate (the number of households interviewed divided by the number of households visited) was 79 per cent for non-migrant households (Table 11.4), 82 per cent for lifetime migrant households (Table 11.5) and 71 per cent for recent migrant households (Table 11.6). In the case of recently arrived migrants, it ranged from 46 per cent in Medan to 95 per cent for single-member households in Makassar.

Some households were not interviewed because a dwelling could not be found, its residents had died or moved away, or its residents were temporarily away and enumerators were unable to contact them after three visits. The combined share of such cases ranged from 11 per cent (for lifetime migrants) to 16 per cent (for recent migrants), with Samarinda having a relatively high proportion of interview failures for these three reasons. There were a few cases where the household consisted of an elderly person who was unable to answer questions. Outright refusal to be interviewed was rare: 3–5 per cent of households in each category refused to be interviewed, with the highest rates of refusal recorded among migrant households (both lifetime and recent) in Makassar.

Some households were not interviewed because their migration status was inconsistent with the status recorded in the listing. It seems likely that the information was incorrect because it was obtained from household members or neighbours who did not know the full migration history of the household head. The protocol adopted by the enumerator in such cases—and therefore the probability of such a household being interviewed—differed across municipalities. In Samarinda and Makassar, households were interviewed regardless of whether or not their migration status was consistent with the status recorded in the listing. In Medan and Tangerang, households whose migration status was recorded incorrectly in the listing, and that were revealed to be non-migrant or lifetime migrant households, were not interviewed. However, households confirmed as being recent migrant households *were* interviewed because of the scarcity of households in this category. Based on the principle that all households in the sample should be interviewed, in 2009 we revisited the households in Medan and Tangerang whose interviews had been terminated and collected information from them.

Among households that were asked about their migration status in 2008, the proportion whose migration status was confirmed as being correct was 86 per cent for non-migrant households, 83 per cent for lifetime migrant households and 68 per cent recent migrant households.[15]

5   SURVEY ORGANIZATION AND TIMELINE

Both the pre-survey listing and the main survey were conducted by the Indonesia Field Survey Project team established within the Faculty of Social and

Table 11.4 *Indonesia: Non-migrant Households Visited and Interviewed by City*[a]

	Medan	Tangerang	Samarinda	Makassar	Total
No. of households in the sampling frame (A)	**2,692**	**2,785**	**1,547**	**1,715**	**8,739**
No. of households visited (B)[b]	378	300	220	182	1,080
Sampling factor ((B) / (A))	0.140	0.108	0.142	0.106	0.124
No. of households not interviewed (C)	79	52	83	16	230
((C) / (B), %)	(20.9)	(17.3)	(37.7)	(8.8)	(21.3)
Reason for not being interviewed					
Dwelling not found	3	7	15	1	26
(%)	(0.8)	(2.3)	(6.8)	(0.5)	(2.4)
Household members died or moved away	38	4	0	1	43
(%)	(10.1)	(1.3)	(0.0)	(0.5)	(4.0)
Household members not found (temporarily away or other reason)	11	4	66	2	83
(%)	(2.9)	(1.3)	(30.0)	(1.1)	(7.7)
Interview was terminated because respondent was elderly	1	0	0	0	1
(%)	(0.3)	(0.0)	(0.0)	(0.0)	(0.1)
Respondent refused to be interviewed	14	21	2	12	49
(%)	(3.7)	(7.0)	(0.9)	(6.6)	(4.5)
Listing-based migration status was incorrect (D)	12	16	0	0	28
(%)[c]	(3.2)	(5.3)	(0.0)	(0.0)	(2.6)
True status = non-migrant	0	0	0	0	0
True status = lifetime migrant	12	16	0	0	28
True status = recent migrant	0	0	0	0	0

No. of households interviewed (E)	299	248	137	166	850
Overall response rate ((E) / (B), %)	(79.1)	(82.7)	(62.3)	(91.2)	(78.7)
No. of households correctly identified in the listing & interviewed (actual status = non-migrant) (F)	277	247	109	124	757
(% among households visited, (F) / (B))	(73.3)	(82.3)	(49.5)	(68.1)	(70.1)
(% among households for which migration status was asked, (F) / [(D) + (E)])	(89.1)	(93.6)	(79.6)	(74.7)	(86.2)
No. of households incorrectly identified in the listing & interviewed (actual status = lifetime migrant) (G)	19	1	24	35	79
(% among households visited, (G) / (B))	(5.0)	(0.3)	(10.9)	(19.2)	(7.3)
(% among households for which migration status was asked, (G) / [(D) + (E)])	(6.1)	(0.4)	(17.5)	(21.1)	(9.0)
No. of households incorrectly identified in the listing & interviewed (actual status = recent migrant) (H)c	3	0	4	7	14
(% among households visited, (H) / (B))	(0.8)	(0.0)	(1.8)	(3.8)	(1.3)
(% among households for which migration status was asked, (H) / [(D) + (E)])	(1.0)	(0.0)	(2.9)	(4.2)	(1.6)

a See the notes to Table 11.2 for a definition of non-migrant, lifetime migrant and recent migrant households.

b The number of households visited was either the entire main sample or the main sample plus the reserve sample. Where the target sample size in a certain municipality and migration category was reached after visiting all households in the main sample, the reserve sample was not used. Both the main and the reserve samples were drawn randomly at the same time.

c In Medan and Tangerang, some households were not interviewed because their migration status was recorded incorrectly in the listing. These households were revisited in the second (2009) round of the survey, so data from future waves of the survey will not be affected by this type of interview failure.

Source: Rural–Urban Migration in Indonesia survey, 2008.

Table 11.5 Indonesia: Lifetime Migrant Households Visited and Interviewed by City[a]

	Medan	Tangerang	Samarinda	Makassar	Total
No. of households in the sampling frame (A)	**1,685**	**2,166**	**2,386**	**1,331**	**7,568**
No. of households visited (B)	378	300	220	182	1,080
Sampling factor ((B) / (A))	0.224	0.139	0.092	0.137	0.143
No. of households not interviewed (C)	68	49	59	20	196
((C) / (B), %)	(18.0)	(16.3)	(26.8)	(11.0)	(18.1)
Reason for not being interviewed					
Dwelling not found	6	15	7	2	30
(%)	(1.6)	(5.0)	(3.2)	(1.1)	(2.8)
Household members died or moved away	20	2	3	1	26
(%)	(5.3)	(0.7)	(1.4)	(0.5)	(2.4)
Household members not found (temporarily away or other reason)	10	1	44	4	59
(%)	(2.6)	(0.3)	(20.0)	(2.2)	(5.5)
Interview was terminated because respondent was elderly	6	1	0	0	7
(%)	(1.6)	(0.3)	(0.0)	(0.0)	(0.6)
Respondent refused to be interviewed	14	14	5	13	46
(%)	(3.7)	(4.7)	(2.3)	(7.1)	(4.3)
Listing-based migration status was incorrect (D)	12	16	0	0	28
(%)	(3.2)	(5.3)	(0.0)	(0.0)	(2.6)
True status = non-migrant	12	16	0	0	28
True status = lifetime migrant	0	0	0	0	0
True status = recent migrant	0	0	0	0	0

No. of households interviewed (E)	310	251	161	162	884
Overall response rate ((E) / (B), %)	(82.0)	(83.7)	(73.2)	(89.0)	(81.9)
No. of households incorrectly identified in the listing & interviewed (actual status = non-migrant) (F)	25	1	49	40	115
(% among households visited, (F) / (B))	(6.6)	(0.3)	(22.3)	(22.0)	(10.6)
(% among households for which migration status was asked, (F) / [(D) + (E)])	(7.8)	(0.4)	(30.4)	(24.7)	(12.6)
No. of households correctly identified in the listing & interviewed (actual status = lifetime migrant) (G)	285	245	108	114	752
(% among households visited, (G) / (B))	(75.4)	(81.7)	(49.1)	(62.6)	(69.6)
(% among households for which migration status was asked, (G) / [(D) + (E)])	(88.5)	(91.8)	(67.1)	(70.4)	(82.5)
No. of households incorrectly identified in the listing & interviewed (actual status = recent migrant) (H)	0	5	4	8	17
(% among households visited, (H) / (B))	(0.0)	(1.7)	(1.8)	(4.4)	(1.6)
(% among households for which migration status was asked, (H) / [(D) + (E)])	(0.0)	(1.9)	(2.5)	(4.9)	(1.9)

a   See the notes to Table 11.4 for a description of the number of households visited and interviewed.

Source: Rural–Urban Migration in Indonesia survey, 2008.

Table 11.6 Indonesia: Recent Migrant Households Visited and Interviewed by Region[a]

	Medan	Tangerang	Samarinda	Makassar 1 Member	Makassar 2+ Members	Total
No. of households in the sampling frame (A)	**68**	**543**	**223**	**269**	**240**	**1,343**
No. of households visited (B)	68	400	214	41	177	900
Sampling factor ((B) / (A))	1.000	0.737	0.960	0.152	0.738	0.670
No. of households not interviewed (C)	37	149	62	2	13	263
((C) / (B), %)	(54.4)	(37.3)	(29.0)	(4.9)	(7.3)	(29.2)
Reason for not being interviewed						
Dwelling not found	2	51	1	0	2	56
(%)	(2.9)	(12.8)	(0.5)	(0.0)	(1.1)	(6.2)
Household members died or moved away	12	8	3	0	0	23
(%)	(17.6)	(2.0)	(1.4)	(0.0)	(0.0)	(2.6)
Household member not found (temporarily away or other reason)	2	2	57	0	0	61
(%)	(2.9)	(0.5)	(26.6)	(0.0)	(0.0)	(6.8)
Interview was terminated because respondent was elderly	0	0	0	0	0	0
(%)	(0.0)	(0.0)	(0.0)	(0.0)	(0.0)	(0.0)
Respondent refused to be interviewed	0	16	1	2	11	30
(%)	(0.0)	(4.0)	(0.5)	(4.9)	(6.2)	(3.3)
Listing-based migration status was incorrect (D)	21	72	0	0	0	93
(%)	(30.9)	(18.0)	(0.0)	(0.0)	(0.0)	(10.3)

True status = non-migrant	8	3	0	0	0	11
True status = lifetime migrant	13	69	0	0	0	82
True status = recent migrant	0	0	0	0	0	0
No. of households interviewed (E)	**31**	**251**	**152**	**39**	**164**	**637**
Overall response rate ((E) / (B), %)	(45.6)	(62.8)	(71.0)	(95.1)	(92.7)	(70.8)
No. of households incorrectly identified in the listing & interviewed (actual status = non-migrant) (F)	**0**	**0**	**31**	**4**	**10**	**45**
(% among households visited, (F) / (B))	(0.0)	(0.0)	(14.5)	(9.8)	(5.6)	(5.0)
(% among households for which migration status was asked, (F) / [(D) + (E)])	(0.0)	(0.0)	(20.4)	(10.3)	(6.1)	(6.2)
No. of households incorrectly identified in the listing & interviewed (actual status = lifetime migrant) (G)	**3**	**3**	**50**	**2**	**37**	**95**
(% among households visited, (G) / (B))	(4.4)	(0.8)	(23.4)	(4.9)	(20.9)	(10.6)
(% among households for which migration status was asked, (G) / [(D) + (E)])	(5.8)	(0.9)	(32.9)	(5.1)	(22.6)	(13.0)
No. of households correctly identified in the listing & interviewed (actual status = recent migrant) (H)	**28**	**248**	**71**	**33**	**117**	**497**
(% among households visited, (H) / (B))	(41.2)	(62.0)	(33.2)	(80.5)	(66.1)	(55.2)
(% among households for which migration status was asked, (H) / [(D) + (E)])	(53.8)	(76.8)	(46.7)	(84.6)	(71.3)	(68.1)

a   See the notes to Table 11.4 for a description of the number of households visited and interviewed.

Source: Rural–Urban Migration in Indonesia survey, 2008.

Political Sciences at Gadjah Mada University, Yogyakarta. This team super-
vised the regional teams established in each of the four municipalities to be
surveyed. Each regional team consisted of a regional coordinator from Gadjah
Mada University, supervisors, field supervisors, enumerators and data entry
staff. The supervisors and enumerators were mainly lecturers, research staff
and students from local universities or research agencies.

The general timeline of the survey was as follows. The questionnaire for
the pre-survey listing and main survey was designed between March 2007 and
February 2008. During this period, Indonesia Field Survey Project staff tested
the questionnaire in Yogyakarta and the survey cities, prepared documentation
(such as a questionnaire manual) and developed survey and data entry protocols. They also carried out two pilot studies in which the main survey was
implemented on a small scale in each of the four municipalities.

Field preparation for the pre-survey listing and main survey began in the
middle of 2007 and continued until early 2008. This included observation of
procedures in the field and supervisor training. The 2007 Susenas list of households was obtained, to be used as the sampling frame. The pre-survey listing
was implemented in January 2008.

The main survey was conducted between March and May 2008 following
set protocols on data collection and quality control. Enumerators were given a
list of the households to be visited together with a map of the area, and asked to
contact their field supervisors by SMS if they struck problems. All interviews
were subject to validation by supervisors. Data entry was controlled by a CS-
Pro program, to ensure a logical flow of data entry and to identify extraordi-
nary outliers (such as a respondent age of 150).

6 QUESTIONNAIRE

The purpose of the RUMiCI study is to gather rich information on labour market characteristics, poverty, health and educational attainment in China and
Indonesia, enabling a wide range of analyses and comparisons. The questionnaire developed for Indonesia consisted of six sections. The first concerned
migration status and household composition. The questions in this section
allowed enumerators to check the household's actual migration status against
its listing-based migration status. The second section consisted of a household
roster, to ascertain the basic socio-economic and demographic characteristics of all household members. The third section inquired into labour market
activities, migration history, migrants' links with and activities in the village
of origin, and labour protection and social security. The questions on labour
market activity identified five categories of workers: (1) salaried employees /
wage workers in the private sector; (2) civil servants (including military and

police); (3) self-employed workers; (4) individuals working for a family business without payment; and (5) unemployed persons or those outside the labour force. The fourth section asked about household income, consumption, assets, liabilities and housing. The questions in this section were quite detailed, to allow an accurate estimate of household welfare. The fifth section asked about the dwelling in the place of origin, the type of identity card held in the current residential municipality, and residents' social networks. The last section was about mental health.

Institutional differences between China and Indonesia are reflected in some features of the questionnaire. For example, in Indonesia it is common for workers, particularly migrant workers, to hold several jobs at once. To capture this characteristic of the labour force, the Indonesian questionnaire asked individuals who held multiple jobs to list all their jobs. It also contained procedures to decide the main job of these individuals. To better understand the characteristics of a worker's main job, the section on labour market activities was expanded to five categories, rather than the three—salaried employees / wage workers, self-employed and unemployed—used in the Chinese survey. In particular, the Indonesian survey separated civil servants from other wage workers on the basis that these two groups receive very different levels of benefits. Unpaid work by family members was also distinguished, because this is distinct from self-employment or wage work, yet crucial for households involved in small-scale enterprises. On the other hand, some information explored in the Chinese questionnaire was not covered by the Indonesian questionnaire. This included information on the siblings and parents of a household head and that person's spouse, and on life events such as births, deaths and marriages.

While carrying out the survey, we found that some of the more subjective and hypothetical questions required additional explanation. Examples included perceptions of the level of income before and after a respondent moved to an urban area, of the wage an unemployed person would have been able to earn had he or she been employed, and of mental health. Some respondents did not understand some of the questions or the reasons for asking them. Also, the responses to some questions appeared to be affected by a measurement error. For instance, while information on both itemized and total expenditure was collected, there were inconsistencies between the two sets of data in some cases. Lessons learned from these issues were incorporated in the design of the questionnaire for the second wave of the survey.

7 CONCLUSION

This chapter has reviewed the basic design of the Indonesia component of the RUMiCI study, including the selection of survey cities, listing and sampling procedures, the organizational structure and timeframe of the survey, and the structure of the questionnaire. The study design provides the basis for a unique, large-scale, longitudinal study of rural–urban migrants in Indonesia and China. Preliminary analysis of the 2008 data, discussed in the other chapters of this book, indicates the broad scope of the analysis enabled by the data. We plan to track as many of the migrant and non-migrant households in the initial sample as possible in the coming years. Data from future rounds of the survey should provide us with additional information to analyse the welfare and behaviour of migrants. In particular, the data will straddle important events such as the 2008–09 global financial crisis, the 2009 Indonesian elections and the socio-economic changes flowing from these events. The RUMiCI study will provide original information on rural–urban migrants, who may be particularly vulnerable to economic shocks and social change.

NOTES

1   The prevalence of circular, seasonal and other types of temporary migration is high in Indonesia (Hugo 1982). To the extent that these types of migrants do not reside in residential structures or register with the relevant local authority, they are less likely to be included in the study.

2   See Cribb (2000) for a historical treatment of the demographic, socio-cultural and economic diversity of Indonesia at the subnational level.

3   These migrants are often referred to as 'lifetime' migrants in the Indonesian context. However, we reserve the use of this term for the specific sense in which it is used later in this chapter.

4   A number of special procedures were introduced in the 2000 census to try and include as many squatters and people living in temporary dwellings as possible. However, Hull (2001) reports difficulties in enumerating some of these migrants because they were reluctant to cooperate with the enumerators.

5   Migrants who had moved from one municipality to another municipality accounted for 33 per cent of long-term migrants and 39 per cent of short-term migrants. It is of interest, but outside the scope of this study, to compare urban–urban and rural–urban migrants.

6   The figures in this section are based on the tables in Resosudarmo, Yamauchi and Effendi (2009).

7   See Surbakti (1995) for a history of the development of the Susenas.

8   The non-migrant category included households that had migrated from another urban area to the urban area in which the household head was currently residing.

9   The most common problems were missing street numbers and the use of abbreviations (or nicknames) for the surname of the household head. Some names are very common in certain areas; Sundanese names such as Cecep and Ujang are often found in West Java, for example, and Daeng is common in Makassar. When both the address and the name of the household head were unclear, it was difficult for the enumerator to identify the listed household. There was a relatively large number of such cases in Tangerang, where the rapid growth of the municipality may have been accompanied by frequent movement of residents and changes in neighbourhood structure.

10 If a dwelling appeared to be unoccupied, the enumerator was instructed to ask the neighbours about the whereabouts of the household. In some cases neighbours confirmed that no one was resident at the address; in others, neighbours did not know whether or not the dwelling was occupied.

11   If a dwelling appeared to be occupied but no one was home, the enumerator was instructed to ask the neighbours about the whereabouts of the household. Some neighbours did not know the household on the Susenas list and could not say whether there was a new resident; some were able to tell us that the previous resident had died or moved away; some knew who was living in the dwelling but did not know the whereabouts of the residents; and some told us that the residents were temporarily away (on a business trip or holiday, for example).

12   The sample was initially allocated across the four cities according to population size, based on the expectation that the two larger cities, Medan (with a population of 2 million) and Tangerang (1.5 million), would have more heterogeneous migrant and non-migrant populations than Samarinda (574,000) and Makassar (1 million). However, later analysis of the 2000 census indicated that large cities did not necessarily have more heterogeneous populations.

13   The proportion of single-member recent migrant households in Makassar was 53 per cent, compared with 17 per cent for the survey's base population.

14   The samples selected for interview during the training period were extracted randomly from the base population together with the main and reserve samples. Thus, the whole sample still consisted of a randomly selected set of households. Inclusion of the training samples in the final dataset is being considered.

15   Weights are being analysed to take account of conventional non-response cases and the cases of households in Medan and Tangerang whose migration status was recorded incorrectly in the listing. That is, the initial sampling factor will be adjusted by incorporating the probability of a household being interviewed given the listing-based and survey-based migration status.

References

Abeyasekere, S. (1987), *Jakarta: A History*, Oxford University Press, Singapore.

All-China Women's Federation (2006), 'Quanguo nongcun liushou ertong gongzuo dianshi dianhua huiyi zaijing zhaokai' [National video conference on rural left-behind children], available at http://www.women.org.cn/manguage/big1.jsp?id=33853.

Athukorala, P. and C. Manning (1999), *Structural Change and International Migration in East Asia: Adjusting to Labour Scarcity*, Oxford University Press, Melbourne.

Au, Chun-Chung and V. Henderson (2006), 'How migration restrictions limit agglomeration and productivity in China', *Journal of Development Economics*, 80: 350–88.

Azis, I.J. (1997), 'The increasing role of the urban non-formal sector in Indonesia: employment analysis within a multisectoral framework', in G.W. Jones and P.M. Visaria (eds), *Urbanization in Large Developing Countries: China, Indonesia, Brazil, and India*, Clarendon Press, Oxford, pp. 109–10.

Bandiyono, S., Mudjiyani and S.S. Purwaningsih (2003), 'Pekerja migran di Kalimantan Timur [Migrant workers of East Kalimantan], Pusat Penelitian Kependudukan (PPK), Lembaga Ilmu Pengetahuan Indonesia (LIPI), Jakarta.

Batbaatar, M., T. Bold, J. Marshall, D. Oyuntsetseg, C. Tamir and G. Tumennast (2005), 'Children on the move: rural–urban migration and access to education in Mongolia', Report No. 17, Childhood Poverty Research and Policy Centre, available at http://www.childhoodpoverty.org/.

Benabou, R. (1993), 'Workings of a city: location, education, and production', *Quarterly Journal of Economics*, 108(3): 619–52.

Bilsborrow, R.E. (1998), *Migration, Urbanization, and Development*, Springer, New York NY.

Bilsborrow, R.E., A.S. Oberai and G. Standing (1984), *Migration Surveys in Low-income Countries: Guidelines for Survey and Questionnaire Design*, Routledge, London.

Bogin, B. and R.B. MacVean (1981), 'Biosocial effects of urban migration on the development of families and children in Guatemala', *American Journal of Public Health*, 71(12): 1,373–7.

Brown, R. (1991), *Society and Economy in Modern Britain, 1700–1850*, Routledge, London.

Budiono, S.H., G. Hart, G. Papanek and A. Partadiredja (1982), 'Technological change, productivity and employment in Indonesian agriculture: an analysis of annual agricultural surveys of the Central Statistical Office with regard to rice agriculture, particularly in Java/Bali', unpublished paper, Gadjah Mada University, USAID and Boston University, Yogyakarta.

Butzer, R., Y. Mundlak and D. Larson (2003), 'Intersectoral migration in Southeast Asia: evidence from Indonesia, Thailand and the Philippines', World Bank Policy Research Working Paper No. 2949, World Bank, Washington DC.

Chan, Emily Y.Y., Sian Griffiths, Yang Gao, Chok Wan Chan and Tai Fai Fok (2008), 'Addressing disparities in children's health in China', *Archives of Disease in Childhood*, 93: 346–52.

Chan, Kam Wing and Li Zhang (1999), 'The *hukou* system and rural–urban migration in China: processes and changes', *China Quarterly*, 160(December): 818–55.

Chan, Kam Wing, Ta Liu and Yunyan Yang (1999), '*Hukou* and non-*hukou* migration in China: comparisons and contrasts', *International Journal of Population and Geography*, 5: 425–48.

Chen, Shaohua and M. Ravallion (2008), 'China is poorer than we thought, but no less successful in the fight against poverty', World Bank Policy Research Working Paper No. 4621, World Bank, Washington DC.

Chen, Yi, S. Démurger and M. Fournier (2005), 'Earnings differentials and ownership structure in Chinese enterprises', *Economic Development and Cultural Change*, 53(4): 933–58.

Cheng, Tiejun and M. Selden (1994), 'The origins and social consequences of China's *hukou* system', *China Quarterly*, 139: 644–68.

Chun, Hyunbae and Injae Lee (2001), 'Why do married men earn more: productivity or marriage selection?', *Economic Inquiry*, 39(2): 307–19.

Collier, W.L., Soentoro, G. Wiradi, E. Pasandaran, K. Santoso and J.F. Stepanek (1982), 'Acceleration of rural development of Java', *Bulletin of Indonesian Economic Studies*, 18(3): 84–101.

Cribb, R. (2000), *An Historical Atlas of Indonesia*, University of Hawaii Press, Honolulu.

Davila, A. and M.T. Mora (2008), 'Changes in the relative earnings gap between natives and immigrants along the U.S.–Mexico border', *Journal of Regional Science*, 48(3): 525–45.

Davin, D. (1999), *Internal Migration in Contemporary China*, Palgrave Macmillan, New York NY.

Day, L. and Xia Ma (1994), *Migration and Urbanization in China*, M.E. Sharpe, Armonk NY.

de Brauw, A. and J. Giles (2006), 'Migrant opportunity and the educational attainment of youth in rural China', IZA Discussion Paper No. 2326, Institute for the Study of Labor (IZA), Bonn.

de Jonge, H. and G. Nooteboom (2006), 'Why the Madurese? Ethnic conflict in West and East Kalimantan compared', *Southeast Asian Journal of Social Science*, 34(3): 456–74.

Démurger, S., M. Fournier and Yi Chen (2005), 'The evolution of gender earnings gaps and discrimination in urban China: 1988–1995', HIEBS Working Paper No. 1116, University of Hong Kong, Hong Kong.

Démurger, S., M. Fournier and Li Shi (2006), 'Urban income inequality in China revisited (1988–2002)', *Economics Letters*, 93(3): 354–9.

Démurger, S., M. Gurgand, Li Shi and Yue Ximing (2009), 'Migrants as second-class workers in urban China? A decomposition analysis', *Journal of Comparative Economics*, 37(4): 610–28.

Deng, Quheng (2007), 'Chengzhen jumin yu liudong renkou de shouru chayi: jiyu Oax-aca-Blinder he quantile fangfa de fenjie' [The earnings differential between urban residents and rural migrants: evidence from Oaxaca–Blinder and quantile regression decompositions], *Chinese Journal of Population Science*, 2: 8–16.

Deng, Quheng and Li Shi (2009), 'What lies behind rising earnings inequality in urban China? Regression-based decompositions', *CESifo Economic Studies*, 55(3–4): 598–623.

Donges, J.B., B. Stecher and F. Wolter (1980), 'Industrialization in Indonesia', in G.F. Papanek (ed.), *The Indonesian Economy*, Praeger, New York NY, pp. 357 405.

Du, Yang (2000), 'Rural labor migration in contemporary China: an analysis of its fea-tures and the macro context', in L. West and Y. Zhao (eds), *Rural Labor Flows in China*, University of California Press, Berkeley CA, pp. 67–100.

Du, Yang, R. Gregory and Xin Meng (2006), 'The impact of the guest-worker system on poverty and the well-being of migrant workers in urban China', in R. Garnaut and L. Song (eds), *The Turning Point in China's Economic Development*, Asia Pacific Press, Canberra, pp. 172–202.

Du, Yang, A.F. Park and Sangui Wang (2005), 'Migration and rural poverty in China', *Journal of Comparative Economics*, 33(4): 688–709.

Dubey, A., R. Palmer-Jones and K. Sen (2006), 'Surplus labour, social structure, and rural to urban migration: evidence from Indian data', *European Journal of Develop-ment Research*, 18(1): 86–104.

Edwards, A.C. and M. Ureta (2003), 'International migration, remittances, and school-ing: evidence from El Salvador', *Journal of Development Economics*, 72: 429–61.

Effendi, T.N. (2000), 'Konflik dan kekerasan sosial' [Conflict and social violence], in *Pembangunan, Krisis dan Arah Reformasi* [Development, Crisis and *Reformasi*], Muhammadiyah University Press, Surakarta, pp. 175–86.

Fields, G. (1975), 'Rural–urban migration, urban unemployment and underemploy-ment, and job-search activity in LDCs', *Journal of Development Economics*, 2: 165–87.

Fields, G. (1982), 'Place-to-place migration in Colombia', *Economic Development and Cultural Change*, 30(3): 539–58.

Fields, G. (1998), 'Accounting for differences in income inequality', unpublished paper, Cornell University, New York NY.

Firman, T. (1997), 'Patterns and trends of urbanisation: a reflection of regional dispar-ity', in G. Jones and T. Hull (eds), *Indonesia Assessment: Population and Human Resources*, Institute of Southeast Asian Studies, Singapore, pp. 101–18.

Firman, T. (2004), 'Demographic and spatial patterns of Indonesia's recent urbanisa-tion', *Population, Space and Place*, 10: 421–34.

Firman, T., B. Kombaitan and P. Pradono (2007), 'The dynamics of Indonesia's urbani-sation, 1980–2006', *Urban Policy and Research*, 24(4): 433–54.

Forbes, D. (1978), 'The peddlers of Ujung Pandang', Working Paper No. 17, Centre of Southeast Asian Studies, Monash University, Melbourne.

Forbes, D. (1984), 'Industrialization and urbanization in Indonesia', paper presented to the fifth national conference of the Asian Studies Association of Australia, Adelaide University, Adelaide.

Forest Watch Indonesia (2001), *Potret Keadaan Hutan Indonesia* [A Portrait of For-estry in Indonesia], Forest Watch Indonesia and Global Forest Watch, Bogor.

Foster, J., J. Greer and E. Thorbecke (1984), 'A class of decomposable poverty measures', *Econometrica*, 52(3): 761–6.

Fraser, N. (2008), 'Can social security be extended to the informal sector: the case of India', unpublished manuscript, University of Edinburgh, Edinburgh.

Gamborg, M., P.K. Andersen, J.L. Baker, E. Budtz-Jørgensen, T. Jørgensen, G. Jensen and T.I.A. Sørensen (2009), 'Life course path analysis of birth weight, childhood growth, and adult systolic blood pressure', *American Journal of Epidemiology*, 169: 1,167–78.

Gardiner, P. (1997), 'Migration and urbanisation', in G. Jones and T. Hull (eds), *Indonesia Assessment: Population and Human Resources*, Institute of Southeast Asian Studies, Singapore, pp. 118–33.

Garip, F. (2006), 'Social and economic determinants of migration and remittances: an analysis of 22 Thai villages', unpublished manuscript, Department of Sociology, Princeton University, Princeton NJ.

Garnier, D., K.B. Simondon, T. Hoarau and E. Benefice (2003), 'Impact of the health and living conditions of migrant and non-migrant Senegalese adolescent girls on their nutritional status and growth', *Public Health Nutrition*, 6: 535–47.

Giles, J. and R. Mu (2007), 'Elderly parent health and the migration decision of adult children: evidence from rural China', *Demography*, 44(2): 265–88.

Goldsmith, P.D., K. Gunjal and B. Ndarishikanye (2004), 'Rural–urban migration and agricultural productivity: the case of Senegal', *Agricultural Economics*, 31(1): 33–45.

Gong, Xiaodong, Sherry Tao Kong, Shi Li and Xin Meng (2008), 'Rural–urban migrants: a driving force for growth', in L. Song and W.T. Woo (eds), *China's Dilemma*, Asia-Pacific Press and Brookings Institute Press, Canberra and Washington DC, pp. 110–52.

Granovetter, M. (2005), 'The impact of social structure on economic outcomes', *Journal of Economic Perspectives*, 19(1): 33–50.

Gustafsson, B. and Li Shi (2000), 'Economic transformation and the gender earnings gap in urban China', *Journal of Population Economics*, 13: 305–29.

Gustafsson, B. and Li Shi (2001), 'The anatomy of rising earnings inequality in urban China', *Journal of Comparative Economics*, 29: 118–35.

Han, Jialing (2003), 'Chengshi bianyuan qunti jiaoyu wenti yanjiu: Beijingshi liudong ertong yiwu jiaoyu zhuangkuang diaocha baogao' [Research on education of the marginalized population: report on migrant children's education in Beijing], in Peilin Li (ed.), *Nongmingong: Zhongguo Jincheng Nongmingong de Jingji Shehui Fenxi* [Peasant Migrants: Socio-economic Analysis of Peasant Workers in the Cities], Social Science Publishing House, Beijing.

Hanson, G.H. and C. Woodruff (2003), 'Emigration and educational attainment in Mexico', unpublished manuscript, University of California, San Diego, available at economics.ucr.edu/seminars/winter04/03-05-04Gordon%20Hanson.pdf.

Hare, D. (1999), '"Push" versus "pull" factors in migration outflows and returns: determinants of migration status and spell duration among China's rural population', *Journal of Development Studies*, 35(3): 45–72.

Harris, J. and M. Todaro (1970), 'Migration, unemployment and development: a two-sector analysis', *American Economic Review*, 60(1): 126–42.

Hazans, M. (2004), 'Does commuting reduce wage disparities?', *Growth and Change*, 35(3): 360–90.

Hetler, C.B. (1989), 'The impact of circular migration on a village economy', *Bulletin of Indonesian Economic Studies*, 25(1): 53–75.

Hill, H. (1996), *Southeast Asia's Emerging Giant: Indonesian Economic Policy Development since 1966*, Cambridge University Press, Melbourne.

Hill, H. (2000a), *Southeast Asia's Emerging Giant: Indonesian Economic Policy and Development*, revised edition, Cambridge University Press, Cambridge.

Hill, H. (2000b), *The Indonesian Economy*, second edition, Cambridge University Press, Cambridge.

Hugo, G. (1978), *Population Mobility in West Java*, Gadjah Mada University Press, Yogyakarta.

Hugo, G. (1982), 'Circular migration in Indonesia,' *Population and Development Review*, 8(1): 59–83.

Hugo, G. (1993), 'International labour migration', in C. Manning and J. Hardjono (eds), *Indonesia Assessment 1993: Labour Sharing in the Benefits of Growth?* Australian National University, Canberra, pp. 108–26.

Hugo, G. (1995), 'Indonesia's migration transition', *Austrian Journal of Development Studies*, 11(3): 285–309.

Hugo, G. (1997), 'Changing patterns and processes in population mobility', in G. Jones and T. Hull (eds), *Indonesia Assessment: Population and Human Resources*, Institute of Southeast Asian Studies, Singapore, pp. 68–100.

Hugo, G. (2000), 'The impact of the crisis on internal population movement in Indonesia', *Bulletin of Indonesian Economic Studies*, 36(2): 15–38.

Hugo, G., T. Hull, V. Hull and G. Jones (1987), *The Demographic Dimension in Indonesian Development*, Oxford University Press, Oxford.

Hull, T. (2001), 'First results of the 2000 population census', *Bulletin of Indonesian Economic Studies*, 37(1): 103–11.

IADB (Inter-American Development Bank) (2004), *Good Jobs Wanted: Labor Markets in Latin America*, 2004 Economic and Social Progress Report, Washington DC.

ILO (International Labour Office) (2000), 'Employment and social protection in the informal sector: ILO activities concerning the urban informal sector: thematic evaluation', GB.277/ESP/1/1, Geneva.

Jellinek, L. (1978), 'Circular migration and the "pondok" dwelling system: a case study of icecream traders in Jakarta', in P.J. Rimmer, D.W. Drakakis-Smith and T.G. McGee (eds), *Food, Shelter and Transport in Southeast Asia and the Pacific*, Australian National University, Canberra.

Jellinek, L. (1991), *The Wheel of Fortune: The History of a Poor Community in Jakarta*, University of Hawaii Press, Honolulu.

Jones, G.W. (1997), 'Introduction', in G.W. Jones and P.M. Visaria (eds), *Urbanization in Large Developing Countries: China, Indonesia, Brazil, and India*, Clarendon Press, Oxford, pp. 109–10.

Katz, E. and O. Stark (1986), 'Labor migration and risk aversion in less developed countries', *Journal of Labor Economics*, 4: 134–49.

Kennan, J. and J. Walker (2003), 'The effect of expected income on individual migration decisions', NBER Working Paper No. 9585, National Bureau of Economic Research, Washington DC.

Knight, J. and Li Shi (1996), 'Educational attainment and the rural–urban divide in China', *Oxford Bulletin of Economics and Statistics*, 58(1): 83–117.

Knight, J. and Lina Song (2001), 'Economic growth, economic reform, and rising inequality', in C. Riskin, Zhao Renwei and Li Shi (eds), *China's Retreat from Equality: Income Distribution and Economic Transition*, M.E. Sharpe, New York NY, pp. 84–122.

Knight, J., Lina Song and Huaibin Jia (1999), 'Chinese rural migrants in urban enterprises: three perspectives', in S. Cook and M. Maurer-Fazio (eds), *The Workers' State Meets the Market: Labour in China's Transition*, Frank Cass, London, pp. 73–104.

Krashinsky, H.A. (2004), 'Do marital status and computer usage really change the wage structure?', *Journal of Human Resources*, 29(3): 774–91.

Krausse, G. (1979), 'Economic adjustment of migrants in the city: the Jakarta experience', *International Migration Review*, 13(1): 46–70.

Lall, S.V., H. Selod and Z. Shalizi (2006), 'Rural–urban migration in developing countries: a survey of theoretical predictions and empirical findings', World Bank Policy Research Working Paper No. 3915, World Bank, Washington DC.

Leinbach, T.R. (1981), 'Travel characteristics and mobility behavior: aspects of rural transport impact in Indonesia', *Geografiska Annaler*, Series B, 63(20): 119–29.

Liang, Zai and Yiu Por Chen (2007), 'The educational consequences of migration for children in China', *Social Science Research*, 36: 28–47.

Liang, Zai, Lin Guo and Charles Chengrong Duan (2008), 'Migration and the well-being of children in China', *Yale China Health Journal*, 5: 25–46.

Lin, Liangming, Xue Gu, Jie Mi and Xiaoyi Shan (2003), 'Health and preventive health care of migrant children', in Liming Zhang and Shunyi Zhao (eds), *Zhongguo Jiu Chengshi Liudong Ertong Zhuangkuang Diaocha Baogao* [Survey Report on Temporary Migrant Children in Nine Cities of China], Office of Women's and Children's Affairs of the State Council and China National Children's Center, United Nations Children's Fund, Beijing.

Liu, Zhiqiang (2005), 'Institution and inequality: the *hukou* system in China', *Journal of Comparative Economics*, 33: 133–57.

Long, J. (2005), 'Rural–urban migration and socioeconomic mobility in Victorian Britain', *Journal of Economic History*, 65(1): 1–34.

Long, L.H. (1975), 'Does migration interfere with children's progress in school?', *Sociology of Education*, 48(3): 369–81.

Lu, Hong and Shunfeng Song (2006), 'Rural migrants' perceptions of public safety protections in urban China: the case of Tianjin', *Chinese Economy*, 39(3): 26–41.

Lucas, R. (1997), 'Internal migration in developing countries', in M. Rosenzweig and O. Stark (eds), *Handbook of Population and Family Economics*, Elsevier BV, Amsterdam, pp. 721–98.

Lucas, R. (2004), 'Life earnings and rural–urban migration', *Journal of Political Economy*, 112(1): s29–s59.

Maloney, P. (1998), *Are LDC Labor Markets Dualistic?* World Bank, Washington DC.

Manning, C. (1987), 'Rural economic change and labour mobility: a case study from West Java', *Bulletin of Indonesian Economic Studies*, 23(2): 52–79.

Manning, C. (1998), *Indonesia in Transition: An East Asian Success Story?* Cambridge University Press, Melbourne.

Manning, C. (2008), 'The political economy of reform: labour after Soeharto', Indonesian Studies Working Paper No. 6, University of Sydney, Sydney, August.

Mansuri, G. (2006), 'Migration, school attainment and child labor: evidence from rural Pakistan', World Bank Policy Research Working Paper No. 3945, World Bank, Washington DC.

Martin-Schiller, B. (1980), 'The green revolution in Java: ecological, socio-economic and historical perspectives', *Prisma*, 18(9): 71–93.

Mather, C.E. (1983), 'Industrialization in the Tangerang regency of West Java', *Indonesia*, 15(2): 2–17.

Mazumdar, D. (1976), 'The rural–urban wage gap, migration, and the shadow wage', *Oxford Economic Papers*, 28(3): 406–25.

Mazumdar, D. (1994), 'Urban poverty and labor markets', in E. Pernia (ed.), *Urban Poverty in Asia: A Survey of Critical Issues*, Oxford University Press, Hong Kong.

McCawley, P. (1982), 'Rural development and rural electrification in Indonesia: problems of helping the poor in developing countries', in G. Hainsworth (ed.), *Village-level Modernization in Southeast Asia: The Political Economy of Rice and Water*, University of British Columbia Press, London and Vancouver, pp. 85–108.

McLeod, R. (2008), 'Survey of recent developments', *Bulletin of Indonesian Economic Studies*, 44(2): 183–208.

Meng, Xin (2000), *Labour Market Reform in China*, Cambridge University Press, Cambridge.

Meng, Xin (2004), 'Economic restructuring and income inequality in urban China', *Review of Income and Wealth*, 50(3): 357–79.

Meng, Xin and Junsen Zhang (2001), 'The two-tier labor market in urban China: occupational segregation and wage differentials between urban residents and rural migrants in Shanghai', *Journal of Comparative Economics*, 29(3): 485–504.

Meng, Xin, R.G. Gregory and Guanghua Wan (2007), 'Urban poverty in China and its contributing factors, 1986–2000', *Review of Income and Wealth*, 53(1): 167–89.

Meng, Xin, R.G. Gregory and Youjuan Wang (2005), 'Poverty, inequality, and growth in urban China, 1986–2000', *Journal of Comparative Economics*, 33(4): 710–29.

Mincer, J. (1978), 'Family migration decisions', *Journal of Political Economy*, 86(5): 749–73.

Montgomery, J.D. (1992), 'Job search and network composition: implications of the strength-of-weak-ties hypothesis', *American Sociological Review*, 57(5): 586–96.

Morduch, J. and T. Sicular (2002), 'Rethinking inequality decomposition, with evidence from rural China', *Economic Journal*, 112: 93–106.

Moretti, E. (2008), 'Real wage inequality', NBER Working Paper No. 14370, National Bureau of Economic Research, Washington DC.

Moriya, Fumio (1963), *Ri Ben Jinji Shi* [An Economic History of Japan], translated from Japanese, Joint Publishing, Beijing.

Muhidin, S. (2002), *The Population of Indonesia: Regional Demographic Scenarios Using a Multiregional Method and Multiple Data Sources*, Population Studies Series, Rozenberg Publishers, Amsterdam.

Murad, A. (1980), '*Merantau*: outmigration in a matrilineal society of West Sumatra', unpublished paper, Department of Demography, Australian National University, Canberra.

Naim, M. (1974), 'Voluntary migration in Indonesia', Working Paper No. 26, Institute of Southeast Asian Studies, Singapore.

NBS (National Bureau of Statistics) (2006a), *China Statistical Yearbook*, China Statistics Press, Beijing.

NBS (National Bureau of Statistics) (2006b), *Zhongguo Tongji Zhaiyao 2006* [China Statistical Abstract 2006], China Statistics Press, Beijing.

NBS (National Bureau of Statistics) (2007), *China Yearbook of Rural Household Survey*, China Statistics Press, Beijing.

NBS (National Bureau of Statistics) (2008), *Zhongguo Tongji Zhaiyao 2008* [China Statistical Abstract 2008], China Statistics Press, Beijing..

Pelly, U. (1994), *Urbanisasi dan Adaptasi: Peranan Misi Budaya Minangkabau dan Mandailing di Medan, Sumatera Utara* [Urbanization and Adaptation: A Case Study of Minangkabau and Mandailing Migrants in Medan, North Sumatra], LP3ES, Jakarta.

Perkins, D. and S. Yusuf (1984), *Rural Development in China*, Johns Hopkins University Press, Baltimore MD.

Pribesh, S. and D.B. Downey (1999), 'Why are residential and school moves associated with poor performance?', *Demography*, 36(4): 521–34.

Ravallion, M., Shaohua Chen and P. Sangraula (2008), 'Dollar a day revisited', World Bank Policy Research Working Paper No. 4620, World Bank, Washington DC.

Resosudarmo, B.P. and A. Kuncoro (2006), 'The political economy of Indonesian economic reform: 1983–2000', *Oxford Development Studies*, 34(3): 341–55.

Resosudarmo, B.P., C. Yamauchi and T. Effendi (2009), 'Rural–urban migration in Indonesia: overview, study design and field report', Australian National University, Canberra.

Roberts, K. (1997), 'China's "tidal wave" of migrant labor: what can we learn from Mexican undocumented migration to the United States?', *International Migration Review*, 31(2): 249–93.

Rosenzweig, M. and O. Stark (1989), 'Consumption smoothing, migration, and marriage: evidence from rural India', *Journal of Political Economy*, 97(4): 905–26.

Rozelle, S., J.E. Taylor and A. de Brauw (1999) 'Migration, remittances, and agricultural productivity in China', *American Economic Review*, 89(2): 287–91.

Rutz, W. (1987), *Cities and Town in Indonesia: Their Development, Current Positions and Functions with Regard to Administration and Regional Economy*, Gebruder Borntraeger, Berlin and Stuttgart.

Sato, H. (2006), 'Housing inequality and housing poverty in urban China in the late 1990s', *China Economic Review*, 17(1): 37–50.

Sen, A.K. (1966), 'Peasants and dualism with or without surplus labor', *Journal of Political Economy*, 74(5): 425–50.

Sheng, Laiyun (2008), *Liudong Haishi Qianyi? Zhongguo Nongcun Laodongli Liudong Guocheng de Jingjixue Fenxi* [Floating or Migration? Economic Analysis of Floating Labor from Rural China], Shanghai Yuandong Press, Shanghai.

Sheng, Laiyun and Liquan Peng (2005), 'Dangqian nongcun waichu wugong de shuliang jiegou he tedian' [The population, structure and characteristics of rural migrant workers], in Department of Rural Survey, National Bureau of Statistics (ed.), *Zhongguo Nongcun Laodongli Diaocha Baogao* [Research on Rural Labour in China], China Statistics Press, Beijing.

Shi, Bonian (ed.) (2005), *Chengshi Bianyuanren: Jincheng Nongmingong Jiating Jiqi Zinü Wenti Yanjiu* [The Urban Marginalized: Research on Migrant Families and Their Children], Social Sciences Academic Press, Beijing.

Shorrocks, A.F. (1999), 'Decomposition procedures for distributional analysis: a unified framework based on the Shapley value', unpublished paper, Department of Economics, University of Essex, Colchester.

Skeldon, R. (1997), 'Rural-to-urban migration and its implications for poverty alleviation', *Asia-Pacific Population Journal*, 12(1): 3–16.

Solinger, D. (1999), *Citizenship in Urban China: Peasant Migrants, the State, and the Logic of the Market*, University of California Press, Berkeley CA.

Sorensen, A. (2004), *The Making of Urban Japan*, Nissan Institute of Japanese Studies, Tokyo.

Standing, G. (1978), *Labour Force Participation and Development*, International Labour Organization, Geneva.

Stark, O. (1976), 'Rural-to-urban migration and some economic issues: a review utilising findings of surveys and empirical studies covering the 1965–1975 period', World Employment Programme Research Working Paper, International Labour Organization, Geneva.

Stark, O. (1991), *The Migration of Labor*, Basil Blackwell, Oxford.

Stark, O. and D. Levhari (1982), 'On migration and risk in LDCs', *Economic Development and Cultural Change*, 31(1): 191–6.

State Council Research Group (2006), *Zhongguo Nongmingong Diaoyan Baogao* [Report on Migrant Workers in China], China Yan Shi Publishing House, Beijing.

Statistics Indonesia (2000), *The Population of Indonesia, Results of the 2000 Census*, Series S2, Jakarta.

Statistics Indonesia (2006), *Penduduk Indonesia: Hasil Survei Penduduk Antar Sensus Tahun 2005* [Population of Indonesia: Results of the 2005 Intercensal Survey], Jakarta.

Statistics Indonesia (2007), *Analisis dan Perhitungan Tingkat Kemiskinan 2007* [Analysis and Calculation of the 2007 Poverty Rate], Jakarta.

Statistics Indonesia Medan (2006), *Medan dalam Angka 2006* [Medan in Figures 2006], Medan.

Statistics Indonesia, Bappenas and UNDP (2001), *Indonesia Human Development Report 2001: Towards a New Consensus*, Statistics Indonesia, National Development Planning Agency (Bappenas) and United Nations Development Programme (UNDP), Jakarta.

Steele, R. (1981), 'Origin and occupational mobility of lifetime migrants to Surabaya and East Java', PhD dissertation, Australian National University, Canberra.

Strauss, J. and D. Thomas (1995), 'Human resources: empirical modelling of household and family decisions', in T.N. Srinivasan and J.R. Behrman (eds), *Handbook of Development Economics*, Volume III, Elsevier, Amsterdam, pp. 1,883–2,023.

Strauss, J., F. Witoelar, B. Sikoki and A.M. Wattie (2009), 'The Fourth Wave of the Indonesia Family Life Survey (IFLS4): Overview and Field Report', WR-675/1-NIA/NICHD, April.

Suharso, A. Speare, H.R. Redmana and I. Husin (1976), *Rural–Urban Migration in Indonesia*, Leknas, Jakarta.

Surbakti, P. (1995), *Indonesia's National Socio-economic Survey: A Continual Data Source for Analysis on Welfare Development*, Central Bureau of Statistics, Jakarta, available at http://www.rand.org/labor/bps.data/manualpdf/susenas/surbakti_1995_review.pdf.

Taylor, E.J., S. Rozelle and A. de Brauw (2003), 'Migration and incomes in source communities: a new economics of migration perspective from China', *Economic Development and Cultural Change*, 52(1): 75–102.

Temple, G. (1974), 'Migration to Jakarta: empirical search for theory', PhD dissertation, University of Wisconsin, Madison WI.

Thee, K.W. (2001), 'The Soeharto era and after: stability, development and crisis', in H. Dick, V.J.H. Houben, J.T. Linblad and K.W. Thee (eds), *The Emergence of a National Economy: An Economic History of Indonesia, 1800–2000*, Allen & Unwin, Sydney, pp. 194–243.

Thorbecke, E. and T. van der Pluim (1993), *Rural Indonesia: Socio-economic Development in a Changing Environment*, IFAD Studies in Rural Poverty No. 5, New York University Press, New York NY.

Tirtosudarmo, R. (2008), 'Bugis migration to Samarinda, East Kalimantan: establishing a colony?', in P. Graham (ed.), *Horizons of Home: Nation, Gender and Migrancy in Island Southeast Asia*, Monash Asia Institute, Clayton, pp. 101–12.

UNDP (United Nations Development Programme) (2005), *China Human Development Report 2005*, China Development Research Foundation and UNDP, Beijing.

Wan, Guanghua (2004), 'Accounting for income inequality in rural China: a regression-based approach', *Journal of Comparative Economics*, 32: 348–63.

Wang, Hansheng and Xiaoqiang Wang (1995), 'Zai liudongzhong shixian jingying yimin' [Migration and migration selection], *Strategy and Management*, 5: 112–20.

Warouw, N. (2006), 'Community-based agencies as the entrepreneur's instruments of control in post-Soeharto's Indonesia', *Asia Pacific Business Review*, 12(2): 193–207.

Weber, B., A. Marre, M. Fisher, R. Gibbs and J. Cromartie (2007), 'Education's effect on poverty: the role of migration', *Review of Agricultural Economics*, 29(3): 437–45.

West, L. and Yaohui Zhao (eds) (2000), *Rural Labor Flows in China*, University of California Press, Berkeley CA.

Widodo, J. (n.d.), 'About Medan: the advent of a North Sumatran modern city', available at http://medan.m-heritage.org/about_medan/index.html, accessed 1 August 2009.

World Bank (1990), *World Development Report*, Washington DC.

World Bank (2001), *China: Overcoming Rural Poverty*, Washington DC.

World Bank (2009), *Reshaping Economic Geography*, World Development Report, Oxford University Press, Oxford.

Xiang, Biao (1996), 'Chuan tong he xin shihui kong jin de sheng cheng' [Mobility, traditional networking, marketization and the development of a 'non-government' controlled space], *Strategy and Management*, 6.

Yap, L. (1977), 'The attraction of cities: a review of the migration literature', *Journal of Development Economics*, 4(3): 239–64.

Ye, Jingzhong, J. Murray and Wang Yi Huan (eds) (2005), *Left-behind Children in Rural China: Impact Study of Rural Labor Migration on Left-behind Children in Mid-West China*, Social Sciences Academic Press, Beijing.

Zahniser, S. (1999), *Mexican Migration to the United States, the Role of Migration Networks and Human Capital Accumulation*, Garland Publishing, New York NY.

Zhang, Kevin H. and Shunfeng Song (2003), 'Rural–urban migration and urbanization in China: evidence from time-series and cross-section analyses', *China Economic Review*, 14: 386–400.

Zhao, Yaohui (1999a), 'Labor migration and earnings differences: the case of rural China', *Economic Development and Cultural Change*, 47(4): 767–83.

Zhao, Yaohui (1999b), 'Leaving the countryside: rural-to-urban migration decisions in China', *American Economic Review: Papers and Proceedings*, 89(2): 281–6.

Zhao, Yaohui (2000), 'Rural-to-urban labor migration in China: the past and the present', in L. West and Y. Zhao (eds), *Rural Labor Flows in China*, University of California Press, Berkeley CA, pp. 15–33.

Zhao, Yaohui (2003), 'The role of migrant networks in labor migration: the case of China', *Contemporary Economic Policy*, 21(4): 500–511.

Zhu, Nong (2002), 'The impacts of income gaps on migration decisions in China', *China Economic Review*, 13(2–3): 213–30.

Index